KANJI FROM THE START

KANJI
FROM
THE START

A Comprehensive Japanese Reader
Martin Lam and Shimizu Kaoru

Kodansha International
Tokyo · New York · London

Distributed in the United States by Kodansha America, Inc., 114 Fifth Avenue, New York, New York 10011, and in the United Kingdom and continental Europe by Kodansha Europe Ltd., 95, Aldwych, London WC2B 4JF.

Published by Kodansha International Ltd., 17-14, Otowa 1-chome, Bunkyo-ku, Tokyo 112 and Kodansha America Inc.

First Edition, 1995
95 96 97 98 10 9 8 7 6 5 4 3 2 1

ISBN 4-7700-1936-X

Calligraphy by Goto Gyokuen
Designed by Masayuki Uchida
Set on a Macintosh in 明朝, Helvetica, Garamond, and **Triplex** by Work Design, Tokyo
Printed in Japan

Library of Congress Cataloging-in-Publication Data
A catalog record for this book is available from the Library of Congress

Contents

◇ ◇ Foreword ◇ ◇

This work was aimed at the MBA students learning Japanese at King's College, London–hence the choice of themes covered in the twelve units. It was designed with hypertext in mind–that is, an electronic version which would enable the learner to access, from the screen, explanations of characters or of grammar points in the displayed text. We are most grateful to Dr Vanessa Davies, Director of Language and Communication at King's, for her encouragement and support for our work, which has been produced, initially, in book form. The British author is also indebted to a succession of motivated teachers, and especially to David Bentliff for his generous advice.

Apart from the future use of hypertext the rationale of this mainly self-contained reader for learners of Japanese can be summarized in four points:

First, the authors think it is shortsighted to begin, as many Japanese primers do, with expressions wholly in hiragana. The learner who continues along this path will never be able to read real Japanese, or will have to retro-fit the characters–which will be frustrating. Some other books expect the learner to master quite difficult kanji from the outset. Here, we begin deliberately with simple kanji and progress to more difficult shapes.

Second, we explain the construction and, where possible, the origin of each kanji as we meet it, emphasizing the role of the radicals in mediating the meaning, and of semantic/phonetic family relationships between kanji. (For reasons of space this aspect will await fuller treatment elsewhere.) Nearly all the kanji are in the primary school list.

Third, we explain the grammar points of each unit as they arise, avoiding technical terms so far as possible. The indispensable terms are included in an Alphabetical Reference Grammar, to which are also attached Tables of Verb and Adjective endings.

Fourth, we give the learner an opportunity to reinforce his or her acquisition of the words and grammar of each unit by means of sentences and themes to be rendered in Japanese. We attach to these a transformation, based on simple rules of thumb, to help the learner to adapt to the Japanese sentence structure.

The work is designed for self-study or for use in class. In either case we recommend that several sessions should be devoted to each unit–but not past the point where the learner becomes satiated. Better to rely on the rule that one does not fully master Unit 1 until one has finished Unit 3. Again, no learner can be expected to know and recognize a kanji or a point of grammar after one meeting. It will take a while for a mnemonic network to build up in the student's memory, and there have to be lapses on the way. We have deliberately duplicated some of our kanji and grammar entries in successive units so as to allow for this normal iterative learning process.

Unit I
THE SECOND-HAND CAR
中古の車

Frontispiece character : 車 kuruma *car*

◇ ◇ Introductory Note ◇ ◇

(Asterisks point to entries in the Alphabetical Reference Grammar)

These first texts are written in the polite* form and are composed mainly of simple characters–and, of course, of inflections*, particles* etc. written in the phonetic hiragana syllabary. Most of the characters used here have just one component, and in many cases this is a radical or classifier–that is, one of the 214 basic shapes by which Chinese characters have traditionally been classified. The radical for each character is identified in the kanji notes to this unit; familiarity with the most common radicals is to be recommended since these are among the primitive shapes out of which the characters are made and mediate some degree of order in what seems at first a kanji jungle. Getting to know the common radicals helps towards the gradual recognition of the trees.

The kanji of this text are used mainly with their original Japanese pronunciation ("kun" reading*), as opposed to the "ON" reading derived from the Chinese. There are, however, a number of compound kanji in the text: 中古CHUUKO, 土曜日 DOYOObi, 東京TOOKYOO, 二回NIKAI, and the kanji in these compounds (except for the "bi" in DOYOObi) have the ON readings (see Unit 4 for further explanation of ON and kun). On a point of detail, in proper names with a long vowel the transliteration (roomaji) uses double letters, but the English translation follows the conventional form: eg Tookyoo but Tokyo.

This first text is annotated with what looks like a large number of grammar points. These are mainly elementary but basic items, including a number of particles, the two types of adjectives*, several tenses* of the verb, participles* and the use of counters*. All these help to get the adult learner started. There are also a few constructions (eg a comparison*, indirect* speech, an indirect* question, a subordinate* clause ending with node, maening *because...*, and the equivalent of a relative* clause) without which the text would be unduly bland. The rationale of our grammar notes and an explanation of the terms used are given below in the pages preceding the grammar notes on this first unit.

For each of the grammar points a superscript letter in the transliteration (roomaji) identifies the summary explanation in the grammar notes following the text.

中古の車

（一）　土曜日です。門のそばに、田中正子さんが立っています。夫の田中一夫さんも出て来ました。ここに住んでいます。この二人には、三才と六才の子供があります。白い、元気な小犬もいます。

正子さんは、今月、三十才になりました。一夫さんは、正子さんより四才年上です。

（二）　田中さんは東京のサラリーマンで、町を出て田舎へ行くのが大好きです。それで、この間、車を買いました。大きな中古の車に、五十万円払いまし

た。高くないと思いました。田中一夫さんのサラリーは月三十五万円で、ボーナスも年二回、サラリーの半年分出るので、車を買うために十分だと思いました。ガソリンが安くない事を知っていましたが、仕方がありませんでした。ガレージがありませんでしたが、戸外に止める所がありました。

（三）　子供は、車でどこへ行くか聞きました。母は、明日、日曜日に、田舎へドライブするつもりだと言って、皆（犬の他）は、サンドイッチを作って、包みました。

CHUUKO NO KURUMA

1 Doyoobi desu[a]. Mon no[b1] soba ni[b1], Tanaka Masako san ga[b1] tatte[c] imasu. Otto no[d] Tanaka Kazuo san mo[b2] dete kimashita[e]. Koko ni sunde[c] imasu. Kono futari[f] ni wa[g], san-sai to[b2] roku-sai no kodomo ga arimasu[g]. Shiroi genki-na[h] ko-inu mo[b2] imasu. Masako san wa, kon-getsu, sanjussai[i] ni[b1] narimashita. Kazuo san wa, Masako san yori, yon-sai toshi-ue[j] desu.

2 Tanaka san wa Tookyoo no sarariiman de[k], machi o dete[k] inaka e[b2] iku no ga[l] daisuki desu. Sorede, kono aida[m] kuruma o[b1] kaimashita. Ookina[n] chuuko no[b1] kuruma ni, gojuuman en haraimashita. Takaku nai to[o] omoimashita. Tanaka Kazuo san no sararii wa tsuki sanjuu-go man en de, boonasu mo nen nikai[f], sararii no han-toshi bun[p] deru node, kuruma o[b1] kau tame ni[q] juubun da to[o] omoimashita. Gasorin ga yasuku nai koto o[r] shitte imashita ga[s], shikata ga arimasen deshita[t]. Gareeji ga arimasen deshita ga[s], kogai ni tomeru[u] tokoro ga arimashita.

3 Kodomo wa, kuruma de[b1] doko e iku ka[v] kikimashita. Haha wa, ashita, nichiyoobi ni, inaka e doraibu suru tsumori da to[o] itte, mina–inu no hoka–wa sandoitchi o tsukutte tsutsumimashita.

THE SECOND-HAND CAR

It is Saturday. Masako Tanaka is standing by the gate. Her husband Kazuo Tanaka has also appeared. This is where they live. The couple have children of three and six years old. They also have a lively white puppy. Masako was thirty this month. Kazuo is four years older than Masako.

Mr Tanaka is a Tokyo office worker, and very much likes to leave the city and get out into the countryside. So they recently bought a car. They paid 500,000 yen for a large second-hand car. They did not think this was dear. Kazuo Tanaka's salary is 350,000 yen a month, and since twice a year his bonus comes out at half a year's salary, they thought this was enough for them to buy a car. They knew that petrol was not cheap, but this could not be helped. They had no garage, but there was a place to keep the car out of doors.

The children asked where they were going by car. Their mother said they intended to go for a drive in to the countryside the next day, Sunday, and they all–except for the dog–made sandwiches and wrapped them up.

Unit I

◇ ◇ How to read the notes on kanji ◇ ◇

(Asterisks denote items in the Alphabetical Reference Grammar)

The kanji are neither an entirely arbitrary collection of shapes nor a fully organised set of symbols, but something between the two. A notion of the component parts and origins of the kanji will help to build an associative mnemonic network to link the kanji in the learner's memory. Shapes which at first seem chaotic are later identifiable as primitive components and/or radicals; not all the primitives are radicals, but the latter are a starting point. Of the traditional 214 radicals about one third are the most common, and the recognition of these will build up quite readily. Recognition of the radicals will also enable the learner to use a dictionary. The first two units introduce, as kanji in their own right, 65 common radicals.

Over the centuries there has been some disagreement about the appropriate radical for a given kanji; this leads to small differences between dictionaries. Indeed the most modern dictionary (Spahn and Hadamitsky) classifies the kanji to only 79 radicals, mainly by segregating into a separate category those kanji which do not boast one of the 79 chosen radicals.

In the following notes the columns from left to right show: the character itself; the number of the radical (in the traditional set of 214); the shape of the radical; the meaning ascribed to the radical. (In a few cases the traditional choice of radical seems arbitrary and is not significant to the meaning or to retrieval; in such cases the number is here shown in parenthesis).

The next column gives the pronunciation, "reading"*, of the character *in the text*. In these first texts usually the native Japanese or "kun" reading, where the character is used on its own; lastly the character's derivation and its meaning in the context.

In the column of readings the stem* or root is shown first, then, after a hyphen, the ending/inflection*, which is written in the phonetic syllabary called hiragana. The so-called Japanese set of adjectives* (which conjugate* partly like verbs*) are shown in full with the basic kanji and the normal -i or -shii ending. Verbs add to the basic root kanji, which bears the meaning, an ending -mu or -gu or -ku etc to give what is here called the dictionary* form. As a reference point it corresponds to the infinitive* in European languages; but in Japanese it is the plain* form of the affirmative* present* tense. In some parts of the verb the final consonant of the stem will be subject to the phonetic changes listed in Verbs and Adjectives Table 2, following the Alphabetical Reference Grammar. In other parts of speech too the basic kanji may be complemented by a suffix in hiragana; for example, in "kawari-ni" (Unit 2; *instead of*) "ka-" is represented by a kanji , but the "wa", the "ri" and the "ni" are in hiragana.

The derivations of the kanji set out here come from different sources; some of these reflect Chinese tradition, some more modern ideas. Many explanations are not entirely satisfactory, but we have tried here to use those which make reasonable sense and thus provide a peg on which to hang the recall of the sign in question and its analogues. If all else fails a mnemonic is sometimes offered, even if it is etymologically without substance.

◇ ◇ Notes on Kanji ◇ ◇

By convention the **ON** (originally "Chinese") readings are in capital letters and the **kun** (native Japanese) readings are in lower case.

In the notes to the kanji of these first units not all the readings are given, but only those which are relevant to the meaning or to the origin of the kanji. If the same kanji occurs later with a different reading this will be signalled.

Notes refer the learner, where appropriate, to the listing of phonetic/semantic families of kanji which follow the main texts.

KANJI	RADICAL			KANJI	
character	no	shape	meaning	reading	derivation and meaning
中	(2)	丨	vertical line	CHUU/na-ka	Arrow in middle of target; *middle*; **naka** means *inside, in the centre of, among* (see Tanaka below).
古	24	十	ten	KO/furu-i	Either ten mouths/generations or a skull: ◆中古 CHUUKO "middling old", *second-hand*.
車	159	車	vehicle	kuruma	Radical: cart with wheels; here it means *car*.
土	32	土	earth	DO/tsuchi	Radical: pile of earth or a plant, *earth*.
曜	72	日	sun	YOO	At first sight one of the most off-putting of the common kanji, but readily responds to treatment. Right-hand side (RHS) has on top two simplified versions of radical 124, a feather, and below, radical 172, "short-tailed bird". With the sun radical on LHS said to have meant sun, moon and planets. (Perhaps because they shine like a bird's tail.) Thus used as a suffix for the European days of the week.

KANJI	RADICAL			KANJI	
character	no	shape	meaning	reading	derivation and meaning
日	72	日	sun	NICHI/hi	Radical: squared pictorial of sun: the kun reading hi,which becomes bi in compounds and means **day**. ◆土曜日 DOYOObi *Saturday.*(Mnemonic–many house-owners spend Saturday digging the soil.)
門	169	門	gate	MON	Radical: pictorial of a *gate.*
田	102	田	ricefield	ta	Radical: pictorial, with irrigation. *Ricefield, paddy.*
中	(2)	|	vertical line	naka	See CHUU above. ◆田中 Tanaka, a common family name.
正	1	一	horizontal line	SEI/SHOO/ tada-shii/ masa	Top added to leg symbol. Means *direct, right.* The reading masa is used as part of a name and means *honest.*
子	39	子	child	ko	Radical: wrapped-up baby, *child.* A common suffix for girls' first names. ◆正子 a woman's first name Masako
立	117	立	stand	ta-tsu	Pictorial radical: man *standing* on ground.
夫	(4)	ノ	(slash)	otto	From ookii below; or a man with a hat. *Man, husband.*
一	1	一	horizontal line	ICHI/ hito-tsu/ hito-ri	Radical: one. Kazu is reading used as part of a proper name meaning *first.* ◆一夫 Kazuo is a given name indicating first son.

KANJI		RADICAL		KANJI	
character	no	shape	meaning	reading	derivation and meaning
出	2	丨	as above	de-ru	Foot with shoe, or plants sprouting. *Go out, leave.* See Unit 2 for reading da-su, transitive*, meaning *to bring out, give out*.
来	(4)	ノ	(slash)	ku-ru	Originally cereal stalk; borrowed to mean *come*.
住	9	亻	person	JUU/su-mu	Phonetic JUU from RHS. Image of lamp with a flame, meaning house-holder; *to reside*.
二	7	二	two lines	NI/futa-tsu/ futa-ri	Radical: two. Just as ICHI (*one*) above has native Japanese equivalent forms hito-tsu (for things) and hito-ri (for people), so the native Japanese numeral for *two* is futa-tsu and futa-ri means the *couple*.
人	9	人	person	hito/JIN/NIN	Radical: by itself pronounced chto (*ch* as in German *ich*). A *man, person*. Here read, exceptionally, as the ri of futa-ri.
三	1	一	(line)	SAN/mit-tsu	Pictorial, meaning *three*. Mittsu is the Japanese numeral, like hitotsu and futatsu above.
才	(6)	亅	(vertical line)	SAI	Originally a stream with a dam. Normally means *talent*, but also used, as here, as simplified form of counter* for years of age.
六	8	亠	lid	ROKU/ mut-tsu	Originally house or cave, but borrowed to mean *six*. There was a binary element in the native Japanese series of numbers: thus mittsu 3 and muttsu 6; yottsu 4 and yattsu 8. Less obviously hitotsu 1 and futatsu 2.
供	9	亻	person	tomo	Phonetic: RHS two hands meaning an offering together; with person radical on LHS. As suffix added to ko (above).

KANJI character	RADICAL no	shape	meaning	reading	KANJI derivation and meaning
					◆子供 kodomo *child, children.* (Mutation of initial unvoiced consonant to voiced, as here t to d, is usual in compounds; cf bi for hi in DOYOObi above.)
白	106	白	white	shiro-i	Radical: traditionally from inside of acorn; *white.*
元	7	二	two lines	GEN/moto	Big head and two legs, leading to meaning chief, hence *origin.*
気	84	气	breath	KI	Steam rising hence *spirit.* ◆元気 GENKI-na *healthy, lively.*
小	42	小	small	chii-sai/ko	Radical: three dots meaning *small.* (Unusually, this kanji has two kun readings.)
犬	94	犬	dog	inu	Radical: animal with tail; *dog.* ◆小犬 ko-inu, *puppy.* (Compound with both components in their kun reading.)
今	9	人	person	KON/ima	Top triangle is a primitive meaning union (cf KAISHA in Unit 3); with lower stroke, (pointer of sun-dial?)*now.*
月	74	月	moon	GETSU/ tsu-ki	Radical: squared pictorial of moon; hence also means *month* (cf *monthly* below). ◆今月 KONGETSU, *this month.*
十	24	十	(ten)	JUU/too	Radical: borrowed to mean *ten.* ◆三十 SANJUU, *thirty.*
四	31	口	enclosure	SHI/yon	Either borrowed from sound of breathing out or a shape easily divided into two, eg four fingers *–four.*

KANJI	RADICAL			KANJI	
character	no	shape	meaning	reading	derivation and meaning
年	(4)	ノ	(slash)	NEN/toshi	Origin traditionally from 千 SEN/chi meaning 1,000 + sign for grain/harvest; *year*.
上	(25)	卜	(oracle)	ue/nobo-ru	Symbolic: a line over the horizon, *above*; as verb noboru, *to climb*.
東	(4)	ノ	(slash)	TOO/higashi	Sun behind trees: *east*.
京	8	亠	lid	KYOO	House on a hill: *capital*. ◆東京 TOOKYOO Tokyo–Eastern capital. (Cf 京都 KYOOto and 北京 Beijing–Northern capital).
町	102	田	paddy	CHOO/ma chi	Road junction, or field staked out for building, or from phonetic ON reading of RHS CHOO (a block of buildings); *town*.
舎	9	人	person	SHA	Place to stretch out in; barracks, dormitory. This is one of the few anomalous compounds, with pronunciation special to the kanji (ateji); here ricefield + building = 田舎 inaka *countryside*. See short list of these anomalous readings in Appendix 3.
行	144	彳	go	i-ku	Radical: stepping forward with two feet, or crossroads; *to go*.
好	38	女	woman	su-ki	LHS is character for woman and the RHS is the character for child (see above). *Liked, what one likes.*
大	37	大	big	TAI/DAI/ ooki-i	Large man; *big, much*. The reading ookii is the one used when standing alone. *Large.* (See below.)

| KANJI | RADICAL | | | | KANJI |
character	no	shape	meaning	reading	derivation and meaning
					◆大好き DAIsu-ki *what is liked very much.*(Note that in this compound DAI has the ON reading but suki the kun.)
間	169	門	gate	aida	Light through a door. Space, interval in time or space. Idiom*–この間 kono aida means *recently, the other day.*
買	122	罒	net	ka-u	Top is string bag; below is shell (rad 154) meaning money; *to buy.*
五	(1)	一	(line)	GO	A spool, borrowed, or five fingers of a hand; *five.*
万	(1)	一	(line)	MAN	Said originally to be floating weed; *ten thousand.*
払	64	扌	hand	hara-u	RHS simplified: original RHS was phonetic; with hand radical, meant *to wipe away.* Now also means *to pay.*
円	13	冂	contain	EN/maru-i	Simplified sign easier to remember than its derivation: was inscribed in a circle and meant round. *Japanese yen.*
高	189	高	high	taka-i	Radical: building with two floors; *high, tall*; here it means *dear* or *expensive.*
思	102	田	paddy	omo-u	Top was not field but a head or skull + heart below; *think.*
回	31	囗	enclosure	KAI	Was two circles, thus round and round, *times.* ◆二回 NIKAI *two times, twice.* Cf 今回 KONKAI *this time.*

KANJI character	RADICAL no	shape	meaning	reading	KANJI derivation and meaning
半	(3)	丶	(comma)	HAN	Origin not clear: best remembered as shape easy to divide in two, *half*. ◆半年 HANtoshi *six months* (*half-year*). (Another mixture of ON and kun readings).
分	12	八	eight	BUN/BU/FUN/wa-keru/wa-karu	Bottom is radical 18, knife: hence what is divided eg *a minute*; here it means *a part*. Wakeru means *to divide*; wakaru means *to distinguish* or *to understand*. ◆十分 JUUBUN (see JUU above) *enough* (mnemonic 10/10 = full marks) .
安	40	宀	roof	AN/yasu-i	Roof over woman; *peace*: cf 天安門 TIEN AN MEN Square in Beijing. Here Japanese meaning of yasui is *cheap*.
事	(6)	亅	(vertical line)	JI/koto	Best to remember with 書く kaku *write* (Unit 3). Both contain a primitive for hand ⇒ but, fittingly, kaku has it at the top (radical 129), and underneath is a pen with, below, a writing or ink block. JI/koto, however, has the hand at the bottom, as if it were holding on to something–not a brush, but something concrete, *a fact* or *a matter*. Here koto is part of the grammatical shorthand for "the fact that..." as object of shiru to *know*.
知	111	矢	arrow	shi-ru	LHS is arrow radical: with mouth RHS implies words going straight to the point; *know*.
仕	9	亻	person	SHI /tsuka-eru	Phonetic: RHS is 士 SHI *important person*–sage or samurai, sitting straight; with radical for person on LHS; *to serve*.
方	70	方	direction	kata	Origin said to be a spade; now means *direction*, or *way* (of doing something; thus 読み方 yomikata "reading" of

KANJI	RADICAL			KANJI	
character	no	shape	meaning	reading	derivation and meaning
					a character in Unit 4). ◆仕方 SHIkata (ON and kun) *method, means*.
戸	63	戸	door	KO/to	Radical: shape of *a door*.
外	36	夕	evening	GAI/soto/hoka	RHS is divination by cracks and LHS is a crescent moon. Together, for unclear reasons, they mean *outside*. See below for an alternative kanji with kun reading hoka, *other, apart from*. ◆戸外 KOGAI (literally) *out of doors*.
止	77	止	stop	to-meru	Radical: a foot at rest; *to stop*.
所	63	戸	door	tokoro	RHS is an axe and a pound weight: meaning *place* probably phonetically based. Mnemonic–use your axe to make the door.
聞	169	門	gate	ki-ku	Origin phonetic, but mnemonic is "to listen at a door" and it means *to hear* (main meaning of kiku); however the same verb is used, as here, to mean *ask*.
母	80	母	mother	haha	Radical: woman with breasts, *mother*.
明	72	日	sun	aka-rui	Combination of sun and moon meaning *light, bright*. ◆明日 ashita *tomorrow*. Another expression with anomalous readings – cf inaka above and Appendix 3. ◆日曜日 NICHI YOOBI *Sunday*.

KANJI	RADICAL			KANJI	
character	no	shape	meaning	reading	derivation and meaning
言	149	言	speech	i-u	A mouth + words/sound waves coming out; *to say*.
皆	81	比	compare	KAI/mina	Radical 81 is two people side by side which means *to compare*; not clear why with addition of white radical below (see 白い shiroi above) it becomes *all*. Cf 皆さん minasan *Ladies and Gentlemen*.
他	9	イ	person	TA/hoka	Taken directly from "he" in Chinese: several signs got confused. We have seen above another kanji 外, with kun reading hoka and meaning "outside". The meaning of this kanji, however, is rather *third person* or *other than*, though the two meanings tend to overlap.
作	9	イ	person	tsuku-ru	RHS perhaps was carving; with person radical on LHS, *to produce*.
包	(4)	ノ	(slash)	tsutsu-mu	Originally gestation, now means *to wrap up*.

Unit I

◇ ◇ Guide to the grammar notes ◇ ◇

1. In the grammar notes to each unit we comment on specific points in the text. By contrast the words marked with an asterisk are items in the Alphabetical Reference Grammar which follows the units and provides a general key to grammatical terms and Japanese usage. Attached to the reference grammar are Tables which set out the inflexions* (word endings) of verbs* and of one kind of adjective*.

2. In the grammar notes to each unit we explain, as characteristic of Japanese:

> (a) **word-endings**: these are written in hiragana and added to the kanji which carries the basic meaning. The words which mainly rely on endings (inflexions*) to indicate their full meaning are the *verbs**, which in all languages indicate actions like *swim, hit, be, become*; and in Japanese some *adjectives**–the descriptive words like *deep, red* –which also have certain endings in common with verbs. The verb endings are set out in Tables 1-6 and those of the adjectives in Table 7. *Adverbs**, that is, words which describe not things but actions, like *deeply, well, badly*, are regarded by the Japanese as a form of the adjective; their characteristic endings are also shown in Table 7.

> (b) the use of the **particles*** which, in Japanese, show the role of the word in the sentence and also mediate connections between words.

> (c) how the various parts of the sentence fit together–sometimes called the *syntax* (a word now used in computing to describe the formal structure of software instructions).

3. As to (a) it is a prime characteristic of Japanese that *verbs* have two full sets of endings, corresponding to plain* and to formal* speech. The Japanese verb does not change with number (singular/plural) or with person (I, you, he/she, we, they) or with gender, but as in European languages the verbs, and, in Japanese as noted above, one kind of adjective, change their endings:

> with tense* (present/future, past),

> according as the statement is affirmative* or negative*; Japanese verbs have a complete set of negative forms to match the affirmative set (both appear in the Tables),

> according to whether the statement is part of an "if/when" hypothetical* clause (if/when he arrives, if the weather were bad),

> according to whether the verb is active* or passive*,

according to whether a verb is part of a general statement about the action in question (he wins races) or continuous* (he is winning this race). In the latter case "winning" is both in English and in Japanese the present participle* of the verb "to win",

to convey an order: the imperative*, in all languages, denotes a command or exhortation*–"do this"; "do not do that"; "let us have a drink". Japanese has several forms for such expressions.

4. Japanese also has verb forms, derived from the basic root, which express **to want to do something** (desiderative*), **to cause someone to do something** (causative*), **to be able to do something** (potential*). These derived verbs are included in Tables 1-5.

5. Our Tables show in adjoining columns the two main sets of Japanese verb endings, of which one corresponds to formal speech or writing (alternatively labelled the "polite" form) and the other–called the plain form. The plain form is normally used in most subordinate* clauses–that is, in those parts of the sentence which are subsidiary to the so-called main* clause which makes the principal statement. For example, "He will eat (main clause) **when he arrives** (subordinate clause)".

6. Because Japanese grammatical perceptions are different from the European conventions there is sometimes a dilemma about how to label one form or another. For example when we look up a French or German verb in the dictionary we see the infinitive*–*aller, gehen*–which translates as "to go". In Japanese verbs are given in the dictionary* form ending in -u; this is essentially the plain form of the present tense, though it also has some features in common with the European infinitive. In our notes we follow convention and call it the "dictionary form".

7. Verbs which need a noun* (as an object*) to complete their sense are transitive* (the dog chases *the cat* = object); verbs which do not need an object are intransitive* (the dog barks). Japanese verbs often come in pairs, both using the same kanji, but with one of the pair transitive and the other intransitive. Some of these pairs are set out in the Introduction to the Tables, with examples of a few verbs which can be used both transitively and intransitively.

8. In all languages a verb can be used as a noun: I hate *shaving* ; *to err* is human. The result is called a verbal* noun; we shall see several ways in Japanese of making a verb into a noun. A whole clause can also be used as if it were a noun (eg it is believed "that Japanese is dif-

ficult"); this is a particular instance of a subordinate clause.

9. As to the *particles* – point (b) in para 2 above – Japanese has particles of two kinds. One kind is, as it were, a tag added on to a word to distinguish the topic of the sentence, the subject and the object of a verb. (The dog [subject]chases the cat [object]). Many of these particles will be used and explained in Unit 1. Their attribute is that they can be removed from the sentence (and often are in colloquial* use) without affecting the sense.

10. However, there is in Japanese another set of particles which by their nature cannot normally be left out without losing the sense. Many European languages have prepositions*–on, towards, of–which explain the relation between two concepts and which go in front of a noun, for example "*on* the table". Japanese has particles which do the same job, but which come after the noun and thus can be called post-positions*. Because they are basic tools of the language many of them are used and explained in Unit 1.

11. As to (c) in para 2 – *syntax* – the key point is that in all languages the main statement being made is embodied in a *main clause*. We then have conjunctions* as words which link two statements. Sometimes these statements are of equal weight: he was drinking *and* eating; tired *but* happy. As we shall see in Unit 1, Japanese, unlike most languages, does not readily place such clauses in parallel, but instead often puts the first verb in the form of the participle or of the "-masu stem*" (see Appendix 2).

12. One over-riding feature of Japanese syntax is its reliance on word order: *words or clauses which comment on another word or clause have to come before the word or clause they refer to.* You cannot say in Japanese "He drank after he had eaten"; it has to be "After he had eaten he drank". In practice, therefore, the main verb nearly always lands up at the end of the sentence. In our grammar notes we deal in some detail with the consequences of this rule for the comprehension of written Japanese.

13. We have tried to keep our grammar notes reasonably short and have avoided grammatical jargon except where it is more effective to use it than not. The Alphabetical Reference Grammar offers definitions of the terms commonly used and also deeper explanations where required.

◇ ◇ **Grammar Notes** ◇ ◇

A Desu *is*, in the polite form (plain form–da–see Note O below). Because it joins or links two concepts (Kazuo *is* a man, Tokyo *is* a capital) this verb is often called the copula* in Japanese, to distinguish it from the two verbs "to be" in the sense of exist: as we shall see these are iru when the subjects* are animate and aru (see Note G) for inanimate subjects.

B1 Japanese relies on adding particles* *after* a word (sometimes called post-positions*) to do the work done in many other languages by using prepositions* (which by definition precede the noun). A number of post-positions figure in this paragraph.

The particle ga is the tag used here to mark the subject of the verb. Wa (see just below) is the tag for the topic of the sentence; it may or not also be the subject of a verb.

The particle no after a noun usually means possession ("of") but no is also used, as here in mon no soba ni, to link what we would call an adverb of place (*near*) with a noun. No can also link two nouns so as to make the first one adjectival, as in the title of this unit chuuko no kuruma "car of second hand" (Cf French *voiture d'occasion*).

Ni is the particle which indicates the place at which someone or something is, stays, lives, stands; thus here mon no soba ni *near / by the gate* (stands Masako Tanaka). Similarly, just below, with koko ni sunde imasu. (Ni after the noun can also indicate the person to whom something is given (see futari ni wa below) and the agent* by whom something is done).

To summarise this initial description of Japanese particles:

wa   topic of sentence

ga   subject of verb (in 'we buy a car'–we is the subject)

o   object* of verb (kuruma o kaimashita *they bought a car*; car is the object)

no   possession—of what or of whom—and a link between an adverb and a noun: mon no soba *near the door*, ki no shita *under the tree*; or between two nouns—chuuko no kuruma

ni   to whom, and place in or on, as here in mon no soba ni and (see below) after naru *become*.

de   instrument* with which (kuruma de *by car*) and also place at which an action takes place.

Unit I

B2　Other particles, which also come after the noun, include:

    to, ya and

    e   towards (inaka e–below)

    mo   also (inu mo imasu–below).

C　**Tatte** is the present* participle* of **tatsu** *to stand* (for the change of consonant in **tatsu** to **tatte** see Verb Table 2). The participle used with the present of **iru** (*to be*) forms the present continuous*–the English "is standing". Cf **sunde imasu** below.

D　**Otto no** uses **no** to link two nouns (said to be in "apposition*") "Her husband, Mr. Tanaka".

E　**Dete kimashita**; **kimashita** is the past tense of **kuru** (Verb Table 4). Here the two verbs used together, of which the first is in the form of a participle (going out + come), mean "appear".

There is no exact equivalent in Japanese of the English tense ("has come") but the past tense here implies that Tanaka had come out while we were watching.

F　For the numbers up to ten there are two parallel number* systems: thus here **futa-ri** *two* (persons) in the native Japanese system, while **san** and **roku** *three* and *six* in the "Chinese" system. One and two in the Japanese system each have two forms incorporating different counters (see Note I below); for these numbers alone the ending/counter* in **-ri** is for people, and the ending/counter in **-tsu** is for things: **hitori, hitotsu; futari, futatsu**.

G　**A ni (wa) B ga arimasu** is a common way of saying *A has B*. Normally, as with **ko-inu** below, the verb to be with animate subjects is **iru**. However, all language is subject to exceptions, and in Japanese enumerations like those of the members of a family, as here, use not **imasu** but **arimasu**.

H　We have in **shiro-i** and **genki-na** examples of the two main sets of adjectives* in Japanese. Those with the ending **-i** are the original Japanese adjectives. They have negative forms, a plain form past tense, and other forms like those of verbs (see Table 7)

The other class, sometimes called pseudo-adjectives*, are made by the addition to the basic form (or "adjectival noun*") of the suffix **-na** when the adjective is used attributively*–ie right next to a noun. The basic form is used by itself in other cases; for example genki *having good health* (cf the greeting "genki desu ka?"). But "a healthy person" requires the addition of -na, genki-na hito. The -na adjectives do not conjugate* like verbs.

I   *Thirty* is sanjuu, but there is a phonetic change to short u here because sanjuu is followed by a counter* for years. Counters* are used regularly in Japanese but exceptionally in English–as in "head" of cattle, "cloves" of garlic. A few of the Japanese combinations of number and counter are subject to phonetic changes.

J   In conformity with the Japanese rule (see Guide to the Grammar Notes para 12) that what qualifies* or modifies* something has to come before the thing which is qualified or modified, the objects being compared (comparison*) must, in Japanese, come before the adjective carrying the attribute; eg age or size. Thus M yori K wa ookii desu or K wa M yori ookii desu both mean "K is bigger than M". Here ue means above; thus "three years above (ie *older than*) Masako".

K   As pointed out in the introduction to these notes, when English has two clauses* in parallel Japanese often uses a participle for the verb of the first clause. Thus, here, de is the participle of desu, and dete is the participle of deru (*go out*). See also tsukutte in para 3 below.

L   An important construction–formation of the verbal noun*; that is, the verb used as a noun (eg *shaving* is a bore, *drinking* is dangerous). Daisuki desu "is very likeable" is the main verb and, as usual, is at the end of the sentence. Its subject is the verbal noun iku no ga "going", formed from the dictionary form* of the verb iku + no + (in this case) ga because the verbal noun is the subject of the verb – the copula desu.

M   Kono aida (literally "this interval of time") *recently*. Ko- used above in koko (*here*) and kono futari (*this couple*) is the syllable which determines a set of demonstrative* pronouns and adjectives indicating *this* ie what is near both to the speaker and to the person being addressed.

N   Ooki-na is anomalous: ookii is one of the group of so-called Japanese adjectives; it is the other group–the "pseudo" adjectives (Note H above)–that take na after them when used together with the noun they describe; eg kirei-na (*pretty*), shizuka-na (*quiet*). However, ookii is one of just a few "Japanese" adjectives that sometimes take -na.

O A simple case of reported speech; the original statement would have been takaku arimasen/nai desu *it is not dear* (for the negative form of the adjective, based on the adverbial form ending in -ku, see Table 7). To make this into a noun-clause*–object of omoimashita *they thought*–the verb remains in its original tense* (present) but goes into the plain form nai, and the particle to (in a different usage from that in B2 above) is added; *they thought it was not dear.*

Similarly, just below, the direct* statement was juubun da *it is enough*; the indirect* statement becomes juubun da to omoimashita.

P Han is a *half*, bun is a *part* or *portion*; hanbun *a half*. Hantoshi bun "half-a-year portion". Node means *as, because* with the plain form of the verb.

Q Tame ni is an important phrase meaning *in order to* ; kau tame ni *in order to buy* (the car).

R Another example of reported/indirect* speech, with a slight difference. The original statement would be "yasuku arimasen" or "yasuku nai desu" *it is not cheap*. As in Note O above the direct speech is reported, in Japanese, with the same tense as in the original, and using the plain form of the verb, yasuku nai. However, the difference is in the choice of tag. Whereas English regards all noun clauses as roughly equivalent (He thinks he is Napoleon; he knows that he is tall) the Japanese tend to use the particle to after omou (*to believe*), but after shiru (*to know*) they look for something more concrete. Thus here the tag attaching to the noun clause is koto o. Koto *thing* or *fact* ; it has added to it, according as the noun clause is the subject or object of a verb, either ga or, as here, o. The phrase means, therefore, *they knew (the fact that) petrol was (is) not cheap.*

One further point is the use here of shitte imashita. Instead of "they know" Japanese says "they are knowing"; thus "they knew" becomes "they were knowing"...

S Ga here is not the same as the subject tag, but acts as a conjunction* joining two statements, often, as here, with a meaning intermediate between "and" and "but".

T Shikata ga nai/arimasen is a set phrase or idiom*; the basic meaning of shikata is "way of doing something". Thus shikata ga nai roughly means *No way* ! but in the sense of *There is no other way* or *It can't be helped.*

U Importantly, this is the Japanese equivalent of a relative* clause, as in "(the man) who was here", "(the house) that Jack built." The neat adjectival phrase* **kogai ni tomeru** *to park outside* comes before the noun (**tokoro**) to which it refers: "the 'park outside' place".

V   Here we have more reported* speech, this time an indirect question*. It was put directly by the children as "(To) where are we going by car?" **Kuruma de doko e iki-masu ka?** As reported in English the question becomes "The children asked where they were going by car"–ie the tense changes (from present to past). In Japanese the tense remains what it was in the original, and the particle **ka** (almost equivalent to the question mark) also stays. The only difference is that the verb changes from the polite form **ikimasu** (assuming that this is what the children used) to the plain form **iku**.

Unit 1

◇◇ Japanese Proper Names ◇◇

Japanese names of families and also of companies, except where these are abbreviations, are often derived from native Japanese words, particularly those implying a geographical feature identifying landmarks or the place where the family lived. (As in English Fieldhouse, Whetstone). As a caution it should be borne in mind that some names can be rendered in several ways by the use of different characters.

Here are some names based on the simple roots used in this Unit 1.

Root	Kanji name	Transliteration	Meaning
ta/da	町田	Machida	town ricefield
	前田	Maeda	front field
	住田	Sumita	ricefield home (sumu *to reside*)
	森田	Morita	forest ricefield
	上田	Ueda	upper ricefield/above the ricefield
	安田	Yasuda	safe field
chiisai/ko/o	小松	Komatsu	little pine
KO/furui	古田	Furuta	old field
	古川	Furukawa	old river
	古口	KOguchi*	old entrance
taka	高木	Takagi	high tree
	高石	Takaishi	high stone
GAI/soto	外山	Sotoyama	outer mountain

*Because Japanese names are of Japanese (Yamato) origin almost all the elements in these names have the native (kun) reading. Anomalously, the KO in Koguchi has the ON reading.

◇ ◇ Practice Sentences and Themes ◇ ◇

It is important for the learner to have an opportunity of reinforcing his/her acquisition of the words and syntax of each unit. One path to this end is that of translation from English to Japanese using the material in each unit.

This can be initially discouraging, however, since the pattern of Japanese is so very different from that of English, and the new structure has to be learnt. To set out these changes in the form of rules, as needs to be done for machine translation, would be too intricate a task. However, to help in the learning of the new patterns we give, after each set of English sentences, an intermediate version which conveys an idea of the transformations required in the process of moving from English to Japanese.

There is no entirely satisfactory representation of such a text, but we have chosen these conventions:

1   Where an English word is not needed in the Japanese it is in square brackets. (For example "the" and "a" and very often the subject of a verb.)

2   Where a Japanese particle or postposition takes the place of an English preposition and comes after the noun, the phrase affected is hyphenated. (For example, "of-[their]-children" indicates **kodomo no**.)

3   Whereas the English conjunctions like when, while, after, before, because, come at the beginning of the phrase or clause they introduce, the Japanese equivalent comes at the end of its phrase or clause. "After [they] left" is **dete kara**. Inconvenient though this method is, we show this as "[they] left after".

4   Where a single Japanese verb form is to be used, the equivalent English phrase is hyphenated. (For example, "is-done" (passive) is **sareru**.)

5   To accustom the learner to the use of the Japanese particles, these have at this stage been inserted in hiragana in the transformed English text.

6   "Is" and "are" represent the Japanese copula **da/desu**; when **iru** or **aru** need to be used the English *is* "exists".

7   The question mark at the end of an English sentence is retained, but it has to be replaced in Japanese by the particle **ka**.

◇◇ English into Japanese ◇◇

Sentences and Themes

1. Masako and Kazuo Tanaka (the family name comes first in Japanese) have two children and a dog, so they bought a large car.

2. One (一人 hitori) of their children (of the children one) is six years old.

3. The car they bought ("the they bought"–買った katta–car) was cheap.

4. They did not think the car they bought was dear. (For reported speech* add と to. "They did not think" goes at the end of the sentence.)

5. Office workers like very much to leave Tokyo (For "to leave Tokyo" use dictionary form + のが no ga).

6. They intend to go for a drive on Sunday.

Transformation

1. Tanaka Maskao san と Kazuo san は of-children two と dog exist, therefore [they] large car を bought.

2. Of-[the]-children one は six (+ counter) is.

3. [The] [they] bought car は was-cheap (using cheap in its own past tense).

4. [The] [they] bought car は dear is (plain form) と [they] did-not-think.

5. Office-workers は Tokyo を to leave (dictionary form + のが) very-much-liked is.

6. On-Sunday drive to-make (dictionary form) intention is.

Unit 2
THE PICNIC

ピクニック

Frontispiece character : 森 mori *forest*

◇ ◇ **Introductory Note** ◇ ◇

We continue to use simple characters, still including some which are also radicals, but there are in addition a number of composite kanji; though these are chosen for their relative simplicity. By composite kanji, we mean those single characters which have at least two components, one of which is the radical by which the character can be distinguished from its homophones. The radicals are given emphasis in these first units as a first step towards recognising the patterns of the kanji.

We also introduce a few simple compounds (combinations of two kanji):

国土 KOKUDO, 地図 CHIZU, 気分 KIBUN, 大分 DAIBU,
竹林 CHIKURIN, 毎日 MAINICHI, 谷川 tanigawa, 夕方 yuugata.

Several important constructions are repeated for reinforcement–including the Japanese equivalent of the relative* clause (the man *whom I saw*), a clause* giving a reason (because…), more indirect/reported speech*, and the further use of particles.

As new points of grammar we have a noun clause* as the subject of a verb, the simultaneous* form of the verb ending in nagara (while doing…), nouns formed from adjectives, a subordinate clause using "although", the use of participle* + shimau ("finish up by…"), participle + kara meaning "after", the use of the - masu* stem* with verbs meaning to start or stop doing something, the desiderative* form of the verb (I want to…), a first example of the passive*, and the first use of a hypothetical* = if/when clause.

あって、雲は一つもありません。向こうの高い山には、まだ白い雪が見えます。田中さんは、毎日の忙しさを忘れ始めました。

（五）それから、谷に下りて、虫がいない谷川のそばへ行きました。皆（犬の他）が作ったサンドイッチの包みを出して、草の上で食べました。

（六）子供は、川に入りたいと言ったのに、母は水が汚いと言って許しませんでした。それで、言われたようにしました。代わりに、兄と妹は、川で手を洗うだけでした。

（七）雨になったら、家に帰って、子供はテレビを見て、父はビールを飲みながら夕刊を読んで、母はお茶を入れたでしょう。でも、一日中、好い天気で、夕方、東京へ向かいました。今日は、良い日でした。

ピクニック

（一）日本は、国土の七十五パーセントが、百五十の火山を入れて、山です。それで、日本人の田中さんが、山と森が大好きだと言う事は、ちょうどよいです。

（二）今日は日曜日でドライブをします。まだ朝早いですが、外はもう明るいです。皆は、地図をみながら、北の方へ向かいました。

（三）女の子が気分が良くないと言ったので、車を止めましたが、吐いてしまいました。それで、少し休みました。

（四）又、大分走ってから、やっと車を止めて、林の中の道を歩きました。丘に上って辺りを見下ろしました。牛がいる畑の角に竹林があります。木々の上は風が少し

PIKUNIKKU

1 Nihon wa, kokudo no nanajuugo paasento ga[a], hyakugojuu no kazan o irete, yama desu. Sorede, Nihonjin no[b] Tanaka san ga, yama to mori ga dai-suki da to iu koto[c] wa, choodo ii desu.

2 Kyoo wa nichiyoobi de doraibu o shimasu. Mada asa hayai[d] desu ga, soto wa moo akarui[d] desu. Mina wa, chizu o minagara[e], kita no hoo e mukaimashita.

3 Onna no ko ga kibun ga yoku nai to itta node[f], kuruma o tomemashita ga, haite shi-maimashita[g]. Sorede, sukoshi yasumimashi-ta.

4 Mata, daibu hashitte kara[h], yatto kuruma o tomete, hayashi no naka no michi o[i] aruki-mashita. Oka ni nobotte atari o mioroshi-mashita. Ushi ga iru[j] hatake no kado ni chikurin ga arimasu. Kigi no ue wa kaze ga sukoshi atte, kumo wa hitotsu mo[k] arimasen. Mukoo no takai yama ni wa, mada shiroi yuki ga miema-su. Tanaka san wa mainichi no isogashisa[l] o wasure[m] hajimemashita.

THE PICNIC

Seventy-five percent of Japan's territory is moun-tain, including 150 volcanos. So it is just as well that the Japanese, of whom Mr Tanaka is one, like mountains and forests.

Today is Sunday and they are going for a drive. It is still early morning, but it is already bright outside. Keeping an eye on the map they head-ed northwards.

Because the (little) girl said she was not feeling well they stopped the car, but she still ended up by being sick. So they rested for a bit.

After going on for some time they at last stopped the car and walked along a road in a wood. They climbed a hill and had a view of their sur-roundings. At the corner of a field where there were cattle there was a bamboo wood. Above the trees there was little wind, and not even a single cloud. On the high mountains over there some white snow could be seen. Mr Tanaka started to forget his daily routine. (Literally "being busy").

5 Sorekara, tani ni orite, mushi ga inai[n] tani-gawa no soba e ikimashita. Mina–inu no hoka–ga tsukutta[n] sandoitchi no tsutsumi o dashite, kusa no ue de[o] tabemashita.

They then went down into the valley and came to a (place) near a stream where there were no insects. They got out the parcel of sandwiches they had all made, apart from the dog, and ate them on the grass.

6 Kodomo wa, kawa ni hairitai[p] to[q] itta no ni[r], haha wa mizu ga kitanai to[q] itte yurushimasen deshita. Sorede, iwareta[s] yoo ni[t] shimashita. Kawari ni, ani to imooto wa, kawa de te o arau dake[u] deshita.

Although the children said they wanted to go in the river the mother said the water was dirty and did not allow it. They did what they were told. Instead, the elder brother and his younger sister only washed their hands in the river.

7 Ame ni nattara[v], uchi e kaette, kodomo wa terebi o mite, chichi wa biiru o nominagara[x] yuukan o yonde, haha wa ocha o ireta deshoo[w]. Demo, ichi-nichi juu, ii tenki de[y], yuu-gata, Tookyoo e mukaimashita. Kyoo wa, ii hi deshita.

If there had been rain they would have gone home and the children would have watched television, their father would have read the evening paper while having a beer and the mother would have made tea. However, the weather was good all day, and in the evening they turned back towards Tokyo. Today had been a good day.

Unit 2

◇ ◇ Notes on Kanji ◇ ◇

As with Unit 1, only those readings are shown at this stage which are relevant to the meaning in the text or to the derivation of the kanji.

KANJI	RADICAL			reading	KANJI
character	no	shape	meaning		derivation and meaning
日	72	日	sun	NICHI/hi	Radical: pictorial of sun; *day*.
本	(2)	｜	line	HON	Derived from tree + earth line, hence becomes trunk of tree; *origin*. ◆日本 NIHON/Nippon–origin of sun, *Japan*.
国	31	口	enclosure	KOKU/kuni	A simplified character; now = jewel (**tama**) within a boundary = *country*. (?Mnemonic: "…precious stone set in the silver sea…this England"–*Richard II*).
土	32	土	earth	DO/tsuchi	Radical: pile of earth, and hence, *soil*. ◆国土 KOKUDO *national territory*.
七	(5)	∟	vertical line with loop	SHICHI/na-na	Mnemonic: 7 upside down; (pronounced *shchi*–like cabbage soup in Russian); *seven*. ◆七十五 nana JUU GO *seventy-five*.
百	(1)	一	line	HYAKU	Phonetic, with an added line, derived from sign for *shiroi* (white) above, **ON** readings of which are **HAKU, BYAKU** (both are "bai" in Chinese). ◆百五十 HYAKU GO JUU *one-hundred and fifty*.
火	86	火	fire	KA/hi	Radical: pictorial of *fire*.
山	46	山	mountain	ZAN/yama	Radical: pictorial of *mountain*. ◆火山 KAZAN *volcano*.

KANJI	RADICAL			KANJI	
character	no	shape	meaning	reading	derivation and meaning
入	11	入	enter	i-reru/hai-ru	Radical: pictorial of entrance door; *go in* (hairu and iru), *put in* (ireru). Here **irete** is participle of transitive **ireru**; *including*. (See also end of this text, where **ireru** means "pour in" the tea).
森	75	木	tree	mori	Pictorial: a lot of trees = *forest*.
事	(6)	⌡	line	koto	The lower part is a hand, writing; box at the top is something more concrete; thus it means an event or thing worth recording (see also Unit 1).
今	9	人	person	KON/ima	Unclear origin; top half often implies coming together (as in **kai** of **kaisha** = company). Here and now? Or bottom as pointer of sun-dial? Mnemonic: "today's meeting is at seven". ◆今日 **KYOO** *today*. This is another of the anomalous readings referred to in Unit 1 (ref **inaka**). But **KONGETSU** in Unit 1 para 1, (this month) is a normal reading, and so is the salutation 今日は **KONNICHI** wa.
朝	130	月	moon	asa	Phonetic lost with change of radical in simplified version: as it stands, mnemonic is plus sun plus moon, and so, *morning*.
早	72	日	sun	haya-i	Derived from the sun rising over horizon; *early*.
明	72	日	sun	akaru-i	Sun and moon; *bright*. (Cf **ashita** in Unit 1). Chinese sign for Ming dynasty.

| KANJI | RADICAL | | | KANJI | |
character	no	shape	meaning	reading	derivation and meaning
地	32	土	earth	CHI	Origin unclear because several primitives were confused: (hence TA/hoka in Unit 1). RHS phonetic CHI used also for lake; *land*.
図	31	口	enclosure	ZU	A simplified kanji: plan of a plan; sketch, *map*. ◆地図 CHIZU *a map*.
見	147	見	to see	KEN/mi-ru/ mi-eru/mi- seru	Radical: eye on legs: miru = *see*, mieru = *be visible* – (para 4 below), and miseru = *to show*.
北	21	匕	spoon!	HOKU/kita	In spite of the radical = two persons back to back, apparently facing North and South: this sign = *north*.
方	70	方	direction	HOO/kata	See SHIkata in Unit 1: here, sign has basic meaning of direction. (Cf also yuugata, towards evening, in para 7 below).
向	(2)	丨	vertical	mu-kau/mu- koo	A window facing outwards. Mukau = to turn towards; mukoo = on the other side of; in para 4 below = "over there".
女	38	女	female	onna	Radical: female silhouette; *woman*.
良	138	艮	undefined	i-i/yo-i	Origin obscure: gift from heaven? or a measure? or washed grain and a spoon?. Whatever the origin, here it means *good*. Cf taberu below.
吐	30	口	mouth	ha-ku	Neatly pictorial: mouth + ground; *be sick, vomit*.

Other Compound ◇気分 KIBUN *state, mood*. (Cf GENKI and BUN in Unit 1 .)

KANJI	RADICAL			KANJI	
character	no	shape	meaning	reading	derivation and meaning
少	(4)	ノ	(slash)	suko-shi	The slash is added to sign for 小さい chiisai, small (three dots or lines):hence, *a little* (pron. *skoshi*).
休	9	亻	person	yasu-mu	Classic derivation: man + tree; *to rest.*
又	29	又	hand	mata	Radical: used mainly as component of kanji, here by itself–no doubt in the spirit of "on the one hand, on the other"– *again, also.*
走	156	走	run	hashi-ru	Radical: one of several signs with feet or legs; the basic sign 止 (radical 77) is said to show a leg, foot and toes at rest, and is used as tomeru (stop) in Unit 1 and here. SOKU/ashi = leg (radical 157) is another of the family, and the present character is related to it, possibly showing the man (on top) bending as he *runs.*
林	75	木	tree	RIN/hayashi	Two trees; smaller than 森 mori above; *a wood.* As Hayashi, a common family name (corresponding to Lin in Mandarin).
道	162	辶	motion forward	DOO/michi	Main component is radical 185, a head; with forward motion radical > heading, direction > *road.* (Cf 柔道 JUUDOO and 神道 SHINTOO = "soft way" and "gods' way").
歩	77	止	stop	aru-ku	Base is either the top part (radical 77) reversed > both feet, or it can be seen as sukoshi (see above): in which case, to "stop a little"; *walk.*
丘	(4)	ノ	(line)	oka	Two peaks and hence, *a hill.* (Very common in place names).

Other Compound ◇大分 DAIBU *quite a lot, for some time.* (Cf DAI and BUN in Unit 1 .)

Unit 2

KANJI character	RADICAL			KANJI	
	no	shape	meaning	reading	derivation and meaning
上	(25)	卜	(oracle)	nobo-ru	Same sign as ue (over) in Unit 1, and here in para 5 "on the grass": as verb, it means *climb*. See contrasting sign 下 for shita just below.
辺	162	辶	motion	HEN/ata-ri	A simplification of earlier kanji, apparently meaning to walk over the edge; *district*.
下	(1)	一	(line)	KA/GE/shita/o-riru/o-rosu/kuda-ru	Spacial converse of ue in (Unit 1): orosu = to drop; oriru = go down (para 5 below); among other readings are shita (eg ki no shita = under a tree), and kudasai = "please". Here miru + orosu becomes miorosu; *look down at*.
牛	93	牛	ox, cow	GYUU/ushi	Radical: originally with two horns, one is now crumpled; *cattle*.
畑	86	火	fire	hatake	Not borrowed, but a kanji made in Japan: fire radical + paddy; *a field* which is cleared by burning. (Fire radical not to be confused with water–see mizu below).
角	148	角	corner, horn	KAKU/kado/tsuno	Radical: can be seen as radical 130 肉 = meat, (hanging up?) + horns. Reading tsuno only means *horn*. (In English too, horn and *corner* are related).
竹	118	竹	bamboo	CHIKU/take	Radical: plant with branches drooping. ◆竹林 CHIKURIN or takebayashi *bamboo wood or copse*.
木	75	木	tree	ki	Pictorial; kigi is collective, cf hitobito, people. Note once more change of consonant k to g, as in, tomo to domo, hayashi to bayashi.

KANJI	RADICAL			KANJI	
character	no	shape	meaning	reading	derivation and meaning
々					This sign (almost, but not quite, the same as **ma** in katakana マ) indicates the repetition of a syllable; it can be given the addition ゛ when, as here, the repeated consonant is voiced.
風	182	風	wind	kaze	Radical: inside said to be a snake (but cf **mushi** below); outside = a sail; mnemonic could be insects carried along by *the wind*?
雲	173	雨	rain	kumo	Top is rain radical; the base represents layers of mist or *cloud.*
雪	173	雨	rain	yuki	Rain radical + radical 58 彐 (pig's head > broom?); *snow.*
見	147	見	see	mi-eru	See above; here **mieru** = *is visible.* (Cf 聞こえる ki-koeru = to be heard).
毎	80	母	mother	MAI	Perhaps "woman with hair-do" or mnemonic "everyone had a mother"; *every.* ◆毎日 MAINICHI *every day.*
忙	61	忄	heart (short form)	BOO/isoga-shii	RHS top is, plausibly, a lid with someone or something under it, and so, hiding or getting lost; it means, by itself, to die: as BOO, this sign finds its way into several kanji. Here the phonetic, with heart radical in its short form; *busy.*
忘	8	亠	lid	BOO/wasu-reru	See above entry: oddly, the connection here is semantic, as well as phonetic; *forget.*

Unit 2

KANJI	RADICAL			KANJI	
character	no	shape	meaning	reading	derivation and meaning
始	38	女	woman	haji-meru	RHS by itself is a platform: (cf 台所 DAIdokoro kitchen–place with a plinth). This sign, thanks to shaky phonetics, becomes *begin*. ?Mnemonic: one *begins* by putting the lady on a pedestal.
谷	150	谷	valley	tani	Radical: water gushing between banks; *valley*.
下	(1)	一	(line)	o-riru	See miorosu above.
虫	142	虫	insect	mushi	Radical: cf creature in kaze (above); pictorial; *insect*.
川	47	川	river	kawa	Radical: symbolic of water flowing; *river*. (See also proper names). ◆谷川 tanigawa *valley stream.*
草	140	艹	plant	SOO/kusa	Typical case of phonetic derivation; bottom half is hayai (early, as in para 2 of this text). The ON reading of hayai is SOO; "grass" has the same ON reading SOO, but the meaning is distinguished by adding here the radical for plants; *grass*.
食	184	食	eat	ta-beru	Radical: a kanji to be learnt; said to have once represented rice, bowl and spoon, with lid to keep it hot; can be mnemonically associated with yoi above–"good to *eat* under a roof"; *eat*.
水	85	水	water	mizu	Radical: similar to KA (fire), but differentiated from it by the two side components ending in roughly horizontal lines, instead of leaping flames; *water*.

KANJI	RADICAL			KANJI	
character	no	shape	meaning	reading	derivation and meaning
汚	85	氵	water (radical form)	kitana-i	RHS meant spoon or concavity; with water radical, it becomes a puddle; now means *dirty*.
許	149	言	speech	KYO/yuru-su	Phonetic; ON reading from RHS is KYO–a tool to pound with (pestle); same sign also borrowed for 午 GO midday; here, with speech radical, *to allow*.
代	9	亻	person	ka-wari	Origin vague; RHS is radical 56 弋 javelin, no obvious connection with meaning of substitution. Here, *instead* (of this).
兄	30	口	mouth	ani	Plausibly, a big-head or mouth on legs; *elder brother*.
妹	38	女	woman	imooto/MAI	Origin probably phonetic: RHS alone = MI (not yet), shown as a tree with a line near the top meaning "not yet grown"; *younger sister*.
手	64	手	hand	te	Radical: pictorial of fingers; *hand*.
洗	85	氵	water	SEN/ara-u	Another clear phonetic derivation; RHS is SEN = in front or senior. With water radical, it means *wash*.
雨	173	雨	rain	ame	Radical: pictorial, with sky above; *rain*.
家	40	宀	lid, roof	ie often read as uchi though strictly this is another kanji 内 NAI/uchi *inside*.	Base is radical 152, a pig; with roof radical on top, it means *house, home*.

KANJI character	RADICAL			KANJI	
	no	shape	meaning	reading	derivation and meaning
帰	58	ヨ	pig's head (broom)	kae-ru	Simplified, but still hard. Top RHS is a broom (cf yuki above); LHS is residual of a leg. ?Mnemonic: "Golden lads and girls all must, like chimney-sweepers, come to dust." (*Cymbeline*) (Note: in Japanese, you cannot say to go home (iku); it has to be kuru (come) or kaeru *return*. By itself, kaeru can mean *go home* or *leave*).
父	88	父	father	chichi	Radical: regrettably, hands wielding a stick; *father*.
飲	184	食	eat	no-mu	RHS primitive (radical 76) for having mouth open; LHS is taberu (above): mnemonic–after eating you open mouth *to drink*.
夕	36	夕	evening	yuu	Radical: crescent moon; *evening*. ◆夕方 yuugata (see HOO/kata in para 2), *evening*.
刊	51	干	shield?	KAN	LHS phonetic; with RHS = cutting tool, becomes to carve letters, thus, *publish*. ◆夕刊 yuuKAN *evening edition* (anomalous compound of kun and ON readings).
読	149	言	words	yo-mu	RHS 売 = sell (mnemonic: man [SHI as in SHIgoto; see Unit 1] + desk). LHS speech radical implies that words are being sold; *read*.
茶	140	艹	plant	CHA	Said to be phonetic, but mnemonic is tree + roof + radical for plant: sitting in a house drinking *tea*.
天	(1)	一	(line)	TEN/ame	What is above man: heaven. ◆天気 TENKI ,*weather*. (If a kanji is used with TENKI to mean good [weather], it has to be 好き suki [see above], but it is pronounced ii).

◇ ◇ **Grammar Notes** ◇ ◇

A   Another example of the idiomatic* **wa...ga...** construction that we saw in Note G of Unit 1. "Japan **wa**, 75% of its territory **ga** is mountain".

B   **No** is used here to link two nouns, rather as in **otto no Kazuo Tanaka** in Note D of Unit 1. Here "of the Japanese Mr Tanaka..." = Mr Tanaka as one of the Japanese.

C   This is a foretaste of the regular, but at first somewhat opaque, Japanese construction where a long noun* clause* is the subject* of a verb. It can perhaps be seen as an open sandwich: the bread, the main clause which holds the structure together, = **choodo ii desu** = *is just as well*. The smorgas on the sandwich, the subject of the main verb, is the whole noun clause "**...Tanaka san ga yama to mori ga dai-suki da to iu koto wa**" = *the fact that Mr Tanaka very much likes mountains and woods.*

We have already seen in Unit 1, the use of **to** and of **koto o** appended to a phrase to turn it into indirect speech*. Here is a third way of making a noun clause, by adding "**to iu koto**" to the phrase. **Iu** means "to say", so literally the phrase implies "the fact that one can say that..." It is often used in expressions like this, where the emphasis is on the judgement made.

D   **Hayai** is a true Japanese adjective* (see Note H of Unit 1) and therefore contains its own plain form copula* (ie by itself it means "It is early"). However, the polite form, which we are using, requires the addition of **desu**. Similarly with **akarui desu**.

E   **Mina̲gara** (emphasis on the **na**) is the simultaneous* form of the verb, used to mean that the action is performed at the same time as another–while doing A they did B. Cf **nomina̲gara** in para 7 below. **Mi-ru** is, of course, a Group II* verb (see Table 3 following the Alphabetical Reference Grammar).

F   **...kibun ga yoku nai to itta node: node** is a conjunction*, coming at the end of its clause, meaning "because", and hence, *because she said...* What she said (direct* speech) was **kibun ga yoku nai/arimasen** = "feeling is not good" and thus, *I don't feel well.* To make this into indirect/reported* speech, the verb stays in its original tense* (English changes the tense and says "that she *was* not feeling well") using the plain* form (**nai**) with the addition of **to** showing it is a quote.

G   Haite is the participle* of haku (to be sick) just as kaite is the participle* of kaku (Table 1). The idiomatic* use of shimau with a participle is very typical of Japanese; it implies a discontinuity–*ending up by* doing something, often unpleasant or surprising.

H   Kara is a post-position* used after nouns* to mean "from" and with the participle, as here, to mean "*after…*". By contrast, with an adjective* or a different part of the verb kara = *because.*

I   In Japanese, the road you walk or go along is the object* of the verb of motion and thus takes the tag o–…michi o arukimashita.

J   Another example of the Japanese equivalent of the relative* clause. Ushi ga iru = *where there are cattle,* qualifying* hatake (*field*). Note that the verb "to be" is iru for cattle (as animate) but aru for the copse and the wind.

K   Mo, as a particle*, = *also,* but hitotsu + mo + negative = *there is not even one…* Incidentally, the mixture of present and past tense found in this paragraph is quite normal in Japanese, making the narration more vivid.

L   The adjective isogashi-i = *busy.* The suffix -sa is added, like our -ness, to give the corresponding noun: high is takai (with stem* taka) and takasa = height. As it happens we cannot, in English, say "busyness", but that is literally what isogashisa means.

M   We have noted that there is no infinitive* as such in Japanese. Thus to begin to do something, or to finish doing something, or to continue to do something, requires in Japanese that form of the verb conveniently called the -masu stem*–that is, the form of the verb to which the endings masu and mashita are added. This is a Group II verb in -eru–wasureru–so the -masu stem is wasure. (See Tables).

N   Yet another example of the equivalent of the relative clause. Here, tanigawa (valley stream) is qualified* by the adjectival* clause mushi ga inai = the "there are no insects" valley stream, using the plain form inai–the negative present tense of iru, used with animate objects, even flies,to mean there is, there are–and here, there are not.

This sentence exemplifies the general rule in Japanese that what qualifies a noun, verb or adjective must come in front of the noun, verb or adjective. It is because of this rule, that the main verb is commonly at the end of the sentence–since all the adjectival, noun and adverbial phrases, and indeed the object* of the verb, have to be got out of the way first.

The same relative* construction again in mina ga tsukutta (*which they had all made*) qualifying sandoitchi.

O   We saw in Unit 1 that the particle/post-position ni is used to mean 'at' a place where you are standing, or living; but when some action is being performed (here = eating) the particle/postposition* used is de, as it is just below, with te o arau.

P   The desiderative* form of the verb–meaning "want to...". It is in fact an adjective, and, standing alone, counts as a plain form (see next note); in polite* speech it would be followed by desu (or 'n desu).

Q   Two more examples of indirect/reported* speech; the plain form of the verb is used + the quote particle to. In the first case, the child said "...hairitai" and in the second case the mother said "Mizu ga kitanai". In reported speech the phrases are left just as they were in direct speech, with no change of tense* but are followed by to.

R   No ni at the end of the phrase means "although". Once more, because this is a subordinate* clause, the verb used–itta–is the plain past of iu = to say (cf para 3 above).

S   Iwareta is a passive* form–the passive plain past tense (literally "was said", from iwareru, passive form from the root iu = "to say"). (The w, lost from some forms of a number of verbs of which the stem now appears to end in a vowel, reappears in the past and the negative. Hence, for example, iwanai–negative present of iu to say; kawanai is the negative present of kau, to buy–originally kawu; see also Table 2).

The passive is used here idiosyncratically in the same way as the English passive "the children were told..."–a convenient construction not possible in European languages apart from English.

T ...yoo ni = *as, in the way that...*, followed by a plain form verb, as noted several times, because it is the verb of a subordinate* clause.

U The dictionary* form arau (wash) followed by dake desu (it is only) is the normal way of saying in Japanese (they) only wash... "I only <u>speak</u> Japanese" (ie I can't read it) would be "watashi wa Nihongo o hanasu dake desu".

V An "if/when" clause. <u>Na</u>ttara (emphasis on the na) is a hypothetical* = "if/when" (sometimes called the conjunctive*) form of the verb naru (to become). Naru needs after it the adverbial form of an adjective (takaku naru = to become tall) and with a noun complement it takes the particle -ni. Thus, the phrase means "if it came to rain = if there were rain", or "if there had been rain". (We shall see later other ways of expressing "if/when" clauses.)

W There is no tense in Japanese corresponding to the English or French conditional* for the follow-up main verb after an "if" clause–"...they would have done this or that...". The ordinary present or past (as here) is used instead, sometimes with the addition of deshoo to a verb to give it the meaning "might have...".

X Nomi<u>na</u>gara, from nomu (to drink), (emphasis on the na) is, like minagara in para 2, what we have called in the verb tables the simultaneous* form of the verb. Here, the father is reading the paper while drinking beer.

Y "Ii tenki de" is, once more, the first component of a sentence with two main verbs in English, but where Japanese makes the first into a participle*–here de from da or desu.

◇◇ Japanese Proper Names ◇◇

Root	Kanji name	Transliteration	Meaning
kawa	早川	Hayakawa	fast river
	立川	Tachikawa	rise of river
	田川	Tagawa	ricefield river
	白川	Shirakawa	white river
	大川	Ookawa (long oo)	big river
	小川	Ogawa (short o)	small river
yama	山田	Yamada	hill ricefield
	山本	Yamamoto	origin (= foot) of mountain
	小山	Koyama	little mountain
	森山	Moriyama	forest mountain
	山一	Yamaichi (Securities)	first mountain
CHUU/naka	中川	Nakagawa	between rivers
hata	畑	Hata (+ fire = where the stubble is burnt)	cultivated field
hane	羽田	Haneda (the airport)	wing field (the airport)
ha	羽田	Hata (Prime Minister in 1994)	bird field
MOKU/ki	木田	Kida	tree paddy
RIN/hayashi	小林	Kobayashi (Note change of h to b)	little wood

Root	Kanji name	Transliteration	Meaning
KOKU/tani	谷 谷口	Tani Taniguchi	valley mouth of valley
CHIKU/take	竹下	Takeshita	under the bamboo
shita	松下	Matsushita	under the pine
shir-	白井	Shira-i	white well

◇◇ English into Japanese ◇◇

Sentences and Themes

1. They left Tokyo in the early morning by car.

2. Because (ので node at the end of the clause) they had a map they went towards the mountains.

3. After stopping the car in a wood and climbing a hill they saw fields and cattle.

4. While walking (歩きながら ...nagara) they looked at the countryside.

5. The weather was good, and there was not a single cloud, but there were insects. (Remember when to use ある aru and いる iru.)

6. The children said they liked the sandwiches they had made on Saturday.

7. Mr Tanaka likes to drink beer while watching television.

8. It was a good thing that they bought a car.

Transformation

1. [They] morning early (adverb) by-car Tokyo を left.

2. [A] map が existed because (ので) mountains' direction へ [they] went.

3. Of-[the]-wood inside で car を stopping, hill を climbing after (から), fields で cattle を saw.

4. While-walking [they] [the] countryside を looked at.

5. Weather good being, cloud は one even も did-not-exist, but insects existed.

6. [The] children は [the] on-Saturday [they] made sandwiches が likeable are と said.

7. Tanaka san は TV を while-watching, beer を to drink (dictionary form + のが) likeable is.

8. [A] car を [they] bought 買ったこと (the fact that) was good (past tense of yoi + desu).

Unit 3
A DAY IN THE LIFE OF MR TANAKA

田中さんの一日

Frontispiece character : 社 SHA *company*

Unit 3

◇◇ Introductory Note ◇◇

This text has more composite kanji, comprising not just one shape but a combination of several shapes, always including a radical–eg 机 tsukue the sign for *desk*, with the tree/wood radical. This unit begins, however, to rely more on compounds, that is, combinations of kanji which, together, add up to a meaning which is more than the sum of their parts. For example: 会社 KAISHA *company, corporation* is a compound of 会 KAI "coming together" and 社 SHA "a Shinto shrine or social group". (This does not imply worship of the firm; the Chinese original already meant the abode of the local earth god and the community which recognised it). 大学 DAIGAKU "big learning" means *university*. Most abstract concepts in Japanese, as indeed in Chinese, are conveyed by such two syllable compounds, many more of which will occur in later units.

In terms of grammar, the unit includes: more reported/indirect* speech, the frequentative/iterative* form of the verb, ending in -ari, the pseudo-adjective*, the hypothetical* "if/when…" form in -eba, the use of the verb + to as a general condition, the n' desu construction, the standard translation of obligation* = I/you/he etc *must, have to…*; the translation of "too (excessively)…" using as suffix the verb -sugiru; constructions relating to time–when (in the past), since when, and for how long.

KANJI FROM THE START | 61

らず、家へすぐ帰りません。代わりに、会社の友達とバーに入って、ビールなどを飲みます。

（四）田中さんは、どんな生活をしているんでしょうか。仕事の目的は、多くのお客に仕えて、会社を助ける事です。田中さんにとって、長が付く人は大切です。会社では、自分は課長で、すぐ上のボスは部長です。部長の上には社長がいます。子供が通う学校では、校長先生と時々話します。奥さんの古里に行くと、お父さんがその家の長です。家長は、若いときの話を長々とします。田中さんは、じっと聞かなければなりません。

（五）休みには、町から出たいのですが、スポーツはやりません。ゴルフは高すぎます。子供の時、スポーツをやりましたが、止めたのでかなり太りました。

田中さんの一日

（一）　田中さんがサラリーマンだと言う事は、もう分かりました。彼は、十年間、同じ会社で働いています。丸一日、机の前にいて、色々な手紙を読んだり、たくさんの手紙を書いたり、時々、ただ考え事をしたりします。

（二）　英語を上手に話す事が出来るので、よく外国へ手紙を送ったり、電話をしたりします。そんな電話は朝早くします。そうでなければ、相手は起きていません。夜中もいいです。

（三）　田中さんを助けている二、三人の人は、大学の時から知っています。田中さんは、ほとんどの日本の男の人のように長時間働きます。それにもかかわ

TANAKA-SAN NO ICHINICHI

1 Tanaka san ga sarariiman da to iu koto wa[a], moo wakarimashita. Kare wa, 10 nen kan[b], onaji kaisha de hataraite imasu[c]. Maruichinichi tsukue no mae ni ite[d], iroirona tegami o yon-dari, takusan no tegami o kaitari, tokidoki, tada kangae-goto o shitari shimasu[e].

2 Eigo o joozu ni[f] hanasu koto ga dekiru[g] node, yoku gai-koku e tegami o okuttari, denwa o shitari shimasu[e]. Sonna[h] denwa wa asa hayaku shimasu. Soo de nakereba[i], aite wa okite imasen. Yonaka mo ii desu.

3 Tanaka san o tasukete iru ni, san nin no hito wa[j], daigaku no toki kara[k] shitte imasu. Tanaka san wa, hotondo no Nihon no otoko no hito no yooni choojikan hatarakimasu. Sore ni mo kakawarazu[l], uchi e sugu kaerimasen. Kawari ni, kaisha no tomodachi to baa ni haitte, biiru nado[m] o nomimasu.

A DAY IN THE LIFE OF MR TANAKA

We have already learnt that Mr Tanaka is an office worker. He has been working for the same firm for 10 years. The whole day long, he is behind a desk (J = in front of), reading various letters, writing a number of letters, and sometimes just thinking.

Because he can speak English well, he often sends letters and makes telephone calls to foreign countries. He makes such calls early in the morning. Otherwise, his partners would not be awake. The middle of the night is all right too.

Mr Tanaka has known, since university, the two or three people who assist him. Mr Tanaka, like almost all Japanese men, works long hours. In spite of this, he does not go straight home. Instead, he goes into a bar with friends from his firm and drinks beer or whatever.

4 Tanaka san wa, donna[h] seikatsu o shite iru n'[n] deshoo ka? Shigoto no mokuteki wa, ooku no okyaku ni tsukaete, kaisha o tasukeru koto[o] desu. Tanaka san ni totte, choo ga tsuku hito wa taisetsu desu. Kaisha de wa, jibun wa kachoo de, sugu ue no bosu wa buchoo desu. Buchoo no ue ni wa shachoo ga imasu. Kodomo ga kayou gakkoo de wa, koochoo sensei to tokidoki hanashimasu. Okusan no furusato ni iku to[p], otoosan ga sono ie no choo desu. Kachoo wa, wakai toki no hanashi o naganaga to shimasu. Tanaka san wa, jitto kikanakereba narimasen[q].

5 Yasumi ni wa, machi kara detai no[n] desu ga, supootsu wa yarimasen[r]. Gorufu wa taka-sugimasu[s]. Kodomo no toki, supootsu o yari-mashita ga, yameta node[t] kanari futorima-shita.

What kind of life does Mr Tanaka lead? In his company, he looks after a lot of clients and his objective is to help the company. Seniority is important to him. In the company, he himself is a section head, and his immediate boss is a divisional head. Above him is the company president. Mr Tanaka sometimes talks to the head teacher of the school his children go to. When he visits his wife's home, her father is head of the family. As such, he talks at length about his youth and Mr Tanaka has to listen attentively.

For recreation, he wants to get out of the city, but he does not go in for sport. Golf is too expensive. When he was a boy, he used to go in for sport, but because he gave it up, he has got rather fat.

◇ ◇ Notes on Kanji ◇ ◇

In contrast to the notes on the kanji of Units 1 and 2, the notes below, and those on all the succeeding texts, give the main ON readings as well as the kun readings*.

The kanji used in compounds mainly have the **ON** reading. In the simple case of 上手 **JOOZU** in this unit, one of the two kanji involved is the one we met in Unit 2 with the **kun** reading **ue** = on or above; the other is the kanji for hand, for which the **kun** reading, when the word is used alone, is **te**. (If disconcerted by this phenomenon of two or more pronunciations for a given kanji, the learner can reflect that English uses a number of words like hippodrome, cavalry, equitation, and horse all referring to the same animal. At least in Japanese (and Chinese too, for that matter) though different terms would be used, the horse sign or radical would be found somewhere in all these expressions).

KANJI	RADICAL			KANJI	
character	no	shape	meaning	reading	derivation and meaning
分	12	八	eight	BUN/FUN/ wa-ka-ru	Comprising the sword 刀 together with the radical for eight, which the Chinese regarded as easily divisible, means a fraction (**juubun no ichi** = a tenth) and a division of time = a minute (**fun**). As a verb **wa-ka-ru**, it means to distinguish one thing from another, thus as here, *to understand.*
彼	60	彳	stride	HI/kare	Phonetic: RHS (also radical 107) is HI/kawa = skin (image of a hide hanging up); with LHS, walking radical, meaning of HI transferred to HI/kare; *he* (also a possible mnemonic?).
年	(4)	ノ	slash	NEN/toshi	Probably contracted from equivalent of 千 SEN (1,000) + 禾 grain of cereal (radical 115) and so 1,000 grains make a harvest; *year.* (See also Unit 1.)
間	169	門	gate	KAN/aida	See also Unit 1; sunlight glinting through opening, and thus, *time interval.* ◆十年間 JUUNENKAN *for ten years.*

◇ ◇ Notes on Kanji ◇ ◇

KANJI	RADICAL			KANJI	
character	no	shape	meaning	reading	derivation and meaning
同	13	冂	enclosure	DOO/ona-ji	?Mnemonic: a cover fitted to a vase (hence the mouth sign) or strips of wood with identical apertures; *same*.
会	9	入	person	KAI/E/a-u	Same lid motif as– in ima = now and **KYOO** = today (Unit 1): simplified base = people? *meeting*.
社	113	礻	altar	SHA	LHS is a form of the radical 礻 a sign from heaven or an altar; with the earth radical 32 土 , it means *Shinto shrine; company*. ◆会社 KAISHA *company; cf* 社会 SHAKAI *society*.
働	9	亻	person	hatara-ku	A Japanese-made kanji, combining the person radical, with 重 heavy + 力 strength, and so it means *to work*.
丸	(4)	ノ	slash	GAN/maru	The sign for nine 九, with an added stroke, somehow came to mean round and here, *whole;* familiar, too, in the designation of ships.
日	72	日	sun	NICHI/hi	Cf the kun reading hi in Unit 2 para 7. Here the **ON** reading is used; *day*.
机	75	朩	wood	tsukue	RHS is stool or small table; with wood radical, it means *desk* (pron: tskue).
前	12	丷	eight	ZEN/mae	Distortion of original; *before.* ?Mnemonic: a cut (lower RHS is a knife) through time (lower LHS) under a lid with two handles, indicating past and present.
色	139	色	colour	SHIKI/iro	Origin obscure; possibly erotic> colour> characteristic. (々 is sign for repetition–see Unit 2.) ◆色々な iroiro na *various*.

KANJI	RADICAL			KANJI	
character	no	shape	meaning	reading	derivation and meaning
手	64	手	hand	SHU/te	Pictorial with fingers; *hand*.
紙	120	糸	thread	SHI/kami	Phonetic: LHS = radical 120 (cf radical 52 above) shows cocoons, and gives thread /fibre. RHS is phonetic (SHI = clan (radical 83) and this gives **ON** reading of this kanji, which means *paper*. **Kun** reading is kami (gami). This ka<u>mi</u> has a higher tone on the second syllable, whereas k<u>a</u>mi, meaning god, starts high and comes down on the second syllable. (Ka<u>mi</u> also = hair.) ◆手紙 tegami (kun readings) *letter*.
書	129	聿	brush	SHO/ka-ku	As noted in Unit 1, top is hand with pen or brush; base can be seen as tablet or ink container. Has to be distinguished from **JI/koto** (in Unit 1 and below), where the base also recalls a hand holding a writing implement. However, koto includes a "box" as the concrete incident to be recorded (stand-alone meaning of koto is *matter, affair*). **Kaku** means *write*.
時	72	日	sun	JI/toki	Phonetic from JI/tera, one of a family of JI kanji; see Unit 4: RHS 寺 JI is a temple, derived from earth (top) + measurement or pulse below. With sun radical, often implying time, it signifies *time/hour;* as conjunction toki, it means when. ◆時々 repetitive form **toki-doki** (another change of consonant t to d) *sometimes* .
考	125	耂	old man	KOO/ kanga-eru	Variant of phonetic ROO, depicting an old man with a stick; it becomes **KOO** *think,* in sense of consider. (To have an opinion is 思う omo-u involving the heart 心).

KANJI	RADICAL			KANJI	
character	no	shape	meaning	reading	derivation and meaning
英	140	艹	plant	EI	Phonetic; 英 was *centre* of plant, and gives us beautiful; for phonetic reasons it means England in compounds. ◆英国 EIKOKU *Britain*.
語	149	言	speech	GO	Phonetic; (go = 5) + radical 149; *language*. ◆英語 EIGO *English (language)*.
上	25	卜	oracle	JOO	ON equivalent of kun reading ue in Unit 2; *above, upper*.
手	64	手	hand	SHU	ON equivalent of kun reading te (cf tegami above). ◆上手 JOOZU na *skilful, good at* (SH becomes Z).
話	149	言	speech	WA/hana-su	Semantic: RHS is shita, which means tongue; LHS is speech radical, and this gives us the meaning, *talk, speak*. ON reading WA with KAI above, gives 会話 KAIWA *conversation;* see also DENWA below.
出	(2)	｜	line	SHUTSU/ de-ru/da-su	See deru in Unit 1.
来	(4)	ノ	slash	ki-ru	米 is rice and this also signifies cereal; with added line above, somehow borrowed for RAI/ kuru meaning *come*. (See Unit 1). ◆出来る dekiru *to know how to…* ; -u form of verb followed by "…koto ga dekiru".
外	36	夕	evening	GAI/soto/ hoka	Radical (LHS) is 夕 half-moon–cf yuu in Unit 2: RHS said to show cracks in shells for divination. Here, GAI means *foreign;* cf kun readings soto (outside) and hoka (other).

KANJI	RADICAL			reading	KANJI
character	no	shape	meaning		derivation and meaning
国	31	囗	enclosure	KOKU/kuni	A simplified kanji; cf mnemonic offered in Unit 2; *one's country*. ◆外国 GAIKOKU *abroad*.
送	162	辶	move for-ward	SOO/oku-ru	Radical for movement + two hands holding an object; it means *to send*.
電	173	雨	rain	DEN	Rain radical + lightning; *electricity*.
話	149	言	speech	WA	See **hanasu** above; *talk*. ◆電話 DENWA *telephone*.
朝	130	月	(moon)	CHOO/asa	A simplified kanji; as in Unit 2, mnemonic is extension of 早 **hayai**: with two pluses: + sun + moon = *morning*. Cf also 韓国 **KANKOKU** (*Korea*) in Unit 5.
相	75	木	tree	SOO/ai	A combination of tree and eye that is hard to explain semantically: **ON** form **SOO** signifies appearance; here the **kun** reading **ai** has the meaning *mutual*. ◆相手 **aite** *partner*; suffix **te** (hand) used to indicate agent.
起	156	走	walking	KI/o-ki-ru	Phonetic; RHS is **KI** and LHS is rare radical for walk, (same as **hashiru**, to run, in Unit 2), meaning *get up*.
夜	8	亠	lid	yoru	A simplified kanji; now a lid (radical 8) + half-moon (**yuu** in Unit 2); *night*. ◆夜中 **yonaka** *middle of night, small hours*.
助	19	力	force	JO/tasu-keru	Phonetic; LHS is 且 primitive signifying pile up, also pronounced **SO** and **JOO**; radical 19 力, meaning force / strength. ?Mnemonic: pile up the strength; *help*.

KANJI	RADICAL			KANJI	
character	no	shape	meaning	reading	derivation and meaning
学	39	子	child	GAKU/ mana-bu	Top is simplification of original phonetic. ?Mnemonic: child (Unit 1) under a school roof with three gables; *learn*. Or the three strokes, can be read as meaning small children (**ko/chiisai**)–though in fact their slope differs–or even the light of learning! ◆大学 DAIGAKU *university*.
知	111	矢	arrow	CHI/shi-ru	Arrow radical + mouth means getting right to the point; *know*.
男	102	田	paddy	DAN/NAN/ otoko	Rice-field + strength = *male*.
長	168	長	long	CHOO/ naga-i	Seen as old man with long hair meaning *long*. (ON reading used here, because read with next two kanji, which have the **ON** reading). ◆長時間 CHOOJIKAN (see JI and KAN above), *a long period of time*.
家	40	宀	roof	KA/ie/(uchi)	Roof radical with pig radical 豕 underneath gives meaning *house*; anomalously pronounced **uchi** when it means house in the sense of home, as here; see also Unit 2 para 7.
帰	58	ヨ	pig's head/ broom	KI/kae-ru	See Unit 2: not an easy sign but one that has to be learnt; *return*.
友	29	又	hand	YUU/tomo	Two primitives for hand combined gives two hands clasping; *friend*.
達	162	辶	motion forward	TATSU/ TACHI	Original meaning of succeed, reach; traced to sheep radical 羊 + 大 large on top. However, TACHI can also be used in Japanese as plural* suffix for persons (and some-

KANJI	RADICAL			KANJI	
character	no	shape	meaning	reading	derivation and meaning
					times animals). ◆友達 TOMODACHI *friend or friends*. (Here, the compound does not necessarily imply the plural.)
入	11	入	enter	NYUU/ hai-ru/i-ru	Entrance to cave or house. (See Unit 2).
生	100	生	life	SEI/i-kiru/ u-mareru	A grass shoot + a whorl gives the meaning *life, to live*; umareru means *to be born*.
活	85	氵	water	KATSU	RHS shita means tongue (see WA/hanasu above); + water radical signifies *life*. ◆生活 SEIKATSU *life*.
仕	9	亻	person	SHI/tsuka-eru	RHS is SHI 士 radical 33; by itself, means a samurai or a learned man, teacher. ?Mnemonic: sitting with arms folded? With the person radical, it means *serve*. (See also the verb, tsukaeru below.) ◆仕事 SHIGOTO *work*.
目	109	目	eye	MOKU/me	Radical: pictorial meaning *eye*.
的	106	白	white	TEKI/mato	Phonetic RHS (said to be a loaded spoon). Here, with LHS radical 106 (white), it signifies target to shoot at (mato) or a hit. TEKI is also a common suffix for attributes; originally Chinese possessive particle "de"; further extended in Japan, an analogy of English "-tic" (as in pol*itic*), German *-tisch* and French *-tique*). ◆目的 MOKUTEKI *objective*.

KANJI character	RADICAL no	shape	meaning	KANJI reading	derivation and meaning
多	36	夕	evening	TA/oo-i	Repetition implies numerous: why it is 夕 yuu (evening) which is doubled is unclear; *many*.
客	40	宀	roof	KYAKU	Phonetic: base is **KAKU**, which means every; under a roof becomes a guest; thus here, it means *client*.
長	168	長	long	CHOO/ naga-i	See para 3 above; in the compounds used here, it has the meaning of age, ie the title of *senior*.
付	9	亻	person	FU/tsu-ku	RHS is a hand or pulse (cf **JI/toki** above); putting a hand on gives us attach, stick to. Here, it means to whom the title of senior *attaches*.
切	18	刀	sword	SETSU/ki-ru	LHS is phonetic, and radical RHS is a knife or sword; *to cut* ◆大切 **TAISETSU** *important*. ?Mnemonic: "gets a big cut".
自	132	自	self	JI	Pictorial of nose comes to mean *self, oneself*.
分	12	八	eight	BUN	As for kun form **wa-karu** above (para 1). ◆自分 **JIBUN** *himself, oneself*.
課	149	言	speech	KA	Phonetic; RHS is fruit on a tree, **KA**: with speech radical, giving what is assigned, eg a lesson and here a *section* (of an office). ◆課長 **KACHOO** *section head*.
部	163	阝	ward (of city)	BU	?Phonetic from earlier version of LHS, incorporating negative **FU/BU** and a mouth, giving the meaning of interrupting a speaker; with **BUN/wakaru**, above BUBUN is usual word for 'a part'.

KANJI	RADICAL			KANJI	
character	no	shape	meaning	reading	derivation and meaning
					◆部長 BUCHOO *divisional head*. ◆社長 SHACHOO (see SHA in KAISHA above) *head/ president of a company*.
通	162	辶	forward	TSUU/too- ru/kayo-u	Phonetic RHS perhaps related to YOO, meaning a piece of business; with radical 162 usually signifying *go through*. The special **kun** reading **kayou** means to commute and here, *to go to* school.
校	75	木	tree	KOO	Phonetic RHS said to have meant man with crossed legs, which gives us the meaning, exchange; resemblance to 父 chichi (father) coincidental. With wood/tree radical on LHS, it signifies *school*. ?Mnemonic: teacher sitting cross-legged under a tree? ◆学校 GAKKOO *school*. (Cf GAKU above.) ◆校長 KOOCHOO *head teacher*. (CHOO above.)
先	10	儿	legs	SEN/saki	Top is a foot (cf **aruku** in Unit 2) and base is legs radical; go first, and hence *early*. (Cf. phonetically derived SEN/arau (wash) in Unit 2.)
生	100	生	life	SEI/SHOO/i kiru	See SEIKATSU above. ◆先生 SENSEI *teacher*. (Literally, earlier born; in Chinese pronounced *Xian Sheng* (*Hsien Sheng*), and used to mean Mr.)
奥	(4)	丿	slash	OO/oku	Base said to be two hands; the top is what now looks like **kome** (rice) in an enclosure, giving basic meaning of inside (eg of a house). Here **okusan** (pron: oksan) means (someone else's) *wife*. (?Mnemonic: one who stays inside and cooks rice standing up.) One refers to one's own wife, not as **okusan** but as 家内 KANAI, which also means house-within. (See KA/ie/uchi in para 3 above.)

KANJI character	RADICAL no	shape	meaning	reading	KANJI derivation and meaning
里	166	里	village	RI/sato	Rice-field 田 + earth 土 = a unit of measurement and *village*. ◆古里 furusato one's *home district*. (KO/furui = old; Unit 1.)
父	88	父	father	FU/chichi/ (TOO)	Noted already in Unit 1. One's own father is chichi; some-one else's, as here, is the respectful o + TOO (same kanji) + san, giving otoosan. Too is another anomalous reading. ◆家長 KACHOO (not the same as KACHOO above meaning section head in an office) *head of family*. (See KA/ie above.)
若	140	艹	plant	JAKU/waka-i	A simplified kanji; now plant radical above, sign for right-hand 右 below, meaning, *young*. ?Mnemonic: the young play games on grass using their right hand.
聞	169	門	gate	BUN/MON/ ki-ku	Phonetic: outside is gate, MON (Unit 1); inside is an ear (耳 JI/ mimi (radical 128), signifying *to hear, listen*. (Cf Unit 1 for meaning *ask*.)
休	9	亻	person	KYUU/yasu-mu	Man resting under a tree; yasumi means *holiday*. (See also Unit 2.)
高	189	高	high	KOO/taka-i	Pictorial of tower, meaning high, but here it signifies *dear* (in price).
止	77	止	stop	SHI/ ya-meru	See Unit 1 (tomeru).
太	37	大	big	TAI/TA/futo-i/futo-ru	Extension, in all senses of DAI/ookii, large meaning *fat*. Here the verb means *get fat*.

Unit 3

◇ ◇ Grammar Notes ◇ ◇

A   Reported/indirect* speech again; **ga** is the subject tag, the verb is in the plain form, and the reported statement ends with **to**.

B   Time during which often has attached to it **kan**, meaning *period/interval during which…*; also applied spacially.

C   **Hataraite imasu** is in form present continuous*, but it is used here (and below) to mean the perfect* *has been working.*

D   **Ite** is the present participle* of **iru** (to be, used of animate subjects) and is used here instead of, but parallel to, a main verb, as with previous examples.

E   **…kaitari, yondari…shimasu** is a construction using the iterative* or frequentative* form of the verb (see Tables) and nearly always ending up, as here, with a part of the verb **suru**. It implies a sequence of actions.

F   **Joozu ni** is the adverb* of **joozu na** (skilful). This is the second category of adjectives*, sometimes called pseudo-* or noun adjectives, to distinguish them from the so-called Japanese adjectives proper, which end in -i and partly conjugate* like verbs (see Table 7). This second class of adjective can be regarded as consisting of an adjectival noun* (**joozu** = skill) + the suffix **-na** (part of a former auxiliary verb "to be"). The equivalent of the adverb is made from such adjectives by replacing **-na** with **-ni**; thus **joozu ni** = *skilfully* (with skill).

G   **Dekiru** means *to be able to…*; what you are able to do is expressed as the **-u** form of the verb + **koto ga**. This role of **koto** in making a verbal noun* is similar to that in "**to iu koto**" in paragraph 1 of this text and to "**tasukeru koto**" in para 4 below. (See nominalisation*).

H   **Sonna** is one of a set of adjectives* meaning *kind of;* the **so-** corresponds to the demonstrative* **sono** = this and **soko** = here. **Donna** (para 4 below) is the interrogative* adjective of the set, *what kind of…?*

I   **Nakereba** is one form (see Table 6) of the negative "if and/or when" form of **aru**. We have already seen an example of the other form, ending in **-ara** (**nattara**, part of **naru**) in Unit 2 para 7). As noted, this verb is in the negative; the positive form would be **areba**. This, then, is an alternative way of expressing "if/when" clauses. To arrive at the **-nakereba** form you take the negative plain present of a verb, in this case **nai**, and add to its negative stem*, na-, the -kereba ending of the hypothetical* "if and/or when" form. See also kikanakereba below at the end of para 4.

J   Ni san is a normal expression for "two or three". The counter*–nin for persons–has to be used here, because the numbers ni, san are "Chinese". In Unit 1, where the Japanese number futari was used, a separate counter was not required; more precisely, in futa-ri the last syllable is the virtual counter for people. For things, not people, the numeral would be futa-tsu, where tsu is the virtual counter.

K   Daigaku no toki is a convenient way of saying *when at university* (cf wakai toki in para 4 and kodomo no toki in para 5 below). Such a time expression + kara (from) is a regular way of translating 'has been…since…'. Shitte imasu is in the present continuous, like hataraite imasu above, and bears the meaning of the English perfect*–*has known*.

L   Noun/pronoun + ni mo kakawarazu is the usual expression for in spite of…; the -zu is an old negative, and the phrase means *not taking heed of…*

M   Nado; a frequently met word which means *and the like* (that is, "like the other things you have quoted").

N   …no desu or …n'desu is a frequent construction used to give point to the statement being made. In effect, as with the French *c'est que…*, the construction corresponds to "the fact is that…" or "…you see", or even to the caricaturable English "actually…" A classic example in Japanese is okane ga nai n' desu = "the fact is/actually I have no money". As with the French *c'est que je n'ai pas d'argent*, the statement has more emphasis in relation to the speaker's condition than the bald statement okane ga nai desu. The n' desu form is often used to explain an earlier statement or question, rather as German uses *nämlich*. (*Bitte gib mir was zu essen; ich habe nämlich Hunger* = Please give me something to eat, I'm hungry, you see).

There is a further point; plain form + desu or n'desu lie, as it were, between the plain and the polite form of the verb, and can be used in default of the polite form. Adding desu or n' desu to the plain form virtually transforms it into the polite form (as here with iru n'deshoo). Similarly, in para 5 below, detai (like hairitai in Unit 2) is the desiderative* form of the verb, and means "wants to go out". It has no polite form (because grammatically it is adjectival) and, therefore, the addition of desu or n'desu is the way of making it polite.

O   Tasukeru koto desu has already been noted above (Note G) as a further example of an alternative way of making a verb or verb phrase into a noun phrase–nominalisation*. "To help the company" is the noun phrase which states the "objective" in "His objective is…"

P   Iku to is an example of the simplest hypothetical* expression of if or when, using the dictionary form* of the verb* + to. The expression is timeless–it can mean *if/ when he goes* or *if/ when he went*. Compared with the other ways of expressing a hypothesis (the -tara and -eba forms, see Note I above), it is on the whole more general, both as regards time and person. It implies no specific time, it almost means "whenever", and as to person, it is often the equivalent of "if/when *one* does this or the other".

Q   Kikanakereba narimasen is an apparently circuitous, but nevertheless standard, way of expressing obligation*; and means *he has to listen*. Literally, "if he did not listen, it does not come to anything". An alternative to narimasen (from naru) is ikemasen (from iku) = it cannot go. (Cf French: *cela ne va pas du tout* = that won't do!).

To arrive at the -kereba form of the verb, the inflection -kereba is added to the negative stem*. Here the negative present plain form is kikanai, and -kereba is added to the stem kikana-. Japanese adjectives (not the pseudos) also have a positive form in -kereba, made by adding it to their stem. (See Table 7.)

R   Yarimasen is the polite present of yaru; this quite common verb can be regarded as a somewhat derogatory form of suru *to do* or *to make* or *perform*. It is regularly used, as here, for sports and hobbies; it can also mean "to give" to an inferior, eg to an animal.

S   Takasugimasu is the adjective taka-i with the auxiliary* verb -sugiru added to its stem*. By itself, the verb sugiru means to exceed or go past; in combination with an adjective* it is the way of saying "too…"

T   Yameta node: Yameru is a very handy verb meaning *to give up something definitely* (like smoking) or *temporarily* (like trying to phone someone).

◇◇ Japanese Proper Names ◇◇

Root	Kanji name	Transliteration	Meaning
CHOO/nagai (In names ha can be nagai and se can be tani)	長沢 長谷川	Nagasawa Hasegawa	long marsh long valley stream
chiisai/ko/o	小沢	Ozawa	little marsh
TAKU/sawa (the ON reading used in TAKUSAN沢山)	沢田	Sawada	marsh paddy
RI/sato	里見	Satomi	Seen from the village, or place from which you can see the village.

◇◇ **English into Japanese** ◇◇

Sentences and Themes

1. Mr Tanaka entered his present (= "of now") firm after leaving university.

2. When Mr Tanaka and his office friends go into the bar to drink (= in order to = *either* masu stem + ni or dictionary form + ために …tame ni) they talk about work–but sometimes about other things too.

3. Although Mr Tanaka does not go in for (= やる yaru) sport, he walks a little when going to his office or to the companies where his clients work.

4. His wife and children would like to take more holidays* than they do at present–but…**

5. Like all*** ladies, Mrs**** Tanaka makes a lot of telephone calls to her friends.

6. His wife thinks Mr Tanaka is too fat. (… すぎる …sugiru)

> *Translates literally, using もっと休みをとる motto yasumi o toru, but with とる toru in the desiderative とりたい + と思っています to omotte imasu. This is a convenient way of saying "would like to"
> **A frequent Japanese construction using ga, and implying that you do not press the point or cannot after all do the thing you are talking about.
> ***all = すべての subete no; like = のように …-no yoo ni.
> ****Tanaka san could mean either Mr or Mrs Tanaka. To make clear that it is Mrs Tanaka, we can use either 田中夫人 Tanaka fujin (*wife*; rather formal) or else 田中さんの奥さん Tanaka san no okusan.

Transformation

1. Tanaka san は of-now firm に university を leaving after (から) entered.

2. Tanaka san と of-company friends into-bar go when (とき) about-work (about is について) talk, but sometimes about other matters also も talk.

3. Tanaka san は sport を does-not-do although が to [his] company or to [the] [where] [his] clients work companies に go when, a little walks.

4. [His] wife と children は now than more holiday を want-to-take と think, but…

5. All-of ladies like (のように) Mrs Tanaka は to-friends a lot-of telephone calls を makes.

6. [His] wife は, Tanaka san が too-fat-is と thinks.

Unit **4**
THE KANJI
漢字について

Frontispiece character: 漢 **KAN** *China.*

◇ ◇ **Introductory Note** ◇ ◇

This text explains, with examples, two fundamental characteristics of Japanese (as, indeed, of Chinese) writing:

> 1. A given phoneme, of itself, can have a number of possible meanings, each carried by a different kanji. (For example, SHOO has 65; SHI has 48; KAN has 45.) The different meanings are supported by the combination of the basic shape plus a so-called radical or classifier. Some basic shapes can thus be recognised as belonging to semantic/phonetic kanji "families", where the various radicals mediate the meaning.

> 2. Compounds of two or more kanji are typical of Japanese and Chinese (from which many of the compounds were derived). There is usually some commonality of meaning uniting semantic "families" sharing one kanji of the compound; often one kanji serves to identify the precise meaning to be attached, in the context, to the other. Sometimes two kanji in a compound seem to have such similar meanings that the combination is in effect repetitive. In the main, at least, one element in the compounds introduced here will already have been used in the units.

In terms of grammar, this unit instances: the "sandwich" construction of Japanese sentences where the subject* is stated first, the main* verb comes at the end, and noun* clauses and other phrases* are in the middle, indefinites*, like someone, something, the ko- so- a- sets of demonstratives*, meaning this, that, the participle* + arimasu meaning "has been…(bought, opened etc)", and a form of likelihood/probability* expressed by hazu desu.

（三） しかし、多数の漢字は、形からは成り立ちが分かりません。その理由は、漢字の九十パーセント位は、その起源が音に有るからです。つまり、このような漢字は、音を表す部分と、部首と言う部分で出来ていますが、音は沢山の漢字に共通です。それで、意味の区別をする部分が部首です。

（四） このグループの例として、漢字の「寺」と「金」が以下に示してあります。

（五） ほとんどの漢字には、色々な読み方が有って、「音」は昔の中国の読み方です。「訓」は日本の読み方で、二つ以上の漢字から出来た漢語は、ほとんどいつも音読みです。今まで、私達は、主に一つ一つの漢字を使って来ましたが、これからは、漢字の組み合わせも、もっと使用するはずです。

漢字について

　（一）　私達は、日本人が中国から千五百年前入って来た文字を使っている事を知っています。漢字について、面白い事が三つ有って、それは、①その起こり、②一つの漢字に色々な読み方が有る事、③漢字の組み合わせ方、です。

　（二）　漢字のいくつかは、成り立ちが分かり易いです。例えば、「東」は、木の後ろから日が上っている所です。「西」は休んでいる鳥を示すそうです。「右」は、右手が食べるために使われるから、手と口で表します。「左」にも手が付いていますが、「工」の部分も有ります。多分、説明は、右手で仕事をする時、左手で木片を持つのだと言う事でしょう。

Unit 4

KANJI NI TSUITE

1 Watashitachi wa, Nihonjin ga Chuugoku kara sen-gohyaku nen mae haitte kita[b] moji o tsukatte iru koto o shitte imasu[a]. Kanji ni tsuite omoshiroi koto ga mittsu[c] atte, sore wa 1) sono okori, 2) hitotsu no kanji ni iroiro na yomi-kata[d] ga aru koto, 3) kanji no kumiawase-kata[d], desu.

2 Kanji no ikutsuka[e] wa, naritachi ga wakari-yasui desu. Tatoeba, "higashi" wa, ki no ushi-ro kara hi ga nobotte iru tokoro desu. "Nishi" wa yasunde iru tori o shimesu soo desu[f]. "Migi" wa migi te ga taberu tame ni tsukawareru[g] kara, te to kuchi de arawashimasu[h]. "Hidari" ni mo te ga tsuite imasu ga, "koo" no bubun mo arimasu. Tabun, setsumei wa, migi te de shig-oto o suru toki, hidari te de mokuhen o motsu no da[i] to iu koto deshoo.

3 Shikashi, tasuu no kanji wa, katachi kara wa naritachi ga wakarimasen. Sono riyuu wa[j], kanji no 90 paasento gurai wa, kigen ga on ni aru kara desu[k]. Tsumari, kono yoo na kanji wa, on o arawasu bubun to, bushu to iu bubun de dekite imasu[l] ga, on wa takusan no kanji ni kyootsuu desu. Sorede, imi no kubetsu o suru bubun ga bushu desu[m].

THE "CHINESE" CHARACTERS

We know that the Japanese use signs which came from China (HAN) one thousand five hundred years ago. Three interesting points about the kanji are (1) their origin (2) that they can be "read" in several ways (the readings) and (3) the way in which the kanji can be com-bined.

The origins of some kanji are easy to under-stand. For example, east is where the sun rises behind the trees. West is said to be a bird com-ing down to rest. The character for right shows a hand and a mouth, because the right hand is used for eating. Left is also written with a hand (attached), but also with a part that indicates "KOO" meaning carpentry/construction. Perhaps the explanation is that we hold a piece of wood with our left hand while working on it with the right.

However, the origin of most kanji cannot be understood by their shape. The reason is that about 90 per cent of kanji have a phonetic ori-gin. That is, the kanji of this kind consist of one part which represents the sound, and anoth-er part called the radical. Many kanji have a common sound and then it is the radical which distinguishes the different meanings.

4 Kono guruupu no rei toshite[n], kanji no JI to KIN ga ika ni shimeshite arimasu[o].

5 Hotondo no kanji ni wa, iroirona yomikata ga atte, "kun" wa Nihon no yomikata de, "ON" wa mukashi no Chuugoku no yomikata desu. Futatsu ijoo[p] no kanji kara dekita kango wa, hotondo itsumo ON-yomi desu. Ima made, watashitachi wa, omoni hitotsu hitotsu no kanji o tsukatte kimashita ga, kore kara wa, motto kanji no kumiawase mo, motto shiyoo suru hazu desu[q].

As an example of these groups those for JI and KIN are shown below.

Nearly all kanji have several "readings"; the one called kun (river with speech) is the Japanese reading, and the ON (= sound) the onetime Chinese sound or reading. In "Chinese" words with two or more characters, these almost always use ON readings. So far we have been using mainly single characters, but from now on we are also bound to use more combinations of kanji.

◇ ◇ Notes on Kanji ◇ ◇

KANJI character	RADICAL			KANJI	
	no	shape	meaning	reading	derivation and meaning
漢	85	氵	water	KAN	Phonetic: has the water radical because it was the name of a river; extended from sign for HAN dynasty to come to mean *China*. (Also can mean "a chap"!)
字	40	宀	roof	JI	Phonetic from bottom SHI/ko which means child; with roof radical on top. ?Mnemonic: what children learn at school is writing *characters*. ◆漢字 KANJI *Chinese/Japanese characters*.
私	115	禾	cereal	SHI/watashi watakushi	RHS said to derive from a cocoon and so comes to mean self-sufficient; with LHS, it means *my* share of the cereal. Alternatively linked to side view of a nose meaning *personal*. ◆私達 WATASHITACHI *We/me/us*.
千	(4)	ノ	slash	SEN/chi	Obscure; *thousand*. ?Mnemonic: ten has two strokes; this has three, and so ten to the power three?
五	1	一	line	GO/itsu	Originally had five lines; *five*.
百	1	一	line	HYAKU	Phonetic from HAKU/BYAKU/shiro-i (white). See Unit 1; *one hundred*. cf 千五百 SENGOHYAKU *1500*.
文	67	文	writing	BUN/MON	Origin said to be ripples or grain in water or wood. Important character in compounds. ◆文字 MOJI *letter, characters*.
使	9	亻	person	SHI/tsuka-u	Simplest form 史 SHI is a hand grasping a pen meaning a chronicle: with additional line – cynically said to represent an official (SHI) set over the illiterate. Here, with person radical 9, it means a *messenger*. Kun reading tsukau means to use; (see also SHIYOO suru in para 5, below).

Other Compound   ◇中国 CHUUGOKU *China* (middle kingdom).

KANJI	RADICAL			KANJI	
character	no	shape	meaning	reading	derivation and meaning
面	176	面	surface	MEN/omote	A head with mask; *face*. ◆面白い omoshiroi *interesting*. (Unusual compound in that both the readings are kun.)
有	130	月	meat	YUU/a-ru	Hand (cf tomodachi in Unit 3 and migi and hidari–left and right–below) holding meat means possession; *is, are, have*.
起	156	走	walk	KI/o-kiru/ o-koru	See "to get up" in Unit 3; here okori means *origin*.
方	70	方	direction	HOO/kata	As in Unit 1 and Unit 2, originally meant spade, but borrowed for direction, *way* (as here) = *way of reading*.
組	120	糸	thread	SO/kumi	RHS is an important primitive, though not a radical, meaning to pile up, perhaps on shelves; with the thread (ito) radical, it means group; kun reading kumi means *put together*.
合	9	人	person	GOO/a-u/ a-waseru	Cover over an opening, or triangle + a mouth comes to mean *fit*. (Cf 場合 ba'ai in Unit 6 means a case; and お見合 omiai is arranged meeting as a step to marriage. ◆組み合わせ kumiawase *composition*.
成	62	戈	spear	SEI/na-ru	The radical is a spear or halberd; how a single extra loop makes it mean to achieve, and *become* is unexplained. ◆成り立ち naritachi *composition*.
易	72	日	sun	EKI/I/ yasa-shii	Nothing to do with sun 日 radical, but primitive of house-lizard able to change colour *easily;* with verb, as here, means *easy to…*

KANJI	RADICAL			KANJI	
character	no	shape	meaning	reading	derivation and meaning
東	(4)	ノ	slash	TOO/higashi	As in text, sun behind trees means east. Cf 東京 TOO-KYOO (eastern capital).
例	9	亻	person	REI/tato-eru	Of the three radicals which compose this kanji, the one in the middle 歹 (radical 78) represents bones and thus disintegration (to die 死 derives from it). The centre and right together make 列 RETSU which means a row or line. With the person radical, it becomes example, compare. 例えば tatoeba means if you compare "so and so" in English, *for example*.
後	60	彳	stride	GO/nochi/ KOO/ato/ ushi-ro	RHS is two cocoons on top (cf **watashi** above) meaning thread + follow, go slowly, below. With the walk radical, it forms the important sign for after, and here, *behind*.
所	63	斤	door	SHO/tokoro	LHS is radical for door (or at least one wing or leaf of it); RHS is radical 69 斤 = axe. Why in Chinese and Japanese this means *place* is unclear; did one use an axe to make a door for one's own place? (See Unit 1.)
西	146	西	cover	SEI/nishi	See text; *west*.
鳥	196	鳥	bird	CHOO/tori	Pictorial of *bird* + tail.
示	113	示	altar	JI/shimesu	Radical for an altar or sign from heaven: here extended to mean *to show* in general. We have seen this sign compressed as a radical in 社 SHA a shrine (cf 会社 KAISHA).
右	30	口	mouth	YUU/migi	As in text, primitive for hand + mouth radical; *right hand*.

KANJI	RADICAL			KANJI	
character	no	shape	meaning	reading	derivation and meaning
口	30	口	mouth	KOO/kuchi	Pictorial of *mouth*.
表	(2)	丨	line	HYOO/ omote/ arawa-su	Base is radical 145 = clothes, visualised as the sleeves above and the skirts below; (as a radical the shape is different 衤 –<u>not</u> to be confused with radical 113 as above in shimesu). The top of the kanji is the sign for hair/fur (毛 MOO/ke). You wear a skin with the fur outside; thus the whole, plausibly, comes to mean surface, front, and as verb, *express*.
左	48	工	build	SA/hidari	As in text; hand + work/construction radical 48; *left hand*.
工	48	工	build	KOO/KU	Variously an adze or hammer or plumb line or set square; anyhow, it means *construction*.
部	163	阝	ward	BU	As noted in Unit 3 (ref BUCHOO) LHS may be phonetic (from negative prefix 不 FU/BU); RHS is simplified radical for a (walled) city or ward. ◆部分 BUBUN *part*.
説	149	言	speech	SETSU/ to-ku	RHS recalls 兄 ani (elder brother in Unit 2): implausibly, with part of wakaru, it becomes take, strip off, and with speech radical, get something off one's mind. Anyhow, it means *opinion, theory*; verb toku = persuade. ◆説明 SETSUMEI *explanation*.
片	91	片	split wood	HEN/kata	One side of a split piece of wood > what normally comes in pairs: thus 片目 katame means one eye. ◆木片 MOKUHEN *piece of wood*.

KANJI	RADICAL			KANJI	
character	no	shape	meaning	reading	derivation and meaning
持	64	扌	hand	JI/mo-tsu	Phonetic: member of JI family listed after this unit. Here, with hand radical, it means to have, *hold*.
数	66	攵	action	SUU/kazu	A simplified kanji; bottom LHS is a woman; top LHS is now rice; with RHS beating or action radical 66 (hand holding a stick); *number*. ?Mnemonic: "How many times does a woman beat rice?" ◆多数 TASUU *many*.
形	59	彡	hair/stripes	KEI/GYOO/ katachi	LHS ?variant of 井 well or square frame: with radical for hair/ornament; *shape*. Cf. 人形 NINGYOO *doll*.
理	96	王	jewel	RI	Phonetic; RHS is former unit of linear measure (Chinese 'li') derived from paddy field + land; also means sato village: (Cf furusato in Unit 3.) With jewel radical (because gems have to be cut in a regular pattern?) it means *reason, principle*.
由	(2)	丨	stroke	YU/YUU	A pot from which you take things, thus a *source, cause*. ◆理由 RIYUU *reason*.
九	4/5	丿乚	stroke or curl	KYUU/ kokono	No obvious origin; *nine*. ◆九十 KYUUJUU *ninety*.
位	9	亻	person	I/kurai	Person with "stand" radical 117 (Unit 1) means standing, thus *status, rank*. Here as gurai, often used with numbers to mean *about*.
起		走	walk	KI/o-koru	See para 1 above.

	156				

KANJI	RADICAL			KANJI	
character	no	shape	meaning	reading	derivation and meaning
源	85	氵	water	GEN/ minamoto	Even without the water radical, shows a cliff (radical 27) with a spring and indicates *origin*: with water radical this meaning is enhanced. ◆起源 KIGEN *origin*.
音	180	音	sound	ON/IN/oto	Radical 180: same origin as 言 (speech radical); bottom is, strictly, not sun but mouth, with lips closed or showing a tongue; *sound*. (This character supplies the ON of the so-called ON readings.)
首	185	首	head	SHU/kubi	Head with hair means head; (cf michi in Unit 2). ◆部首 BUSHU *radical or classifier*.
沢	85	氵	water	TAKU/sawa	RHS was old measure, shaku: used phonetically with water radical to mean a marsh; here in phonetic compound. ◆沢山 TAKUSAN *many*.
共	(12)	八	eight	KYOO/tomo	Originally two hands which indicate *both, in common* (eg co-education, communism) and kodomo (Unit 1).
通	162	辶	move forward	TSUU/ too-su/ too-ru/ kayo-u	Same as kayou in Unit 3: RHS meant to pierce; with move forward radical means go through; toosu means let through. ◆共通 KYOOTSUU *what is in common*.
意	180	音	sound	I	Top is ON (see above, meaning sound) + heart symbol below, giving us what you hear in your heart; *thought, feeling*.
味	30	口	mouth	MI/aji	Phonetic: RHS is MI = not yet (in compounds). ?Mnemonic: from a new shoot appearing on a tree; with mouth radical, it means *taste*. ◆意味 IMI *meaning*.

KANJI	RADICAL			KANJI	
character	no	shape	meaning	reading	derivation and meaning
区	22	匚	box	KU	A simplified kanji: an enclosed part of a town; *ward, district* (as used in postal addresses).
別	18	刂	sword	BETSU/ waka-reru	LHS is bones (cf 例えば tatoeba above): RHS is cut/separate. ◆区別 KUBETSU *distinction*.
例	9	亻	person	REI/tato-eru	See tatoeba in para 2 above; *example*.
寺	32	土	earth	JI/tera	Bottom was SUN (unit of length) derived from hand > pulse > time > law: top was not necessarily earth radical but sign of possessive case; thus where the law comes from; *temple*.
金	167	金	metal	KIN/kane	Related phonetically to 今 KON\ima now: but best mnemonic is nuggets from the earth under a mine roof; *metal, gold*.
訓	149	言	speech	KUN	Partly phonetic from Chinese equivalent of SEN/kawa river, but with semantics of original meaning of *teaching*; used for the native Japanese reading of a kanji.
以	9	亻	person	I	The radical is on the RHS: hard to assign origins, but is a prefix which derives meaning from the context. ◆以上 IJOO *more than*; *above mentioned*. ◆以下 IKA is the converse, meaning *less than, below*.
昔	72	日	sun	SEKI/ mukashi	Top either dried meat hung up to keep, or recalls kumi-awase (above para 1): with base sun/day implies piling up time and thus mukashi *of old*.

KANJI	RADICAL			KANJI	
character	no	shape	meaning	reading	derivation and meaning
主	8	亠	lid	SHU/nushi/omo	Said to show burning oil lamp and thus the master; omo with na (adj) or ni (adv) means *main(ly)*. (Cf 住む sumu in Unit 1 with person radical 9.)

Other Compounds   ◇漢語 KANGO *"Chinese" word.* (Cf <u>KAN</u>JI above, and EI<u>GO</u> in Unit 3.)
◇使用 SHIYOO *use, usage.*

◇ ◇ Grammar Notes ◇ ◇

A   The noun* clause ending with koto o is the object* of the main* verb **shitte imasu**. The whole sentence is a typical Japanese hierarchical construction, which can be understood more clearly if its elements are represented by symbols. It has the basic form:

<u>Watashitachi wa</u> {A…[B…B]…A} <u>shitte imasu</u>.

Here, the bread of the sandwich (underlined) means "we know". Inside the bread, the main filling {A…A} is the noun clause object of **shitte imasu**:

{<u>Nihonjin ga</u> [B…B]<u>…moji o tsukatte iru koto o</u>}
(the fact) that the Japanese use characters.

Nested* inside this noun clause is the adjectival* clause [B…B] qualifying moji:

[<u>Chuugoku kara sengohyaku nen mae haitte kita</u>]
(which) came from China 1500 years ago.

This sandwich pattern will often be repeated; that is, the bread (main clause) with the subject at the beginning of the sentence and the main verb, whether in the -masu or in the plain form*, right at the end. In the middle of the sandwich, the filling often takes the form of a noun clause with a verb in the plain form. Nested in the middle of the filling, there will be possibly another clause or two, also with a verb in the plain form, qualifying* a noun or modifying* the verb of the noun clause.

B   Haitte kita is like dete kimashita in Unit 1. Tsukatte kimashita at the end of this text means *we have been using*.

C   Mit-tsu is the Japanese number *three*, in which -tsu is a virtual counter*. The Japanese set of numbers* is conveniently used (a) when there are no more than ten objects being counted; and (b) when no specific counter is to be used. Another constraint is that only hitori (one) and futari (two) can be used with persons; the series with -tsu can be applied only to things. See also Grammar Note F in Unit 1.

D   Yomi-kata; kumiawase-kata means *the way of reading (the characters); the way of combining (them)*. The form of the verb used here (ending with -i, or -e for verbs in -eru) is the -masu* stem, shown as such in the verb tables. Another example is wakari-yasui below.

E   Ikutsuka (pronounced ịk(u)tska) is the indefinite* form of the interrogative* ikutsu how many? (With persons o-ikutsu desu ka means "how old are you?") Thus ikutsuka means "some" in the sense of "an indefinite quantity of…" Others in the set of indefinites* derived from interrogatives* include:

dare	who?	dareka	someone
itsu	when?	itsuka	sometime
nani	what?	nanika	something
doko	where?	dokoka	somewhere.

F   Soo desu; much used expression consisting of the adjective* or the plain form* of a verb + soo desu, implying that the content of the preceding phrase* is something one has heard, but does not know for certain. The plain form is soo da.

G   Tsukawareru–passive* of tsuka-u to use–a Group I* verb with stem* ending with an invisible w. The passive is regularly formed by adding -rareru to the active stem of -ru verbs (Group II) and -areru to the Group I stems. (Eg tabe-rareru = is eaten; ka-kareru = is written; see verb Tables.) However, as we saw with iwareta in Unit 1, verbs which appear to have a vowel stem (like i-u, tsuka-u, and ka-u) put back their lost w and thus take on an extra syllable when they form the passive.

H   Arawashimasu from arawasu, an transitive* verb meaning "to express"; as often happens in Japanese the subject* is not expressed but understood–in this case, "we" or "one". (This propensity of Japanese to dispense with the subject of a verb is one of the things that make machine translation more difficult.)

I   No da; this is the plain form (because it is in the subordinate noun clause* ending to iu koto) of the n' desu explained in note N of Unit 3. In this sandwich sentence, the main clause is <u>Tabun, sono setsumei wa</u> {A…[B…B]…A} <u>deshoo</u> meaning *Perhaps the explanation for this is {A…[B…B]…A}.*

The filling {A…A} is the subordinate noun clause {<u>hidari te de mokuhen o motsu n' da to iu koto</u>} which means *the fact that one holds the piece of wood with the left hand.*

[B…B] is a subordinate* clause of time, modifying* motsu, which can be regarded as a flavouring of the filling: [<u>migi te de shigoto o suru toki</u>] indicating *when we are working with our right hand* (toki = when).

J   In <u>sono</u> riyuu and in sono setsumei, sono means not just "this" but "of this". Kono yoo na kanji below means *kanji like this*, where yoo na is an adjectival phrase, meaning "like", linked by no and coming after the thing to which it refers. (Cf English "such like" and dialectal "this like".)

The difference between the three sets: so-no, so-re etc; ko-no, ko-re etc; a-no, a-re etc is that the ko- set means what is near to the speaker; so- means near to the person addressed, and a- means over there—ie not near to the speaker or to the interlocutor. (Latin, Italian and Spanish have a similar usage.)

In a text, either <u>so</u>-no or <u>ko</u>-no can be used to refer to something already mentioned: "The reason for *this* is…".

K   Another sandwich sentence, of which the outside is:

<u>Sono riyuu wa</u> {A…A} <u>desu</u> = *the reason for this is {A…A}.*

The filling {A…A} is {<u>kanji no 90 paasento gurai wa kigen ga on ni aru kara</u>} means *because 90 per cent of kanji have their origin in sound*. The wa…ga… construction is the one referred to in Note G of Unit 1; it is also used above in tasuu no kanji wa…naritachi ga wakarimasen.

Note also that it is bad English, but good Japanese to say, as here "The reason is because… (kara)".

L   The main clause here is: …kanji…bubun to…bubun de dekite imasu which means *such kanji consist of a part which… and a part which…* (The particle to signifies *together with*, and thus, *and*.)

M   The main clause here is: <u>…bubun ga bushu desu</u> *the…part is the radical*. (The thing emphasised comes first in English, but at the end in Japanese.) The subject of desu (with bushu as the predicate*) is bubun. This is qualified by the immediately preceding adjectival clause, [<u>imi no kubetsu o suru</u> (bubun)] meaning *(the part) which makes the distinction "of" their meanings.*

N   Toshite means *"by way of", "as"*. Here, it signifies *by way of (examples of these groups).*

O   Shimeshite arimasu exemplifies an important use of the participle*. We have seen (Note C of Unit 1) that the participle with iru forms the continuous* present tense; however, the participle of a transitive verb + aru is equivalent to a European passive with the meaning "have been …ed". Thus here, shimeshite aru = *are indicated/have been indicated (below).*

P   Futatsu ijoo no kanji; ijoo = *(two) or more*. (Ijoo can also mean *"above"* in a text, just as ika ni in the previous paragraph can mean *below*.)

Q   Hazu desu is a convenient way of expressing probability* or likelihood in the sense of something that is programmed to happen, as with a train due to arrive at a stated time. (Not the same as a moral obligation*, which is beki desu.)

◇ ◇ Japanese Proper Names ◇ ◇

Many names are derived from the sign for KIN/kane meaning metal, money. The origin of the Chinese character is partly phonetic; the top was the same as the sign for KON/ima which means now. This was CHIN in Chinese, and the sign for metal had the same pronunciation. The character is also partly pictorial, with the bottom half showing the earth with dots said to be nuggets. Indeed, the image of a covered mine is an effective mnemonic. Used in names, kane is usually regarded as meaning gold.

Root	Kanji name	Transliteration	Meaning
KIN/kane	金子	Kaneko	golden child
	金山	Kaneyama	gold mountain
	金田	Kaneda	gold paddy
maru	金丸	Kanemaru	round piece of gold?
	石丸	Ishimaru	round stone
	丸山	Maruyama	round mountain
GEN/hara	石原	Ishihara	stone field
			(well-known for his tests for colour blindness)

◇◇ Kanji Families ◇◇

JI

JI/tera: *temple*: earth radical 32 above; inch/pulse radical 41 below.

RADICAL			NEW SIGN		
shape	no	meaning		reading	meaning
扌	64	hand	持	JI/mo-tsu	to hold
日	72	sun	時	JI/toki	hour; time; while, when
亻	9	person	侍	JI/samurai	samurai
彳	60	walk	待	TAI/ma-tsu	wait for
牛	93	cattle	特	TOKU	special
言	149	speech	詩	SHI	poem
竹	118	bamboo	等	TOO/hito-shii/ nado	grade, equal etc; "and the like"(ie of equal importance)

KIN/kane

1 Single character **KIN/KON/kane**: *gold, money* (**kane**):radical 167.

The added signs mainly supply the phonetic.

ADDED SIGN		NEW SIGN		
sign	reading	kanji	reading	meaning
艮	GIN	銀	GIN	silver
同	DOO/ona-ji	銅	DOO	copper
合	EN	鉛	EN/namari	lead
失	SHITSU/ushina-u	鉄	TETSU	iron
岡	GOO/KOO(*hard*)	鋼	KOO/hagane	steel
広	KOO/hiro-i(*wide*)	鉱	KOO	ore
十	Chinese phonetic	針	SHIN/hari	needle

2 Compounds of two kanji including **GIN/KON/kane** and derivatives.

ADDED KANJI			COMPOUND		
sign	reading	meaning	sign	reading	meaning
行	KOO/i-ku	activity	銀行	GINKOO	bank
山	SAN/yama	mountain	鉱山	KOOZAN	mine
火	KA/hi	fire	火鉢	HIBACHI	brazier "hibachi"
水	SUI/mizu	water, liquid	水銀	SUIGIN	mercury
貯	CHO	store up	貯金	CHOKIN	savings
賃	CHIN	earnings	賃金	CHINGIN	wages
現	GEN/arawa-su	present, show	現金	GENKIN	cash
持	JI/mo-tsu	to have	金持	kanemochi	rich
針	SHIN/hari	needle	針金	harigane	wire
料	RYOO	fee/material	料金	RYOOKIN	charge, fee

Further compounds of **KIN**

ADDED KANJI			COMPOUND		
sign	reading	meaning	sign	reading	meaning
資	SHI	resources	資金	SHIKIN	capital, fund
罰	BATSU	punishment	罰金	BAKKIN	fine, penalty
配当	HAITOO	distribute	配当金	HAITOOKIN	dividend
送	SOO	send	送金	SOOKIN	remittance
合	GOO	fit together fix together	合金	GOOKIN	alloy

Unit 4

◇◇ English into Japanese ◇◇

Sentences and Themes

1. Most* people write with the right hand, but a few people use the left hand to write.

2. Many Japanese characters have the Chinese shape and meaning but of course (もちろん **mochiron**) they have a different sound. In Chinese the character JI (JI no **kanji**) has the sound "Zzer".

3. When the samurai have time, they wait in the temple for a special poem. (This is a joke sentence to illustrate the JI family; see the JI listing following this unit.)

4. Silver was used (see text) as money ("money" +...**to shite**) before gold. That is why a bank is GINKOO 銀行 in Japanese and the GINZA (銀座) has this name.

*Note: There is no one-for-one phrase in Japanese, as there is in European languages, to translate "most people". For now, best to use ほとんどの人は **hotondo no hito wa** *almost all*.

Transformation

1. Almost all people は right hand で write, but [a] few people to-write (dictionary form) in order to (ために) left hand を use.

2. Many-of of-Japan characters (に)は of-Chinese-language shape と meaning が exists, but of course [the] sound は is-different.

3. [The] samurai は, time が exists when (とき), in [the] temple [a] special poem を await.

4. Silver は before-gold as-money (お金として) was-used. Therefore "bank" in-Japanese-language で GINKOO is.

Unit 5
THE TWO ISLANDS
二つの島国

Frontispiece character : 島 shima *island*.

◇ ◇ **Introductory Note** ◇ ◇

This unit continues the progression towards more advanced kanji and compounds and introduces some simple concepts relating to geography and trade.

In terms of grammar it shows: how to say "because of", how the Japanese count large numbers*, ordinal* numbers (like first, second), examples of comparisons*, special cases of nominalisation*–ie the translation of noun* clauses in such contexts as "being worried about…", how to say "wherever" and "somewhere", use of the plain intentional* form of the verb + suru, use of the potential* form of the verb, ways of expressing hypothetical*, ie "if/when", clauses, and another use of the -masu* stem.

さは一倍半しかなくて、その上、日本には山がもっと多いです。

（四）人口が多い日本は、主食の米が十分に有るかどうかが心配で、米がいつも手に入るようにしておきたいのです。それで、どこでも土地が平らなら、米を作ろうとします。又、田舎の村には、狭い土地で米を作る人が、あまりにも沢山います。このために、韓国のように、日本は、米がずっと安く売れる米国と争い続けているのです。

（五）両国の比較を続けると、英国には日本より羊が多くて、羊毛を日本より多く使って、羊肉を日本より沢山食べます。さらに、英国は、周りの海の油田に、日本より多くの石油が有ります。両国共、麦を作っています。日本は、ますます小麦を食べるようになり、どちらも大麦からビールを造って互いに売ります。

二つの島国

（一）　日本と英国を比べるのは面白いでしょう。両国は島国で、四方を海に取り囲まれています。多分、このために、日本人と英国人は、昔も今も魚を沢山食べるのでしょう。

（二）　島国の英国は、三億人が住んでいるヨーロッパに有って、主な貿易の相手はヨーロッパです。日本も十二億の人口を持つ中国のすぐ近くに有って、一九九二年には、米国に次いで、中国の第二の貿易相手国に成りました。日本にとって東南アジアは、主な貿易相手の一つですが、そこでは日本の品を売るだけでなく、色々な物を日本国内でより、安く作る事が出来ます。

（三）　日本の人口は、英国の二倍以上ですが、国の広

FUTATSU NO SHIMA-GUNI

1 Nihon to Eikoku o kuraberu no wa omoshiroi deshoo[a]. Ryoo-koku wa shimaguni de, shi hoo o umi ni torikakomarete imasu[b]. Tabun, kono tame ni[c], Nihonjin to Eikokujin wa, mukashi mo ima mo, sakana o takusan taberu no deshoo[a].

2 Shimaguni no Eikoku wa, san-oku[d] nin ga sunde iru Yooroppa ni atte, omona booeki no aite wa Yooroppa desu. Nihon mo juu-ni oku no jinkoo o motsu Chuugoku no sugu chikaku ni atte, 1992 nen ni wa, Beikoku ni tsuide Chuugoku no dai-ni[e] no booeki aite-koku ni[f] narimashita. Nihon ni totte Toonan-Ajia wa omona booeki aite no hitotsu desu ga, soko de wa Nihon no shina o uru dake de naku[g], iroirona mono o Nihon kokunai de yori[h], yasuku tsukuru koto ga dekimasu.

3 Nihon no jinkoo wa, Eikoku no ni bai ijoo desu ga, kuni no hirosa wa ichi bai han shika[i] nakute, sono ue, Nihon ni wa yama ga motto ooi desu.

THE TWO ISLANDS

It may be interesting to compare Britain and Japan. Both countries are islands, surrounded on four sides by the sea. Perhaps this is why the British and the Japanese eat, or used to eat, a lot of fish.

Britain, as an island, is part of Europe, with 3×10^8 inhabitants, and her main trading partner is Europe. Japan is next to China, with a population of 12×10^8. In 1992 Japan became China's second largest trading partner after the United States. South-East Asia is a major trading partner of Japan, and she can not only sell Japanese goods there, but also produce various things there more cheaply than domestically.

Japan's population is more than twice that of Britain, but Japan has only about 1.5 times the area, and also with many more mountains.

4 Jinkoo ga ooi Nihon wa, shushoku no kome ga juubun ni aru ka doo ka ga shinpai de[j], kome ga itsumo te ni hairu yoo ni shite okitai[k] no desu. Sorede, doko de mo[l] tochi ga taira nara, kome o tsukuroo to shimasu[m]. Mata, inaka no mura ni wa, semai tochi de kome o tsukuru hito ga amari nimo[n] takusan imasu. Kono tame ni, Kankoku no yooni, Nihon wa, kome ga zutto yasuku ureru[o] Amerika to arasoi tsuzukete iru no desu.

5 Ryoo-koku no hikaku o tsuzukeru to[p], Eikoku ni wa Nihon yori hitsuji ga ookute[q], yoomoo o Nihon yori ooku tsukatte, yooniku o Nihon yori takusan tabemasu. Sarani, Eikoku wa, mawari no umi no yuden ni, Nihon yori ooku no sekiyu ga arimasu. Ryoo-koku tomo, mugi o tsukutte imasu. Nihon wa, masumasu komugi o taberu yoo ni nari[r], dochira mo oomugi kara biiru o tsukutte tagai ni urimasu.

Japan, with her large population, concerned that there should be enough of her staple food—rice—always want to takes steps to be sure of having it available at any time. Therefore, wherever the land is flat they like to produce rice. There are also so many producers of rice on small plots in country villages. Because of this Japan, like Korea, is in constant dispute with America, which is able to sell rice far more cheaply.

Continuing the comparison of the two countries, Britain has more sheep, uses more wool, and eats more mutton. Moreover Britain has more oil, from oilfields in the sea around Britain. Both countries grow cereals, and Japan is eating more and more wheat. Both make beer from barley—and each sells it to the other.

◇◇ Notes on Kanji ◇◇

NOTE: From this unit onward the radical is shown but its meaning is not .

KANJI character	RADICAL no	RADICAL shape	KANJI reading	KANJI derivation and meaning
島	(4)	ノ	TOO/shima	Phonetic; original radical is 鳥 bird with tail (CHOO/tori). This kanji has the tail feathers replaced by a mountain; *island*.
比	81	比	HI/kura-beru	Two persons side by side; *to compare*.
面	176	面	omo	A head with mask; *face*.
白	106	白	shiro-i	Acorn meaning *white* (Unit 1). ◆面白い omoshiroi *interesting*.
両	1	一	RYOO	Image of balance gives the meaning of pair; *both*.
四	31	口	SHI/yon	Phonetic; sound borrowed from kanji meaning to breathe out; *four*.
方	70	方	HOO	See Unit 2: *direction* . ◆四方 SHIHOO *all four sides*.
海	85	氵	KAI/umi	Phonetic: RHS is **MAI** which means every; + water radical; *sea*.
取	128	耳	SHU/to-ru	LHS is ear radical; RHS is hand radical > "take by the ear"; *take*.

KANJI character	RADICAL no	RADICAL shape	reading	KANJI derivation and meaning
囲	31	囗	I/kako-mu/ kakom-areru (passive)	Phonetic/semantic: ON is simplified version of 井 I (well), inside the enclosure radical, it means *surround*. ◆取り囲まれる torikakomareru *to be surrounded*.
多	36	夕	TA	See Unit 3; *many*.
分	12	八	BUN	See Unit 4 (BUBUN); *part*. ◆多分 TABUN *perhaps* ("more parts than not?").
魚	195	魚	sakana	Pictorial; *fish*.
億	9	亻	OKU	Origin unclear: RHS is 意 I (feeling) in IMI, Unit 4. With additional and shortened heart radical LHS, we get 憶 OKU meaning think, recall. Perhaps borrowed, with LHS person radical, to mean 10^8 or 100,000,000.
主	8	亠	SHU/omo	See Unit 4 para 5.
貿	154	貝	BOO	Radical means shell > money; top is derived from a primitive of door; BOO means *barter, trade*. Trade opens doors?
易	72	日	EKI/I/yasa-shii	Was a lizard able to change its colour > change > exchange; and as adjective (Unit 4), means *easy to…* ◆貿易 BOOEKI *trade*.
近	162	辶	KIN/chika-i	Phonetic from kin meaning axe (radical 69) cf tokoro in Unit 4; *near*. Thus neighbourhood is 近所 KINJO.

Other Compounds ◇人工 JINKOO (people + mouth) *population*.
◇中国 CHUUGOKU *China*.

KANJI character	RADICAL		KANJI	
	no	shape	reading	derivation and meaning
米	119	米	BEI/MAI/kome	Pictorial of raw *rice* grains: the Japanese evolved the phonetic kana in the 9th century but in parallel continued to follow the Chinese, who have no phonetic alphabet and transcribe foreign words by combining syllables having roughly the required pronunciation. Thus in Japan, the rice character is used for the ME of America. (The Chinese invoke the same syllable but, more flatteringly, transcribe it with the sign 美 (MEI) which in Japanese is BI/utsukushii meaning beautiful.) ◆米国 BEIKOKU *USA*
次	15	冫	JI/SHI/tsugi/ tsu-gu	Classified under the "ice" radical, but LHS more plausibly means two; hence meaning of tsugi-no as adjective is *next*. Here as participle of verb, tsu-gu >tsuide, and means *following, after*.
第	118	竹	DAI	Base phonetic: (弟 DAI/otooto younger brother); not clear why the bamboo radical is added to give the sign for ordinal numbers; perhaps because bamboo grows in units. Here 第二 DAINI *second*.
南	24	十	NAN/minami	House to keep plants warm giving the meaning *south* . The top bit may be a plant forcing its way through the roof; or = "half-in", see HAN below. (Cf 南京 Nanjing, in China, means south capital.) ◆東南 TOONAN *south-east*.
品	30	口	HIN/shina	Easy to remember = articles; (上品 JOOHIN elegant, refined; 下品 GEHIN vulgar).
売	32/33	士	BAI/u-ru/u-reru (potential)	A simplified kanji; ?mnemonic: samurai behind table; *sell*. (Cf 読む yomu in Unit 3 – sell words > read.)

KANJI character	RADICAL no	shape	reading	KANJI derivation and meaning
物	93	牛	BUTSU/mono	RHS phonetic: with ox radical, a very common word; *any object/thing*.
内	(2)	｜	NAI/uchi	Entrance to a house; *inside/home*. ◆国内 KOKUNAI inside the country; *domestic*.
安	40	宀	AN = peace/ yasu-i = cheap	(Cf TIEN AN MEN Square in Beijing.) Roof over woman is peace; usual meaning of yasui is *cheap*.
作	9	亻	SAKU/tsuku-ru	RHS =?carving which gives the meaning *produce*. (Cf SAKU (phonetic): 昨年 SAKUNEN last year; 昨日 kinoo yesterday.)
倍	9	亻	BAI	Phonetic: RHS in BUBUN and BUSHU (Unit 4) had sound BU; here and in other characters, it is BAI. With person radical, it means *-tuple*. Thus 二倍 NIBAI *twice as...*
広	53	广	KOO/hiro-i	The roof radical and under it a simplified phonetic: *wide, broad* and with -sa ending (often used to make a noun from an adjective), it means *area* (cf isogashisa in Unit 2).
半	(3)	丶	HAN	May be related to 牛 ox: mnemonic: that it is symmetrical and thus means *half*. ◆一倍半 ICHI BAI HAN *one and a half times* (as much...).
米	119	米	BEI/MAI/kome	Rice grains > raw *rice* (see above).
心	61	心	SHIN/kokoro	Symbolic: *heart*.
配	164	酉	HAI/kuba-ru	Radical, on LHS, is wine-jar: (cf radical 146, with one stroke less, meaning west); here with radical 49 (self), it means *to*

Other Compounds ◇以上 IJOO *more than...* (see Unit 4).
◇主食 SHUSHOKU consisting of SHU/omo (above) and SHOKU/taberu (Unit 2); *main food*.

KANJI character	RADICAL		KANJI	
	no	shape	reading	derivation and meaning
				distribute, share out. (?Mnemonic: one pours out for oneself?) ◆心配 SHINPAI (sharing one's heart) *worry.*
土	32	土	DO/TO/tsuchi	See DOYOObi in Unit 1 and KOKUDO in Unit 2.
地	32	土	CHI/JI	Unclear because several primitives are combined. Here with earth radical, it means *ground.* ◆土地 TOCHI *land, terrain.*
平	1	一	HEI/tai-ra	Floating plant comes to mean *level.*
又	29	又	mata	A radical meaning hand: cf YUU/tomo (friend).
村	75	木	SON/mura	LHS tree radical + RHS hand or measure (cf JI/tera); *village.*
狭	94	犭	KYOO/sema-i/ seba-meru	RHS is phonetic 夾 KYO; LHS is dog radical; unclear what the dog has to do with meaning; *narrow.*
韓	178	韋	KAN	LHS KAN possibly phonetic; several similar compounds read as KAN (cf 乾杯 KANPAI "cheers" as a toast). This radical 178 makes, with radical 162, 違う I/chigau meaning to be different; the top is the geometrical converse of the base. ◆韓国 KANKOKU *Korea.*
争	(4)	ノ	SOO/araso-u	Compising two hands seeking the same object, it mean *conflict, dispute.*

Other Compound ◆十分 JUUBUN *enough.* (Note that 1/10 = JUUBUN no ICHI.)

KANJI character	RADICAL no	shape	KANJI reading	derivation and meaning
続	120	糸	ZOKU/ tsuzu-ku/ tsuzu-keru	Phonetic RHS very much simplified and now same as sign for uru (sell) above (cf yomu (read) Unit 2). With LHS thread radical (ito) it means *continue*. (Pronounced tsu<u>d</u>zuku.) ?Mnemonic: to continue reading?
較	159	車	KAKU	Confused: RHS often has sound of KOO as in 学校 GAKKOO, but not here: relevance of LHS vehicle radical is also unclear; means *to compare*. ◆比較 HIKAKU *comparison*. HI is the same as kuraberu above; this is an instance of two components of a compound which reinforce one another. It also exemplifies the way in which Japanese enriches its vocabulary by drawing on Chinese, as English does on Latin, for expressions, in Japanese usually using suru, with similar meaning to a native word. In English "compare" (Latin root) is almost the same as "liken". In Unit 6, we have 返答 HENTOO (an alternative is 返事 HENJI) suru with a similar meaning to kotaeru = to reply/answer (where, again, "reply" is of Latin origin).
羊	123	羊	YOO/hitsuji	Pictorial of *sheep*.
毛	82	毛	MOO/ke	Pictorial of *wool, hair*. ◆羊毛 YOOMOO *sheep's wool*.
肉	130	肉	NIKU	Pictorial for hunk of *meat*. ?Mnemonic: meat hanging up at home (内 NAI/uchi above). ◆羊肉 YOONIKU *mutton*.
周	13	冂	SHUU/mawa-ri	Radical is a border: inside may be a field with rice plants; meaning what you can go round; here as adverb + no is equivalent of *surrounding*.

KANJI character	RADICAL		KANJI	
	no	shape	reading	derivation and meaning
油	85	氵	YU/abura	Phonetic RHS, from pot, or seed sprouting: with water radical, it means *oil*. ◆油田 YUDEN (DEN is ON reading of ta) *oilfield*.
石	112	石	SEKI/ishi	Pictorial of cliff meaning *stone*. ◆石油 SEKIYU (literally, petra [rock] + oleum) *petroleum*.
共	12	八	KYOO/tomo	Two hands holding something comes to mean *both*. (Cf KYOOTSUU in Unit 4.)
麦	199	麦	BAKU/mugi	A simplified kanji; bottom means going slowly (radical 35) > growing. Top was an ear of *cereal*. ◆小麦 komugi little cereal (ko is variant of chiisai) *wheat*. ◆大麦 oomugi (big cereal; oo is variant of ooki) *barley*.
造	162	辶	ZOO/tsuku-ru	Obscure: RHS alone is KOKU/tsu-geru = report, as in 広告 KOOKOKU advertisement (KOO/hiroi wide). Unclear why, with radical 162, it becomes *produce*. The meaning was, of course, that of the sign taken over from the Chinese; the Japanese had only one verb with this meaning, so once in Japan this sign shared the same kun reading as the sign 作 SAKU/tsukuru in Unit 2, which, in slightly different contexts, also means make, produce. This often happens: several different kanji have the same kun reading, usually for a verb. Conversely a given Japanese verb can be owned by several kanji. This no doubt reflects the small number of native Japanese verbs.
互	(1)	一	GO/taga-i	Two sticks hooked together? Phonetic link with 五 GO 5. In any case, symmetrical and means *reciprocal*.

◇ ◇ Grammar Notes ◇ ◇

A   This usage of **deshoo**, as in Unit 2, implies what might be; sometimes called the presumptive* use of **desu**–the formal equivalent of **daroo**. In Unit 2, **deshoo** was used with a verb in the past tense; here it refers to the present. At the end of this paragraph **taberu no deshoo** is the equivalent form (see Table 6 and footnote) of the **n'desu** described in the notes to Unit 3. This construction can also be used with a verb referring to the future: **ashita kuru daroo** "he may come tomorrow". Idiomatically, **kuru deshoo ka** is the equivalent of "I wonder if they/he/she will   come".

B   **Torikakomarete imasu**: the participle belongs to the passive form **torikakomareru** of the verb **torikakomu** (to surround). (See Table 3 for the passive verbs in **-eru**, which conjugate as Group II*.)

C   **Tame ni** means, here, *because of*; but oddly enough it can also mean "in order to"–eg **ikiru tame ni tabemasu** "we eat in order to live". Once again the demonstrative* pronoun **kono** = of this (cf Unit 3). The <u>ko</u> form is used here (cf Unit 4) referring to something already mentioned (ie *that the two countries are surrounded by sea*); <u>so</u>**no** could also have been used.

D   **San-oku nin ga sunde iru** is the equivalent of a relative* clause, referring to Europe, but it is elliptical in a way which is characteristic of Japanese. No need to say "(the continent) <u>in which</u> 300 million people live"; the simple phrase "300 million people are living" describing "country" suffices to make the point. (Similarly, in Unit 3 **kodomo ga kayou gakkoo**–"children go to" school–meant "the school the children go to".)

   Oku = 10^8: the West tends to think in steps of 10^3 (000's)–one thousand, one million and one billion (one thousand million); the Japanese use steps of 10^4. Thus 一万 (ichi)man = 10^4 (10,000), 一億 oku = 10^8 (100,000,000) and 一兆 CHOO = 10^{12}. 10^{16} is 一京 KEI (rarely used; same sign as KYOO in TOOKYOO). For million, you have to say **hyaku man** = 100 x 10,000.

E   Second largest…after the USA… Ordinal* numbers can be made by adding **me** (eye) after the noun/counter, eg 三年目 **san nen me** meaning third year, **go nin me** = the fifth person. However, when, as here, a ranking is also implied, the alternative form of **dai** in front of the cardinal *number is used. Cf 第一生命 **Daiichi Seimei** "First Life"–an insurance company.

F   To become something in Japanese is noun + <u>ni</u> + naru. If the complement (what follows) is a "Japanese" adjective*, its adverbial form (ending in -ku) is used after naru; pseudo-adjectives* (those requiring -na) become adverbs by the addition of -ni.

G   A dake de naku…B mo… is the way of saying "not only A…but also B…". Naku (from nai) is, here, the equivalent of nakute, which is used as the negative present participle of aru (to be). "Ocha ga nakute, koohi o nomimashita" meaning "there not being any tea we drank coffee" See also nakute below used with shika in para 3.

H   A yori B wa + adjective or adverb is the regular way of expressing comparison* indicating "than A, B cheaper…" ie B is cheaper than A. Or you can say, using the English order with the same meaning, B wa A yori yasui. In either case, the adjective or adverb (here yasuku means cheaply) does not require the equivalent of "more". Similarly at the beginning of paragraph 5 below, the Japanese leaves "more" to be inferred from "much" or "many".

I   The use of shika with a negative verb to mean "only", an alternative to dake, is like the French ne…que–il n'a que deux enfants which means he has only two children.

J   It is not obvious how to translate into Japanese the noun clauses following verbs like "I am sorry that…" "I am worried in case…". This construction (see nominalisation*) is one way of doing it: shinpai de means "it being a worry"; the subject is the noun clause kome ga juubun ni aru ka doo ka–"whether there is enough or how?" = whether or not there is enough rice. Ka, the question mark particle, is retained at the end of indirect* questions, and the verb (plain form) keeps the tense it would have had in the direct* question; doo ka is added with the sense of "or how?" which is the same as "whether or not". Literally, "whether rice is there sufficiently or not is a worry".

K   In yoo ni shite, yoo ni is used with suru to mean "to do things in such a way as to…" Okitai is the desiderative* (cf hairitai in Unit 2 para 6) of oku, an idiomatic verb meaning to do something in advance or with an eye to the future; the accompanying verb is in the form of the participle (here, shite). The sense is "wants to take steps in advance (to have enough rice available)". Another example would be "We are going on a journey tomorrow; let's look at the map (in advance)" = 地図を見ておきましょう chizu o mite okimashoo. We have seen in Unit 2, the parallel idiomatic verb shimau–also preceded by the present participle–and meaning "to end up by…".

L   Doko de mo is the usual way of saying "wherever…" Dokodemo means the indefinite*
     anywhere, just as daredemo means anyone. Where there is a verb phrase, it comes
     between the pronoun and mo; dare ni hanashite mo… whomever you speak to. It is
     these indefinite* dare/nan…mo forms which are used in negative sentences where
     English would use "anyone, anything". Thus, だれにも話さなかった = dare ni mo
     hanasanakatta = I did not speak to anyone.

     The corresponding indefinite phrases "somebody", "somewhere" etc, used in positive
     statements, are rendered by dare<u>ka</u>, doko<u>ka</u>.

     Nara is used here as the "if/when" form of the copula* desu (just as nai and nakute
     (Table 6) are used as negative forms of aru. Nara has to be used to make the "if/when"
     form of taira because taira (na) is a pseudo-adjective*. A "Japanese" adjective could,
     instead, conjugate in its own right (Table 7): for example "if the land were wide
     (hiroi)" could be h<u>i</u>roker<u>e</u>ba or h<u>i</u>rok<u>a</u>tt<u>a</u>ra (emphasis on the syllables shown).
     However, you can also say hiroi nara; the use of nara in such a case is somewhat less
     colloquial*.

M   Tsukuroo to shimasu…–tsukuroo (pron. tskroo) is in the intentional*/volitional
     form of the verb as shown in the verb Tables (cf Note A above, about the corre-
     sponding form of the copula desu). Standing alone this form means I <u>will</u> make,
     eat, etc: tsukuroo, tabeyoo–in the sense of a statement about something you intend
     to do. Used with …to suru, as here, the regular meaning is "they try to…" This con-
     struction with to suru can also mean "to be about to…"

     This form in -oo is the plain form corresponding to the polite form ending in
     -mashoo– 食べましょう tabemashoo (let us eat), and 行きましょう ikimashoo
     (let's go). This is also used in question form 行きましょうか ikimashoo ka (shall we
     go?). The plain form is also used with "…to omoimasu", eg 食べようと思います
     tabeyoo to omoimasu (literally, "I think I <u>will</u> eat" in the sense of I should like to eat,
     etc). (Cf toritai to omoimasu in Practice Sentence 4 after Unit 3).

N   There is no one-to-one translation into Japanese of the European construction
     "…so…that…", eg "he ate *so* much *that* he got fat" or "he was *so* busy *that* he had no
     time." The use of the adverb, amari gets near to it, however, inside a subordinate
     clause ending, typically, with node (because): amari ni mo tabeta node, futorimashita
     which means because he ate so much he got fat. Here, in this Unit, amari nimo
     modifies takusan with the sense of "so many (producers)".

     Amari is most commonly used with the negative to mean "…not very…"

Unit 5

O   Ureru is the potential* (see Tables) of the verb uru (to sell). This is a very usual way of saying "can…", though not as strong as koto ga dekiru (Unit 3). As with koto ga dekiru (Unit 3 para 2) the object of the action is tagged with ga, "…kome ga ureru".

All regular Group I* verbs (as here ur-u, which, like hair-u, is not a Group II* -ru verb, even if at first sight it looks like one) form the potential by adding -eru, -emasu to the stem*. Verbs of Group II (the -ru conjugation) however, add -rareru–eg tabe-rareru; this means that for -ru verbs the potential has the same form as the passive (Table 3).

P   Hikaku o tsuzukeru to recalls (like iku to in Unit 3 para 4) another convenient way of making a hypothetical* statement, ie with the dictionary form of the verb + to; the alternatives are the two hypothetical forms ending in -tara (or ndara depending on the past plain form of the verb) and in -eba, and the dictionary form + nara. The form using -u + to is most used when, as here, the condition/hypothesis being expressed is general rather than particular to a person.

Q   The form of the adjective or adverb ending in -te is sometimes called the suspensive* form, because it leaves the hearer in suspense until the next phrase comes to resolve the sentence. This form has to be used when two adjectives or adjectival phrases are joined. The simplest example would be "this book is long and interesting" = kono hon wa nagakute omoshiroi desu. However, it can also be used where contrast is implied: nagakute omoshiroku nai means long and not interesting and implies "too long to be interesting".

R   Yoo ni has several meanings (cf Unit 2 para 6 and here in para 4); with naru, it indicates something you have "come to" do– eg here, *come to eat more wheat*. Nari is the -masu* stem (the term used in the Tables) of naru; it is the form of the verb which can be used in clauses parallel to those ending with a main verb, like shi for suru, tabe for taberu etc. It is called the root form or the -masu stem, as that form to which -masu (and -tai) are added (nari-masu, tabe-masu). We have seen it used with nouns like kata (yomi-kata = way of reading, in Unit 4) and also find it with such auxiliary verbs as tsuzukeru to continue (+ arasoi in para 4 above); owaru to stop (eg tabe owaru which means to stop eating), hajimeru to begin (eg hanashi hajimeru).

◇◇ **Japanese Proper Names** ◇◇

Root	Kanji name	Transliteration	Meaning
TOO/shima	川島	Kawashima	river with an island
	島田	Shimada	island paddy
BA/uma	馬場	Baba	horse place
		JOO/ba (coincidentally) means a place. Unusually this name uses an ON and a kun reading.	
Nai/uchi	内田	Uchida	inner paddy
	中内	Nakauchi	inner home
	内山	Uchiyama	inner mountain
AN/yasui	安川	Yasukawa	peaceful river
		In modern usage the ON reading mainly means safe and the kun reading yasui means easy, but there is some overlap.	
KOO/hiroi	広川	Hirokawa	wide river
	広田	Hirota	wide field
HEI/taira/hira	平山	Hirayama	flat river
	平田	Hirata	flat field
BEI/kome	米川	Yonekawa	rice river
+ the old reading yone used only in names			
SON/mura	村山	Murayama	village river

◇ ◇ English into Japanese ◇ ◇

Sentences and Themes

1. The Japanese sell abroad (sell to abroad) more goods than they buy.

2. Is it a good thing for Britain to have oilfields? Japan (like Switzerland) (スイス SUISU in katakana) do not have oil ("there not being oil") and have to buy it from other countries.

3. The rice the Japanese produce is dear, but, like the Chinese and the Italians (イタリア人 Itaria in katakana + jin), they eat a lot of it. (the Japanese eat a lot of rice)

4. There is no longer (もう moo) much* fish in the sea round Britain.

5. Europe and America want to sell (desiderative = -masu stem +...-tai) cars to Japan, but this is not easy (易しい yasashii, but using the adverb + the copula in the negative).

*Use the very useful idiom with あまり...ない amari + verb in the negative.

Transformation

1. Japan people は from-abroad goods を buy than to-abroad sell.

2. Britain に oilfields が exist the fact (事) は good is か? Japan は, like Switzerland, oil が not-existing, from-other-countries have to buy.

3. [The] Japan produces rice は dear is but China people と like Italy people [the] Japan people a lot of rice を eat.

4. Britain's round's in-the-sea に, [no] longer much fish は does-not-exist.

5. Europe と America は to-Japan cars を want-to-sell, but this は easily is-not.

Unit **6**
THE MINISTER
大臣

Frontispiece character : 臣 JIN *retainer.*

◇ ◇ Introductory Note ◇ ◇

This unit includes a larger number of compound kanji, that is, combinations of two characters with a specific meaning which corresponds to a single word in Western languages. In such cases it is at least as important to learn the compound as it is to know the discrete kanji.

Most of the compounds used here are fairly simple and comprise kanji already introduced in the previous units or elements which are otherwise manageable. Some, however, are less easy, but appear as an essential introduction to the vocabulary of politics: 政策 **SEISAKU** policy; 関係 **KANKEI** relation (to); 責任 **SEKININ** responsibility; 決定 **KETTEI** decision; 首相 **SHUSHOO** Prime Minister.

In terms of grammar, we shall make closer acquaintance with one of the difficulties of written Japanese, the nesting* of clauses and phrases, each dependent on another. The Grammar Notes will represent these constructions symbolically.

There will also be sentences or clauses where, as often happens in Japanese, the subject* of the verb is not expressed and has to be carried forward from a previous sentence or understood from the context.

The "…koto ga arimasu" construction, meaning "it sometimes occurs that…"–will be used several times (an instance of nominalisation*).

We shall see more of the passive*, and of hypothetical* "if/when" clauses.

The unit also introduces the way in which Japanese expresses the differences between degrees of obligation* or probability*–must, ought to, should; probably will, may (possibly).

臣の秘書官に送ると、担当者は大臣との話し合いに呼ばれるか、大臣の返答の入ったファイルを受け取ります。事務次官が写しを受け取り、意見を述べる事もあります。

（四）大臣自身が決定できない特別な問題が起きると、他の大臣と相談する事があります。問題に直接かかわりがある大臣の意見が一致しない場合は、内閣が決定しなければなりません。そんな場合に、他より有力で、自分の考えを通すのが上手な大臣もいます。

（五）大臣は、当たり役で、人気があって、首相に信用が厚ければ、内閣改造になっても、任務を続け、将来は、元老にまで成るかもしれません。が、失敗すれば、新人に替わるはずです。

大臣

（一）　大臣は大切な人で、もちろん大事なことか行いません。国事が彼の仕事です。国会では部門の政策を説明します。国会で部門に関係がある質問に国会で答弁します。特別な問題については、国会で声明してから、テレビ等で記者会見する事があります。その場合には、記事に何が書かれたかが心配で調べます。

　　（二）　大臣は名声がなければいけません。しかし、名手ではないので、多数の役人が助けます。

　　（三）　すべての役人はそれぞれの責任がどこで始まって終わるか知っていますが、場合によっては、大臣に相談するべきです。まず、担当者が書類を大

DAIJIN

1 Daijin wa taisetsu na hito de, mochiron daiji na koto shika okonaimasen[a]. Kokuji ga kare no shigoto desu. Kokkai de wa bumon no seisaku o setsumei shimasu. Jibun no bumon ni kankei ga aru shitsumon ni kokkai de tooben shimasu[b]. Tokubetsu na mondai ni tsuite wa, kokkai de seimei shite kara, terebi nado de kisha kaiken suru koto ga arimasu[c]. Sono ba'ai ni wa, kiji ni nani ga kakareta ka ga[d] shinpai de shirabemasu.

2 Daijin wa meisei ga nakereba ikemasen[e]. Shikashi, meishu de wa nai node[f], tasuu no yakunin ga tasukemasu.

3 Subete no yakunin wa sorezore no sekinin ga doko de hajimatte owaru ka shitte imasu[g] ga, ba'ai ni yotte wa, daijin ni soodan suru beki desu[h]. Mazu, tantoosha ga shorui o daijin no hishokan ni okuru to[i], tantoosha wa daijin to no hanashiai ni yobareru[j] ka, daijin no hentoo no haitta fairu[k] o uketorimasu. Jimujikan ga utsushi o uketori, iken o noberu koto mo arimasu.

THE MINISTER

The Minister is an important person and, of course, handles only important matters. His job is the affairs of the country. He explains the policy of his department in Parliament. He answers questions in Parliament related to his department. After making a statement on a particular subject, he gives interviews on TV etc and also talks to journalists. In such a case, he is anxious about what may have been written by them and checks it.

The Minister has to be well-known, but because he is not an expert he has a host of officials to help him.

Though every official knows where his responsibility begins and ends, they should, according to the case, consult the Minister. First the responsible official sends the papers to the Minister's private secretary, and then either is called to a discussion with the Minister or receives the file with the Minister's reply. The Permanent Secretary / Director-General may have received copies and may give his opinion.

4 Daijin jishin ga kettei dekinai[l] tokubetsu na mondai ga okiru to, ta no daijin to soodan suru koto ga arimasu. Mondai ni chokusetsu kakawari ga aru daijin no iken ga itchi shinai ba'ai wa[m], naikaku ga kettei shinakereba narimasen. Sonna ba'ai ni, ta yori[n] yuuryoku de, jibun no kangae o toosu no ga joozu na[o] daijin mo imasu.

5 Daijin wa, atari yaku de[p], ninki ga atte[q], shushoo ni shinyoo ga atsukereba[r], naikaku kaizoo ni natte mo[s], ninmu o tsuzuke, shoorai wa, genroo ni made naru kamo shiremasen[t]. Ga, shippai sureba, shinjin ni kawaru hazu desu[u].

If a particular matter arises where the Minister cannot take the decision, he will consult other Ministers. In a case where the Ministers directly concerned with the matter cannot agree, then the Cabinet will have to decide. In such a case, some Ministers have more power than others and are better at getting their way.

If the Minister is effective and popular and if the Prime Minister has confidence in him, in a Cabinet reshuffle he is likely to keep his job, and even one day become an elder statesman. But if he fails, then he is likely to be replaced by a new man.

Unit 6

◇ ◇ Notes on Kanji ◇ ◇

KANJI character	RADICAL no	shape	KANJI / COMPOUND reading	derivation and meaning
臣	131	臣	JIN	Ruler's view of vassal prostrate before him; *retainer*. ◆大臣 DAIJIN *Minister*.
事	6	亅	JI/koto	See Unit 3 for comparison with SHO/ka-ku to write. ◆大事 DAIJI *important*. ◆国事 KOKUJI *affairs of the country*.
行	144	彳	KOO/ i-ku/okona-u	From usual meaning of "go" to reading okonau; *conduct, handle*.
会	9	𠆢	KAI/a-u	See KAISHA in Unit 3. ◆国会 KOKKAI (from KOKU-KAI) *parliament*.
部	163	阝	BU	See Units 3 and 4.
門	169	門	MON	See Unit 1. ◆部門 BUMON *department*.
政	66	攵	SEI	LHS derived from foot (止 tomeru in Unit 1) + line on top > go straight > tadashii; right, correct. Here, + "action" radical 66 = *administration*.
策	118	⺮	SAKU	Bottom phonetic; with bamboo radical to indicate writing material, leads to *plans, measures*. ◆政策 SEISAKU *policy, policies*.
説	149	言	SETSU	Origin not clear: 兄 is ani elder brother (or big-head). The two lines above originally sloped the other way, as in 八 radical 12 meaning separate > get rid of. Here, with the speech radical, it means *story, explain*. (?Mnemonic: get off one's che

Other Compounds ◇大切 TAISETSU *important* (Unit 3).
◇仕事 SHIGOTO *work, job*.

KANJI character	RADICAL		KANJI / COMPOUND	
	no	shape	reading	derivation and meaning
明	72	日	MEI/aka-rui	See Unit 2. ◆説明 SETSUMEI (suru) *explain*.
関	169	門	KAN/seki	A simplified kanji : original sign inside the gate was a bolt with rope and also supplied the phonetic; with gate radical it means boundary, barrier. Cf 関東 **KANTOO** Tokyo region; 関西 **KANSAI** Kyooto region. (One of the common phonemes; 46 **Jooyoo** kanji have reading **KAN**.)
係	9	亻	KEI	Phonetic: RHS **KEI** from radical 120 (ito thread); with line on top (cf **SEI** above) > 系 continuity; with person radical = *connect*. ◆関係 **KANKEI** (aru) *be connected, related*.
質	154	貝	SHITSU	Top is two axes, used as weights, and bottom is radical for shell which means money; sense of evaluation said lead to meaning of *quality*.
問	169	門	MON/to-u	Phonetic from gate radical; with mouth radical *question/ask*. ◆質問 **SHITSUMON** *question*.
答	118	竹	TOO/ kota-e/kota-eru	Top (radical 118) is bamboo and bottom is **GOO**/au meaning fit (see baai and hanashiau below); whole means something that fits; usual verb for *to answer*.
弁	28	ム	BEN	Said to be two hands holding a crown; but now substitutes for several former kanji; one of these implies speech or eloquence. ◆答弁 **TOOBEN** *answer* (formal term). (Note: several former kanji are concealed here, fortuitously **BENTOO** (**TOO** /ataru below) 弁当 is a packed lunch.)

Unit 6

KANJI character	RADICAL no	RADICAL shape	KANJI / COMPOUND reading	KANJI / COMPOUND derivation and meaning
特	93	牜	TOKU	One of the JI/tera family (Unit 4), but like 待 TAI/matsu has aberrant ON reading. Here, with LHS cattle radical 93 it means *special.*
別	18	刂	BETSU/ waka-reru	See Unit 4; *separate, to part.* ◆特別 TOKUBETSU *special, particular*
題	72	日	DAI	Phonetic; LHS variant of ashi leg + sun radical making the kanji TEI = straight, fixed. Here, with RHS radical 181 (頁 head) it means *subject, theme.* ◆問題 MONDAI *subject, problem.* ("mondai ga nai" = "no problem".)
声	32/33	土/士	SEI/ koe=voice	Another simplified kanji; player on top + musical instrument below (guitar?) makes a sound. ◆声明 SEIMEI (for MEI see above) *statement* (see also MEI-SEI below).
等	118	⺮	TOO/ hitishi-i/nado	A kanji from the JI/tera family (Unit 4) with bamboo radical: ?joints of bamboo implying equal, same; here it is nado *and the like.*
記	149	言	KI	Phonetic: RHS 己 KI (self) radical 49; with speech radical it becomes *write, record* (cf below 記事 KIJI *a record, article*).
者	125	耂	SHA/mono	Used (originally in China) as a suffix to change other parts of speech into nouns. Thus in Japanese means "the person who..." or as mono *person.* ◆記者 KISHA *journalist.* ◆会見 KAIKEN *interview;* 記者会見 KISHA KAIKEN is the usual word for *press conference.*

KANJI character	RADICAL		KANJI / COMPOUND	
	no	shape	reading	derivation and meaning
場	32	土	JOO/ba	Phonetic: RHS YOO was sunrise; with earth radical 32 it is the kanji for a (special) *place*. (工場 KOOJOO *factory*; 市場 SHI-JOO *market*.)
合	9	스	GOO/a-u	See 答 above; *fit, join*. ◆場合 ba(w)ai = ba + a-i *a case*.
何	9	亻	KA/nani	RHS phonetic; with radical was Chinese interrogative, taken over into Japanese to mean *what?*.
調	149	言	CHOO/ shira-beru	Phonetic RHS (cf SHUU/mawari in Unit 5 and SHUU week); + speech radical means *check on*.
名	36	夕	MEI/na	Comprising the characters for evening 夕 and mouth 口; calling out one's *name* at night?
声	32/33	圡生	SEI/koe	see SEIMEI above. ◆名声 MEISEI *well-known*.
手	64	手	SHU/te	Pictorial of a hand; often used for an agent (all hands on deck; a dab hand). ◆名手 MEISHU *expert* (could also be 名人 MEIJIN).
数	66	攵	SUU/kazu	Another simplified kanji! See Unit 4. ◆多数 TASUU *large number* (cf TABUN perhaps).
役	60	彳	YAKU/EKI	The RHS (radical 79) is a halberd or lance; with walking radical implies (military) service away from home which leads us to *duty*. ◆役人 YAKUNIN *an official*.

Other Compounds ◇記事 KIJI (see above) *article*.
◇心配 SHINPAI heart-sharing *anxiety*.

KANJI character	RADICAL no	shape	KANJI / COMPOUND reading	derivation and meaning
責	154	貝	SEKI/se-meru	The base is shell radical which indicates money; original meaning was to require something > punish. Thus it now means *responsibility*.
任	9	亻	NIN	Picturesquely, RHS said to be men carrying heavy weight suspended from a pole, burden; + radical means *to entrust*. ◆責任 SEKININ *responsibility*. (Warning: different -NIN in 役人 YAKUNIN and 責任 SEKININ.)
始	38	女	SHI/haji-maru	Several primitives merged in RHS, of which one meant *to begin*. Another means a platform; thus 台所 DAIDOKORO (place with a plinth) kitchen. (?Mnemonic: Start by putting lady on a pedestal?)
終	120	糸	SHUU/o-waru	Phonetic from RHS, **TOO/fuyu** is kanji for winter; LHS is thread radical; *end, finish*. (?Mnemonic: will winter never end?)
相	75	木	SOO/ ai-/SHOO	Comprising a tree + eye; said to imply, oddly, face-to-face. See aite in Unit 3, where ai implies original (Chinese) meaning of mutual. The reading SHOO means Minister; (see 首相 SHUSHOO below *Prime Minister*): (Warning: there are 65 jooyoo kanji with the reading SHOO.)
談	149	言	DAN	The phonetic RHS is a flame; with speech radical means talk. ◆相談 SOODAN *consultation*. (Cf 冗談 JOODAN [superfluous talk] *joke*.)
担	64	扌	TAN/katsu-gu/ nina-u	Phonetic; RHS was **TAN** implying dawn (sun above horizon) in Chinese. With hand radical indicates *load, carry*.
当	42	⺌	TOO/a-taru/ ata-ri	Simplified kanji: basic meaning is hit; thus implies to *be concerned*. (Cf 本当 hontoo *truth*; 当用 tooyoo *everyday*

KANJI character	RADICAL no	shape	reading	KANJI / COMPOUND derivation and meaning
				use (as once applied to the official list of kanji). ◆担当 TANTOO one's charge or *responsibility*.
者	125	耂	SHA/mono	See above. ◆担当者 TANTOOSHA *the responsible person*.
類	181	頁	RUI	Top left is rice; bottom left was a dog; RHS is the head radical. Thus implies "all sorts"; *kind* or *sort*. ◆書類 SHORUI *"the papers" ie the file*. (Cf 新人類 SHIN-JINRUI a new type of Japanese.)
秘	115	禾	HI/hi-meru	Had a change of radical (LHS) from 113 (altar): RHS is HITSU (arrow striking the heart implies must). (Cf 必要 HITSUYOO necessary); *keep secret*. ◆秘書 HISHO *secretary*.
官	40	宀	KAN	A roof over a building was a town hall suggesting government office which implies authority; (in compounds) an *official*. ◆秘書官 HISHOKAN *private secretary*.
送	162	辶	SOO/oku-ru	See Unit 3; *send*.
呼	30	口	KO/yo-bu	Phonetic **KO** RHS is sign for breathe out, and with mouth radical it means *call, invite*.
返	162	辶	HEN/kae-su	RHS phonetic, but also means "send/turn back" (cf 反対 HAN-TAI *opposite*; 返事 HENJI *reply*).
答	118	竹	TOO/kota-e	See 答弁 TOOBEN above. ◆返答 HENTOO *answer, response*.

Other Compound   ◇話し合い hanashiai (from hanasu talk + a-u to meet *to meet and discuss*.

KANJI character	RADICAL no	shape	reading	KANJI / COMPOUND derivation and meaning
受	87	⌒	JU/u-keru	Fingers above and hand below makes *receive*.
取	128	耳	SHU/to-ru	Take someone's ear (LHS) with your hand (RHS) = take (Unit 5). ◆受け取る uketoru *receive, accept*.
務	110	矛	MU/tsuto-meru	LHS (radical) is a halberd (cf YAKU above); with RHS bottom = strength and RHS = action radical; implies *service, work*. ◆事務 JIMU *business, office*. (Cf 事務所 JIMUSHO *office*.)
次	15	冫	JI/tsugi	Origin anomalous: as noted in Unit 5, the radical here stands not for ice (as it does usually), but for the number two, leading to the meaning "next". ◆次官 JIKAN *Vice-Minister* (senior official). ◆事務次官 JIMUJIKAN *Senior official of the Dept.*
写	14	冖	SHA/utsu-su	The radical is a roof; bottom is YO/ataeru = give–said to be based on something given on a spoon. But this sign is probably a simplified phonetic borrowing and means *copy*. (Cf 写真 SHASHIN *photograph*.) 写し utsushi *a copy, copies*.
意	180	音	I	Top is **ON**/oto = sound (Unit 4): with heart radical underneath implies *feeling, thoughts*. ◆意見 IKEN (見 KEN/mi-ru = see) *opinion*.
述	162	辶	JUTSU/ no-beru	Phonetic RHS meant millet: with walk radical implies follow and now means *state, make clear*.
身	158	身	SHIN/mi	Former sign, with large abdomen, shows original meaning of pregnant; extended to mean *body*. ◆自身 JISHIN *oneself*.

KANJI character	RADICAL no	shape	reading	KANJI / COMPOUND derivation and meaning
決	85	氵	KETSU/ ki-meru	RHS phonetic: with water (formerly ice) radical used to = decision; kimeru means *decide*.
定	40	宀	TEI	The bottom is correct, certain; with roof becomes *determine*, *decide*. ◆決定 KETTEI (from KETSUTEI) *decision*.
直	24	十	CHOKU/JIKI/ nao-su	Essentially an eye 目 with vertical and horizontal lines suggesting meaning of straight: fancifully suggested that the sign for ten on the top means that ten eyes were used to check on the squareness of a building; now means *direct*, *honest*; naosu is the verb *repair*. (With tree radical becomes 植 SHOKU = *plant*.)
接	64	扌	SETSU/tsu-gu	RHS variously interpreted as a tatooed female slave (top is a needle) or the daughter of a criminal; Chinese meaning is concubine. With hand radical means *approach, touch, fit together*. ◆直接 CHOKUSETSU *direct*.
致	133	至	CHI/ita-su	(Rare radical. ?Mnemonic: a bird swooping down to earth, therefore to reach.) LHS is radical; RHS is "action" radical, meaning to reach; kun reading itasu is humble equivalent of suru *to do*. ◆一致 ITCHI (from ICHI-CHI) "reach one" *agreement*.
内	2	ǀ	NAI/uchi	See Unit 5.
閣	169	門	KAKU	Phonetic; this sign, inside a gate, means a stately building and, by transfer, a Cabinet of ministers. ◆内閣 NAIKAKU *the Cabinet*.

KANJI	RADICAL		KANJI / COMPOUND	
character	no	shape	reading	derivation and meaning
他	9	亻	TA/hoka	RHS like CHI/ike *lake* but here, with person radical, derived from Chinese TA means *third person*. Tano = *other*. There is some overlap in meaning with 外 GAI/hoka.
有	130	月	YUU/a-ru	Combination of hand + meat (not the moon) said to mean existence > *to have*; cf 有名 YUUMEI *famous*.
力	19	力	RYOKU/ chikara	Derived from a bent arm implying strength. ◆有力な YUURYOKUna *influencial*.
考	125	耂	KOO/ kanga-eru	See Unit 3; *thought, idea*.
通	162	辶	TSUU/too-ru/ too-su(transitive)	See kayou in Unit 3; phonetic base + walk radical suggests pass through and as here means *put through* (transitive*).
気	84	气	KI	Another simplified sign: this radical 84 meant vapour: here, with cross, means *spirit, feeling*. ◆人気 NINKI *popularity*.
首	185	首	SHU/kubi	Cf BUSHU in Unit 4; image of head and neck; (Note that usual word for one's head is 頭 TOO/ZU/atama.) ◆首相 SHUSHOO *Prime Minister*.
信	9	亻	SHIN	A person and his word implies *trust*.
用	101	用	YOO/mochi-iru	A basic shape and radical; said to have represented a wall or fence, but borrowed for any business; use. (Cf 用事 YOOJI a piece of business; 常用 JOOYOO common use–of kanji.) ◆信用 SHINYOO *confidence*.

KANJI character	RADICAL no	shape	KANJI / COMPOUND reading	derivation and meaning
厚	27	厂	KOO/atsu-i	Radical 27 (cliff) has nothing to do with the meaning; the sign inside is both phonetic and also said to indicate something valuable arriving from on high (cf the cargo cult) > generous; thick; here means *ample*. Not, of course the same as 暑 SHO/atsu-i hot (connected phonetically with SHA/mono above.)
改	49	攵	KAI/ arata-meru	LHS originally weaving radical; with "action" radical on RHS unwind, *renew*.
造	162	辶	ZOO/ tsuku-ru =construct	RHS phonetic; with movement radical means *make* or *create*; (in specialised sense; in Units 2 and 5 作 the more usual kanji for tsukuru is used) ◆改造 KAIZOO *reconstruction*.
任	9	亻	NIN	See SEKININ above.
務	110	矛	MU	See JIMU above. ◆任務 NINMU one's duty, *office*.
続	120	糸	ZOKU/tsuzu-ku tsuzu-keru	See tzuzukeru = continue in Unit 5.
将	90	爿	SHOO	Here, the LHS radical, a matching plank (cf mokuhen in Unit 4) is also the phonetic and implies "strong"; the other components, now simplified, include a hand. Strong hand means a leader (cf 将軍 SHOOGUN)–which, apparently, leads to "the future". ◆将来 SHOORAI *the future* (RAI/kuru means come).

KANJI character	RADICAL		KANJI / COMPOUND	
	no	shape	reading	derivation and meaning
元	7	二	GEN/GAN/ moto	Derived from "big-head" on legs thus implies chief. (cf 元気な GENKIna healthy in Unit 1.)
老	125	耂	ROO/ o-iru/fu-keru	Shows bent old man with stick and means *old*. ◆元老 GENROO *elder statesman* (eg an ex-prime minister or very senior in a profession; formerly persons designated as such and filling a constitutional role).
失	(4)	ノ	SHITSU/ ushina-u	Improbably, but in fact, the hand 手 kanji in which the top stroke has slipped; *lose*.
敗	154	貝	HAI/yabu-reru	LHS is radical for shell and also phonetic; RHS is hitting or action radical. ?Mnemonic: pulverising shells/money means ruin? Yabureru means *to be defeated*. ◆失敗 SHIPPAI *failure*.
新	69	斤	SHIN/ atara-shii	LHS is a hazel tree (also phonetic); RHS is radical for axe. Thus freshly cut wood leads to *new*. (Cf 新聞 SHINBUN *newspaper*.) ◆新人 SHINJIN *a new man*.
替	72	日	TAI/ ka-waru/ka-eru	Though distorted, this sign still shows two figures at the top who can substitute for one another; thus means change over, *replace*. (Note that there are also other kanji for 代わる kawaru; eg in Unit 2 meaning instead of.)

◇ ◇ Grammar Notes ◇ ◇

A   Shika + negative verb means "he only…"; as noted in Unit 5, this construction has an analogy in French; here *"Il ne s'occupe que des choses importantes."*

B   The main clause is …shitsumon ni tooben shimasu, with the main verb shimasu at the end of the sentence means *(he) replies to questions in Parliament.* The subject of the verb, he, is understood, not expressed, as often in Japanese. …jibun no bumon ni kankei ga aru is an adjectival clause qualifying shitsumon and therefore preceding it = *(questions) having a relation to his own department.*

C   Koto ga is used with the plain form + arimasu or the corresponding negative to indicate experience or habit. "I have (never) been there" is itta koto ga arimasu/arimasen = the fact of having gone there is (not) so. (Cf koto ga with dekiru in Unit 3). These are extensions of nominalisation*. Once more, "he" as the subject of kisha kaiken suru is not expressed.

D   The main verb is shirabemasu, with he/the Minister as the subject understood from the context. In parallel is the verb phrase shinpai de, where de is the participle of desu = (it) being a worry.

    The subordinate* noun* clause (subject of the worry) is an indirect* question: Kiji ni nani ga kakareta ka. This indirect question *"what has been written by the journalists"* has to end with ka, as would the direct* question ("What was written?").

    However the noun clause (the indirect question) is followed by the tag ga; this is because the whole noun clause is in effect the subject of shinpai de.

E   Nakereba ikemasen: as we have seen in Unit 3, this is the usual way of expressing an obligation* = "if he were not to be well-known it's no go". Ikemasen is in the potential*. An alternative is narimasen = it cannot be(come) so (see below).

F   Meishu da/desu would be the affirmative statement "He is an expert"; the negative would be meishu de wa nai/arimasen. Here the plain* form nai is used in place of arimasen because it is the verb of the subordinate clause ending with the conjunction* node (because). (There is, incidentally, a play on words here in the Japanese, with the contrast between meisei and meishu.)

G   This is a simple "sandwich" sentence:
    A…{B…B}…A, where "A…A" is the outside ("the bread"). "A…A" = Subete no yakunin wa…shitte imasu = *all the officials know…*

The filling {B…B} of the sandwich is what they know; this takes the form of an indirect* question: sorezore no sekinin ga doko de hajimatte owaru ka *where each one's responsibility beginning ends* (begins and ends). The direct question would be "Sorezore no sekinin wa doko de hajimatte owarimasu ka" "Where do their respective responsibilities begin and end?" The only difference in Japanese between the direct and indirect question is that the verb in the indirect question is in the plain form (owaru). The "question mark" ka remains in the indirect question.

H Soodan suru beki desu: the dictionary form + beki desu is a common way of expressing a moral or professional obligation* translated as ought to, should.

I Okuru to: dictionary form + to is a neat expression for the hypothetical* "if/when", particularly in a general case (as here). See also "okiru to" below. (Note that oki-ru is a Group II verb, while okur-u (like ur-u in Unit 5) has to be Group I because Group II verbs can end only in e-ru or i-ru but not in uru).

J Yobareru is the passive* form of yobu "to call". The plain form is used here because it represents the first alternative–ie being summoned. The second alternative, getting the file back, is in the polite form.

K Hentoo no haitta fairu means *the file (into which) the answer has entered.* The equivalent of the relative* clause in Japanese is, as we have seen in Unit 1 ("a place to keep the car"), conveniently elliptical in this way. No is often used in place of ga in such adjectival* phrases.

L This is an open sandwich: (C…C) [B…B]…A…A, where A…A is the main clause ta no daijin to soodan suru koto ga arimasu = *to consult with other Ministers is what sometimes happens* using the nominalising* construction in Note C above.

[B…B] is a subordinate hypothetical* clause: tokubetsu na mondai ga okiru to = *if/when a special subject comes up* (using the construction in Note I above).

(C…C) is a subordinate adjectival clause describing mondai: Daijin jishin ga kettei dekinai. Kettei suru means to take a decision; kettei dekiru means to be able to take a decision. Thus kettei dekinai means not to be able to take a decision. Once again we have the neat equivalent of a relative clause "a not to be able to take a decision (subject)". Dekinai is in the plain form because it is the verb of a subordinate clause.

Soodan suru (consult) is preceded here by the particle to (together with), coming after the persons with whom there is consultation: ta no daijin <u>to</u> = *with other Ministers*. (In para 3 the corresponding particle was ni, as in English "I consulted the doctor").

M   The formula is (C...C) [B...B] A...A, where the main clause A...A is naikaku ga kettei shinakereba narimasen = *the Cabinet has to decide*.

[B...B] is the long phrase, daijin no iken ga itchi shinai ba'ai wa = *in the case that Ministers' opinions do not agree*. Ba'ai is, strictly, a noun, but here it is used like a conjunction, just as "in case" is in English.

(C...C) is an adjectival phrase: mondai ni chokusetsu kakawari ga aru = *having direct concern with the matter*. This phrase describes Ministers and therefore precedes "daijin". *"The Cabinet will have to decide in a case which the Ministers directly concerned with the matter cannot agree."* (Note that in Japanese it is not the Ministers but the Ministers' <u>opinions</u> (iken) that cannot agree).

N   Ta yori (than others). In this common way of expressing comparison*, no comparative form in the English sense is needed. Thus "than others influence is" = "has more influence than others".

O   Joozu na is the adjective meaning skilful at. What you are good at takes the tag ga, as if it were the subject of the clause; hence ga is added to the verbal* noun toosu no <u>ga</u>. (If the verbal noun were the object it would be "toosu no <u>o</u>".)

P   Atari yaku de... TOO/a-taru is a very useful root implying hitting something accurately. Here, it means *effective at his job*. The de here is the usual participle of desu (as in shinpai de above), but in this case it is in parallel with, and equivalent to, not a main verb but the hypothetical* form atsukereba (Note R below).

Q   Ninki ga atte: ninki is a noun meaning popularity; thus *popularity being there*. Here, as in Note P, atte is parallel and equivalent to the hypothetical form, ie as if it had been areba.

R   Shinyoo ga <u>atsukereba</u>: we should not be alarmed to see atsui conjugated* not as a verb but as a "Japanese" adjective* put into the hypothetical form (Table 7) = *if confidence is/were firm*.

S   ...Ni natte <u>mo</u>: *even if it comes to...* With naru (become), an adjective takes the adverbial form, but nouns take the post-particle ni, as with "genroo ni naru" below.

Unit **6**

T   (Naru) kamo shiremasen; *may (for all I know) even become an elder statesman.* Literally, "I cannot know (potential) whether…" A common way of expressing a certain (or uncertain) degree of probability*. (Cf U below).

U   Dictionary form + hazu desu means he will probably…, or it can be expected that… In the past tense, hazu datta, and in the negative, hazu wa nai/arimasen (can hardly be expected to…).

Summary of Conditions and Obligations

NOTE 1   We have now met four ways of expressing a condition–if/when: (a) -eba, (b) -ara (Unit 2–ame ni nattara), (c) dictionary form of the verb + nara, and (d) infinitive + to.

NOTE 2   The three shades of probability* are: (a) ame ga furu <u>deshoo/daroo</u> = it may possibly rain, (b) ame ga furu <u>ka mo shiremasen/shirenai</u> = it may rain. More literally: I can't know (have no way of knowing) whether rain will fall. (c) ame ga furu <u>hazu desu/da</u> = can be expected to (eg as forecast).

NOTE 3   The degrees of compulsion or obligation* are (a) dictionary form + <u>beki desu/da</u> = should, ought to, (b) (shi)<u>nakereba ikemasen/ikenai</u> or (shi)<u>nakereba narimasen/naranai</u> = I have to do it; I must do it.

◇ ◇ English into Japanese ◇ ◇

Sentences and Themes

1. It is the Minister who talks to the Press about the affairs of his department. (Note word order; try to get 大臣です daijin desu at the end.)

2. The Minister cannot know everything that is done in his department, but he gladly (よく yoku*) takes responsibility** for what officials have done well.

3. The Prime Minister has to be a person who is good at getting his way (kangae o toosu).

4. Officials in all countries do not want to handle matters which do not concern*** them.

5. The Prime Minister must have the confidence of the Cabinet and of the country.

*This is the adverb (ending in 〜く ku) of an adjective which means "with good grace".
** "take responsibility for…" is (quite literally) …に責任をとる …ni sekinin o toru. (Here 事に責任 をとる koto-ni sekinin o toru.)
***Idiomatically "to concern…" = …に関係がある = …ni kankei ga aru; the negative is …に関係が ない …ni kankei ga nai.

Transformation

1. [The] Department's affairs about (…について) to-journalists to-talk person [the] Minister is.

2. [The] Minister は of-his-own Department inside are-done all things を [he] not-knows but [he] officials が well did things-about (については) gladly responsibility takes.

3. [The] Prime Minister は getting his way (dictionary form + のが) good-at person has to be (なければいけません).

4. All countries' officials は directly concern [them] not-exist things を do-not-want-to-handle.

5. [The] Prime Minister （に） は [the] Cabinet と [the] country の confidence が has-to-exist.

Unit 7
TOWARDS THE "STANDARD MODEL"

標準モデルへ

◇ ◇ **Introductory Note** ◇ ◇

The good news is that the constructions of scientific Japanese are normally simple. This is just as well if machine translation is to flourish in this area. It is a commonplace that routine Japanese, in which the subject of a sentence is often not expressed, and in which clauses are nested within clauses, can make machine translation impossible without prior editing.

The verbs, moreover, are normally in the plain form in scientific texts.

However, there is still an extensive vocabulary to be tapped, and there is no space to give examples of all technical fields. This one, relating to the atom, should prove less esoteric than it might seem at first sight, since the names of many of the particles end with 子 SHI, and some of the other terms used are often transliterations of Western words into kana. Of course, as the last sentence suggests, there are always new developments, and the physics will be outdated before the language.

This unit has further examples of the usage whereby the -masu* stem of the verb is used suspensively* in parallel with a main verb, some examples of the passive, including the past tense*, instances of fairly complex sentences, common in Japanese writing, which the reader can unravel only by teasing out the relation between clauses and phrases which depend on one another. We continue to represent such sentences symbolically in the Grammar Notes; we also see the idiom by which the intentional*/volitional form of a verb + suru = try to.

In the "derivation and meaning" column in the kanji notes, the black diamond indicates, as in Units 1–6, compounds, derived from a kanji introduced in the unit. From this unit the white diamond indicates compounds of kanji dealt with previously in this or earlier units.

標準モデルへ

1) 19世紀に、物体とエネルギー（電気や光）は別々の実体だと考えられていた。物質は分子から、分子は原子から成り、原子はそれぞれ異なる元素を表した。今世紀初頭、原子は、正の電気を持つ陽子から成る原子核と、その周囲を運動する、負の電気の電子から構成される事が発見された。1930年代に、原子核には、質量はあるが電気を帯びない中性子も存在することが実証された。

2) 一方、アインシュタインの相対性理論は、物質は、もはや、エネルギーと別個だとみなされない事を証明していた。質量とエネルギーの関係は、有名な公式$E=mc^2$（cは光の速度）で示される。

3) 次の一歩は、原子核の内部構造を研究する事だった。ここに、70年代から、標準モデルという理論の展開があり、基本粒子と、それを結び付ける力を見つけだそうとしてい

る。標準モデルの実証のためには、巨大なエネルギーを原子ターゲットに加えて、粒子を加速させることが必要だ。現在のモデルで、基本粒子には6種のクォークと6種のレプトンがある。クォークの複合には中性子と陽子が、レプトンの複合には電子、ミュー粒子、タウ粒子、ニュートリノがある。

4) 力は、エネルギーの束の交換が媒体になって生じるとみなされる。例えば、光子は電磁場を担う光エネルギーの束だが、70年代末、新しい数理論によって、原子核を結びつけ、W^+、W^-、Z^0粒子が担う弱い力に統合され、電弱力と呼ばれる。強い力は、中性子を構成するクォークを結び付け、所謂グルオンが担う。重力だけは、標準モデルの見地からは説明されていない。

5) 万有理論（即ち、真の統一理論）を求めて、研究は続く。

Unit 7

HYOOJUN MODERU E

1 Juukyuu seiki ni, buttai to[a] enerugii—denki ya[a] hikari—wa betsubetsu no jittai da to kangaerarete ita[b]. Busshitsu wa bunshi kara, bunshi wa genshi kara nari[c], genshi wa sorezore kotonaru genso o arawashita. Konseiki shotoo, genshi wa, sei no denki o motsu yooshi kara naru genshikaku to, sono shuui o undoo suru, fu no denki no denshi kara koosei sareru koto ga hakken sareta[d]. 1930 nendai ni, genshikaku ni wa, shitsuryoo wa aru ga denki o obinai chuuseishi mo sonzai suru koto ga jisshoo sareta.

2 Ippoo, Ainshutain no sootaisei-riron wa busshitsu wa, mohaya, enerugii to bekko da to minasarenai[e] koto o shoomei shite ita. Shitsuryoo to enerugii no kankei wa yuumei na kooshiki $E=mc^2$ (c wa hikari no sokudo) de shimesareru.

3 Tsugi no ippo wa, genshikaku no naibu koozoo o kenkyuu suru koto datta. Koko ni, nanajuu-nendai kara, hyoojun moderu to iu riron no tenkai ga ari, kihon ryuushi to, sore o musubi-tsukeru chikara o mitsuke-dasoo to shite iru[f]. Hyoojun moderu no jisshoo no tame ni wa, kyodaina enerugii o genshi taagetto ni kuwaete, ryuushi o kasoku saseru[g] koto ga hitsuyoo da. Genzai no moderu de, kihon ryuushi ni wa roku-shu no kuooku to roku-shu no reputon ga aru. Kuooku no fukugoo ni wa chuuseishi to yooshi ga, reputon no fukugoo ni wa denshi, myuu-ryuushi, tau-ryuushi, nyuutorino ga aru.

TOWARDS THE "STANDARD MODEL"

In the nineteenth century matter and energy, like electricity and light, were thought to be separate entities. Matter was made of molecules, and molecules of atoms, each of which represented a different element. Early in this century, it was discovered that atoms consisted of a nucleus of positively charged protons, circled by negatively charged electrons. In the 1930's it was shown that the nucleus also contains neutrons, which have mass but no charge.

Meanwhile, Einstein's theory of relativity, had shown that matter would no longer be regarded as distinct from energy. The relation between mass and energy is shown in the famous formula: $e = mc^2$ (where c is the velocity of light).

The next step was to research the inner structure of the atom. Hence the development, from the 1970's, of the Standard Model, which tries to identify the basic particles and the forces which bind them. Verification of the model requires accelerating particles with ever greater energy into atomic targets. In the current model the basic particles are six kinds of quark and six leptons. Combinations of quarks compose the neutron and the proton; the leptons are the electron, muon, tau and neutrinos.

4 Chikara wa, enerugii no taba no kookan ga baikai ni natte shoojiru to minasareru. Tatoeba, kooshi wa denjiba o ninau hikari enerugii no taba da ga[h], nanajuu-nendai matsu, atarashii suuriron ni yotte[i], genshikaku o musubi-tsuke W^+, W^- Z^0 ryuushi ga ninau yowai chikara ni toogoo sare, denjakuryoku to yobareru. Tsuyoi chikara wa, chuuseishi o koosei suru kuooku o musubi-tsuke, iwayuru guruon ga ninau. Juuryoku dake wa, hyoojun moderu no kenchi kara wa setsumei sarete inai[j].

5 Banyuu riron (sunawachi, shin no tooitsu riron) o motomete, kenkyuu wa tsuzuku.

As for the forces, these are regarded as mediated by the exchange of bundles of energy. The photon, for example, is the bundle of light energy which carries the electro-magnetic field. In the late 1970's a new mathematical theory combined this with the weak force, which holds the nucleus together and is carried by the W^+, W^- and Z^0 particles, and is now called the electro-weak force. The strong force which binds the quarks inside the neutron is carried by so-called gluons. Only the force of gravity has not yet been explained in terms of the standard model.

Research continues for a "theory of everything", in other words, a truly unifying theory.

◇ ◇ **Notes on Kanji** ◇ ◇

KANJI character	RADICAL no	shape	reading	KANJI / COMPOUND derivation and meaning
標	75	木	HYOO	Phonetic: cf 要 YOO/i-ru meaning need. RHS HYOO (vote, tag); looks like radical 146 (west) over radical 113 (altar); here, with wood radical LHS indicates *sign* or *mark*.
準	24	十	JUN	Phonetic; (meant falcon, derived from short-tailed bird with a '+' sign); with water radical, used to mean *level*, *norm*. ◆標準 HYOOJUN *standard*.
世	(2)	|	SEI/SE/yo	Originally with three strokes meant 30, implying a generation. Cf 二世 NISEI 2nd generation of Japanese.
紀	120	糸	KI	RHS phonetic (己 KI means self): cf KI/o-kiru = get up in Unit 3 and KISHA = journalist in Unit 6. LHS means continuity. ◆世紀 SEIKI *century*.
物	93	牛	BUTSU/mono	See Unit 5.
体	9	亻	TAI/karada	Replaces a complicated kanji: conveniently seen as a person and a tree/cylinder; *body*. ◆物体 BUTTAI *matter*.
電	173	雨	DEN	See Unit 3: rain + field gives lightning and thus *electricity*. ◆電気 DENKI *electricity*.
光	42	⺌	KOO/hikari	Shows a man holding up fire and means *ray, light, shine*.
別	18	刂	BETSU	See Unit 4 区別 KUBETSU and Unit 6 特別 TOKUBETSU ◆別々 BETSUBETSU *separate*.

KANJI character	RADICAL		KANJI / COMPOUND	
	no	shape	reading	derivation and meaning
実	40	宀	JITSU/mi	A simplified kanji: original sign had the shell radical below = money, ie what is real! Thus the kanji meant reality, truth. **Kun** reading mi means *fruit*. ◆実体 JITTAI (with 体 TAI above) *entities*.
質	154	貝	SHITSU	Means quality. (Cf 質問 SHITSUMON in Unit 6.) ◆物質 BUSSHITSU *material, matter*.
子	39	子	SHI/ko	See ko-domo (child) in Unit 1; here, used to mean small object. ◆分子 BUNSHI *molecule*.
原	27	厂	GEN/hara	A spring under a cliff gives us source; *plain* (name 石原 Ishihara = stone plain). ◆原子 GENSHI *atom*.
成	62	戈	na-ru	See Unit 4; here *consist of*.
異	102	田	I/koto-naru	Though the sign is classified under radical 102, the top is not a paddy field; it may be a pile of money on a table which two hands push away because the parties have not agreed; or even a mask; *be different*.
元	7	二	GEN/GAN/ moto	See GENROO in Unit 6: big-headed man = chief which leads to first; = 元 *origin*, *source* (cf Unit 1 GENKIna = healthly).
素	120	糸	SO	Pure silk from radical 120 (thread); gives meaning of *origin*. ◆元素 GENSO *element* (cf 水素 SUISO hydrogen; SUI is ON reading of mizu = *water*).
表	(2)			HYOO/ arawa-su	Means *represent*. (See Unit 4.)

KANJI character	RADICAL no	RADICAL shape	reading	KANJI / COMPOUND derivation and meaning
今	9	人	KON/ima	See Unit 1; here means *this* (century). Cf 今日 KYOO, KON-NICHI today.
初	145	衤	SHO/haji-me	Radical for clothing, <u>not</u> identical with radical 113 (altar), + knife leads to cutting cloth suggesting meaning *to start*.
頭	151	豆	TOO/ZU/ atama	Oddly, phonetic ZU is the sacrificial dish of beans represented by the radical on the LHS, while the RHS is radical 181; *a head*. ◆初頭 SHOTOO *beginning* (eg of a century).
正	(1)	一	SEI/SHOO/ tada-shii	See **Masa** in Unit 1; correct: here used to mean *(electro) – positive*.
持	64	扌	JI/mo-tsu	Means *have*. (See JI/tera family in Unit 4.)
陽	170	阝	YOO	RHS top is sunrise on the horizon and base could be rays of light, supplying the phonetic YOO but also a semantic contribution; with the hill radical on LHS > a sunny place >favourable; *(electro)-positive*. Note: this is also the yang of Chinese yin and yang. ◆陽子 YOOSHI *proton*.
核	75	朩	KAKU	RHS phonetic: may have meant a pig; with tree/wood radical means kernel or, as here *nucleus*. ◆原子核 GENSHIKAKU (atomic) *nucleus*.
周	13	冂	SHUU/mawa-ri	See Unit 5; cf CHOO/shiraberu in Unit 6: core meaning is *going round*.
囲	31	囗	I/kako-mu	Cf torikakomu in Unit 5: *enclosure* surrounding a well. ◆周囲 SHUUI *surroundings, circumference*.

KANJI character	RADICAL		KANJI / COMPOUND	
	no	shape	reading	derivation and meaning
運	162	辶	UN/hako-bu	Basic phonetic (and mnemonic) is a vehicle with lid GUN and means army: with radical 162 = *move, transport*, and, oddly, *fortune* (不運 FU UN bad luck).
動	19	力	DOO/ugo-ku	Sign on LHS can be visualised as "four wheels on one axle" = omo-i (heavy; see ref to RYOO below): with strength radical, means *to move*. ◆運動 UNDOO *movement, exercise* (suru).
負	154	貝	FU/ma-keru	Shows person on shell radical (money) which gives (for no obvious reason) burden, defeat, *minus, and here (electro)-negative.* ◇電子 DENSHI *electron.*
構	75	木	KOO/kama-eru	One of 64 KOO's, RHS is a timber frame: with wood radical, means *construction*. ◆構成 KOOSEI *composition* (with 成 SEI/na-ru in Unit 4 and above).
発	105	癶	HATSU	Radical shows two legs apart: base has been simplified; *begin*. ◆発見 HAKKEN (with 見 KEN/mi-ru) *discovery*. ◇年代 NENDAI *era, decade*: 年 year + 代 DAI/ka-waru in Unit 2 *era/replace*.
量	72	日	RYOO	The top is not really the sun, but perhaps grain; base was omo-i (heavy; see DOO above) which leads to meaning of *quantity*. ◆質量 SHITSURYOO *mass*.
帯	50	巾	TAI/o-biru	Radical 50 is a cloth: this kanji represents the 帯 obi, sash worn round the kimono. By extension, here the verb 帯びる obiru means *carry*.

KANJI character	RADICAL no	shape	reading	KANJI / COMPOUND — derivation and meaning
性	61	忄	SEI/SHOO	Phonetic: RHS means life, birth (**SEI** above and as in 先生 **SENSEI**, and 生活 **SEIKATSU**–Unit 3). With LHS "heart" radical, it is the sign for *nature, quality*; as suffix makes abstract nouns. ◆中性 **CHUUSEI** (middle sex) *neuter*. ◆中性子 **CHUUSEISHI** *neutron*.
存	39	子	SON/ZON	The child radical is clear enough, but the LH sign surrounding it (and similarly in 在 **ZAI** below) is less obvious, but is said to be a variant of 才 **SAI** (talent), used in Unit 1 for years of age (三才 **san-sai**): *existence*.
在	32	土	ZAI	See above; here with the earth radical the idea is of being in a particular place. ◆存在 **SONZAI** *existence*.
証	149	言	SHOO	RHS mainly phonetic: with speech radical LHS means *proof*. ◆実証する **JISSHOO suru** *prove* (**JITSU** fact, truth; see above).
				◇一方 **IPPOO** (**ICHI** + **HOO**–direction) *on the one hand, on the other hand, while.* (Note, however, 一歩 **IPPO** below.)
対	67	文	TAI/TSUI	Simplified; the original was said to compare one written statement with another: the present version, happily, still does this by using radical 67, which as a character, means a text. The basic meaning is that of *a pair* and/or *two things in opposition*. Thus 反対 **HANTAI** opposite and 対する **TAI suru** vis-a-vis. ◆相対性 **SOOTAISEI**: (**SOO** in Unit 6 + 性 **SEI** above making the abstract, *relativity.*

KANJI character	RADICAL no	RADICAL shape	reading	KANJI / COMPOUND reading / derivation and meaning
理	96	王	RI	RHS is phonetic (Chinese "li") and with the jewel radical means a *principle* or *theory*: see Unit 4.
論	149	言	RON	RHS partly phonetic but shows an ordered collection of bamboos(?) or of documents. With the speech radical LHS means discussion. ◆理論 RIRON *theory*.
				◇最早 (in the text in hiragana もはや mohaya; motto(mo), + haya in Unit 1) *already*.
個	9	亻	KO	RHS phonetic is KO/kata-i = hard (in turn from 古 KO/furu-i = old (Unit 1)): with person radical, it means *individual*. ◆別個 BEKKO *distinct*.
				◇証明 SHOOMEI *proof*. ◇証明する SHOOMEI suru *to prove*. ◇関係 KANKEI *relation* (see Unit 6). ◇有名な YUUMEIna *famous*.
公	12	八	KOO/ooyake	The base of this sign, whether a nose or a cocoon, is taken to mean private. How to reconcile this with the meaning of the full sign–public, official? One interpretation is to see the top as opening up the base which was closed, thus suggesting *public*, *official*.
式	56	弋	SHIKI	Possibly phonetic: RHS radical for a dart (or peg to hang plans on) + construction radical gives the sign for *ceremony*, *style*. ◆公式 KOOSHIKI *formula*.
速	162	辶	SOKU/haya-i	Phonetic: RHS (see below under SOKU/taba) = wood tied with rope; with LHS movement radical means *fast*.

KANJI	RADICAL		KANJI / COMPOUND	
character	no	shape	reading	derivation and meaning
度	53	广	DO/tabi	Origin obscure, but most useful concept is that of a hand 又 holding a measure: *degree*. ◆速度 SOKUDO *velocity*.
次	15	冫	JI/SHI/tsugi	See Units 5 and 6; *next*.
歩	77	止	HO/aruku	ON reading of aru-ku (walk) in Unit 2. ◆一歩 IPPO (ICHI-HO) *a step*; cf 散歩 SANPO stroll. ◇内部 NAIBU (see Unit 5 for NAI and Unit 3 for BU) *inner*.
造	162	辶	ZOO/tsuku-ru	RHS is s baffling combination, used as phonetic, of ox on top and mouth below: alone, 告 KOKU mean to report; with motion radical on LHS; it means *to build, produce*. (<u>Not</u> the same sign as the tsukuru with similar meaning in Unit 1 (making sandwiches) but the same as in Unit 5 (making beer)! ◆構造 KOOZOO *structure*.
研	112	石	KEN/to-gu	RHS primitive KEN = to polish; stone radical provides a mnemonic and enhances meaning; *grind, polish* (and to wash rice).
究	116	穴	KYUU/kiwa-meru	The base is phonetic = numeral 9: top is KETSU/ana = hole or cave. ?Mnemonic: to drill nine bore-holes = to investigate. ◆研究 KENKYUU *research*.
展	44	尸	TEN	Radical is a body; base is clothes sign (radical 113). Hard to interpret what is between; the whole means *to spread*. ◆展開 TENKAI *development*. (Cf also 展覧会 TENRANKAI an exhibition.)

KANJI character	RADICAL no	RADICAL shape	KANJI / COMPOUND reading	KANJI / COMPOUND derivation and meaning
基	32	土	KI/moto/motoi	Phonetic: top said to have been a sieve on a support; with earth radical, means *origin*, *basis*. ◆基本 KIHON *basic* (see HON in Unit 2).
粒	119	米	RYUU/tsubu	RHS phonetic is a stand (an ON reading of 立つ tatsu in Unit 1): with LHS rice radical; it means *grain of cereal*. ◆粒子 RYUUSHI *particle*.
結	120	糸	KETSU/ musu-bu	RHS phonetic (a sage speaking): with LHS thread radical means to *bind*; cf 結婚 KEKKON *marriage*.
付	9	亻	FU/ tsu-ku/tsu-keru	RHS is a hand; with person radical gives *put hand on*; *attach*, *stick*. ◆結び付ける musubi-tsukeru *to bind together*.
				◇見つけ出す mitsuke-dasu (to find and bring out) *identify*. ◇実証 JISSHOO (see above) *verification*.
巨	22	匚	KYO	This sign is used phonetically in several kanji, but origin obscure: ?mnemonic, perhaps, the one-eyed cyclops; *giant*. ◆巨大な KYODAI na *enormous*.
加	19	力	KA/kuwa-eru	LHS is force + RHS is mouth = emphasise; *add*. ◆加速 KASOKU (see SOKU above) *acceleration*.
必	(3) or 61	⼼	HITSU/ kanara-zu	Not connected with 心 kokoro *heart*, but this may be the best mnemonic for the basic meaning of *certain*, *necessary*.
要	146	西	YOO/i-ru	Top said to show hands and a waist or head: several primitives have been assimilated into radical 146 (west). ◆必要 HITSUYOO *necessary*.

KANJI character	RADICAL no	RADICAL shape	reading	KANJI / COMPOUND derivation and meaning
現	96	王	GEN/arawa-su	Phonetic RHS is **KEN/miru**: with jewel radical means what shows up and therefore *the present*. ◆現在 GENZAI(GEN + 在 ZAI above) *present*.
種	115	禾	SHU/tane	RHS phonetic **JUU/omoi** + LHS cereal radical; *variety, seed*.
複	145	衤	FUKU	Phonetic RHS: with LHS clothes radical gives us double lined; *double, manifold, again*. ◆複合 FUKUGOO *combination*. (See GOO/a-u in Unit 4 組み合わせ kumiawase.)
束	(4)	ノ	SOKU/taba	See above **SOKU** (fast); **taba** is wood tied together; *bundle*.
交	8	亠	KOO/ka-wasu	Looks like the sign for father with a lid: however the crossed legs motif indicates *exchange*. (Cf also KOO in 学校 GAKKOO, with the tree radical added, school.)
換	64	扌	KAN/ka-eru	LHS another **KAN** phonetic, with origin said to be childbirth: with hand radical same sound; *change over*. ◆交換 KOOKAN *exchange*. (Cf 交換手 KOOKANSHU telephone exchange operator.)
媒	38	女	BAI	RHS has radical 99 (sweet) on top, and a tree beneath: it has the sound **BOO** and (for no obvious reason) means a certain (person/place). With the woman radical, reading becomes **BAI** *in between*.
介	9	人	KAI	The two vertical lines suggest a gap thus *in between*; also provides phonetic for 界 KAI (world).

KANJI character	RADICAL		KANJI / COMPOUND	
	no	shape	reading	derivation and meaning
				◆媒介 BAIKAI *mediation*. (Also in sense of go-between in sense of marriage broking.)
生	100	生	SHOOjiru	SHOO is alternative reading of SEI/u-mareru above; SHOO-jiru is an intransitive verb meaning *to be caused, to be the result*.
例	9	亻	REI/tato-eba	See Unit 4; *for example*.
				◇光子 KOOSHI (see KOO/hikari above) *photon*.
磁	112	石	JI	Main component (RHS) consists of a doubled thread motif with the plant radical above it; this is the phonetic, with original meaning luxuriant: here, with the stone radical; *magnet*.
場	32	土	JOO/ba	Same phonetic origin as YOO in YOOSHI above: with earth radical means a place or here, a *field*. (Cf 場合 ba'ai case, in Unit 6.) ◆電磁場 DENJIba *electromagnetic field*.
担	64	扌	TAN/ katsu-gu/nina-u	RHS is the phonetic (dawn with the horizon): with hand radical LHS means *take on, carry*. Cf 担当 TANTOO in Unit 6 means the person who is charged with the matter (Spanish *encargado*).
末	(4)	ノ	MATSU/sue	A tree with a mark on its tip, said to signify *end*. (Cf 週末 SHUUMATSU weekend.) <u>Not</u> the same as 未 MI (not yet).
				◇数理論 SUURIRON *mathematical theory*. (数 SUU/kazu number in Units 4 and 6.)

KANJI	RADICAL			KANJI / COMPOUND
character	no	shape	reading	derivation and meaning
弱	15	冫	JAKU/yowa-i	Arguably two bows + ice radicals: also suggestive of two wings 羽 (hane); reminiscent of bow motif in tsuyo-i strong (see below); in any case means *weak*.
統	120	糸	TOO/su-beru	RHS alone JUU/a-teru = fill. (Cf 充分 JUUBUN enough.) With metal radical (167), it becomes 銃 JUU (gun). Here, with thread radical LHS *domination, control*. ◆統合する TOOGOO suru *combine*.
				◇電弱力 DENJAKU-RYOKU *electro–weak force*.
呼	30	口	KO/yo-bu	See Unit 6; *call*.
強	57	弓	KYOO/GOO/ tsuyo-i	Originally a beetle (see mushi in Unit 2) with a hard shell; *strong*.
謂	149	言	I/iwa-re	Not a common-use (常用 JOOYOO) kanji, but fairly frequently met: phonetic RHS is the sign for stomach showing a belly-ful of meat. SHO/tokoro sign 所 used as a relative, meant "to say". In Japanese, as 所謂 いわゆる iwayuru, *so-called*. It is often written in hiragana.
重	(4)	ノ	JUU/CHOO/ omo-i	No satisfactory derivation. ?Mnemonic: four wheels on one axle to carry a heavy load. (See DOO/ugoku above.) ◆重力 JUURYOKU *gravity*.
				◇見地 KENCHI *viewpoint*.
万	(1)	一	MAN/BAN	Was weed growing luxuriantly on a pond; came to mean 10,000 (MAN): BAN as variant; *all*. ◆万有 BANYUU *everything*.

KANJI	RADICAL		KANJI / COMPOUND	
character	no	shape	reading	derivation and meaning
即	138 or 26	艮/卩	SOKU/ sunawa-chi	RHS is or was an official seal; not easy to see why kanji now means *immediate* (no connection with す ぐ sugu). Here kun reading means *ie, in other words*.
真	24	十	SHIN/ ma/makoto	We can take our choice between a head upside down and a spoon, on top, used to fill a kettle on the tripod below. The meaning is *truth, sincerity*; the kun reading ma is used with adjectives to indicate extremely, as in 真っ白 masshiro (dead white), and 真四角 mashikaku (square) and the given name 真 Makoto.
				◇統一 TOOITSU *unification*. (See TOO/suberu above.)
求	(3)	丶	KYUU/ moto-meru	Apparently represented a hide, but sign then borrowed for homophone; *to seek*.
続	120	糸	ZOKU/tsuzu-ku/ tsuzu-keru	See Unit 5: *continue*.

◇ ◇ **Grammar Notes** ◇ ◇

A   A simple point, but important: whereas the use of **to** meaning "and" implies that the things you are joining are all there is (as with 物体とエネルギー **buttai to enerugii**), when there may be more things than you have mentioned then **ya** is used. Thus in Japanese 電気や光 **denki ya hikari** means electricity and light. But **ya** shows that these are not exhaustive, ie that there are other forms of energy (eg magnetism). Thus the English says "*like electricity and light*".

B   考えられていた **kangaerarete ita** is the past continuous passive of 考える **kangaeru** translated as *was thought, believed* (ie for a period of time).

C   なり **nari** is the -masu stem of **naru**; this form of the verb is often used suspensively* to mean, as here, *being made of matter and energy...* This replaces a main verb where several clauses or statements are roughly parallel, ie none is subordinate to another. This is in contrast to the construction using the participle (ending in **te** or **de**) where the statement ending with the participle is often in some way subordinate. Cf あり **ari** in para 3.

D   We know that many Japanese verbs are made by using する **suru** with a word borrowed originally from Chinese: thus here 構成する **koosei suru** (to compose), and 発見する **hakken suru** (to discover). Thus, it is no surprise that in the passive, these expressions use される **sareru** (passive) meaning to be made. Thus 構成される **koosei sareru** is translated as *to be made of*, and 発見される **hakken sareru** as *to be discovered*. Similarly with 実証された **jisshoo sareta** in the next sentence.

This whole sentence is a six element sandwich, the upper and lower halves of which are roughly symmetrical. Symbolically:

A...{B([CC]DD)...B...([EE]FF)B}...A
今世紀初頭、{原子は、([正の電気を持つ]陽子から成る)原子核と([その周囲を運動する]負の電気の)電子から構成される}事が発見された。

kon-seiki shotoo {genshi wa ([sei no denki o motsu] yooshi kara naru) genshikaku to ([sono shuui o undoo suru] fu no denki no) denshi kara koosei sareru} koto ga hakken sareta.

A...A, the main clause is 今世紀初頭...事が発見された Konseiki shotoo...koto ga hakken sareta *At the beginning of this century...the fact was discovered*

B...B = the main filling (the noun clause saying what fact was discovered) = 原子は、([C...C]DD) 原子核と ([E...E]FF) 電子から構成される}

{genshi wa ([C...C]DD) genshikaku to ([E...E]FF) denshi kara koosei sareru} *{that atoms are made up of/consist of ([C...C]D) a nucleus and ([E...E]F) electrons.}*

C...C = flavouring (i) = [正の電気を持つ] [sei no denki o motsu] = [having a positive charge] is an adjectival phrase qualifying 陽子 yooshi (protons), which is part of the phrase D...D.

D...D = flavouring (ii) = (陽子から成る) (yooshi kara naru) = *consisting of protons)*; this clause in turn qualifies 原子核 genshikaku (nucleus), part of the noun clause {B...B}.

We have now dealt with that half of {B...B} which ends with 原子核 genshikaku to: in the second half we have:

E...E = flavouring (iii) [その周囲を運動する] = [sono shuui o undoo suru] = [*circled by...*] This is not quite symmetrical with the first half, since here E...E and F...F are in parallel, both qualifying 電子 denshi (the electrons) which brings us back to the noun clause {B...B}.

F...F = flavouring (iv) is (負の電気の) (fu no denki no) = *negatively charged.* This phrase, as noted, qualifies 電子 denshi = the electrons.

E   みなされない minasarenai is the negative of the passive of みなす minasu meaning *would not be regarded as...* The subject of minasarenai is the noun 物質 busshitsu (matter), and the complement, what they cannot be regarded as, is the phrase 別個だと bekko da to *is that they are different.* However, みなされない minasarenai is followed by koto o because the noun clause ending with minasarenai is in turn the object of the main verb 証明していた shoomei shite ita (*had proved*).

示される shimesareru is the passive of 示す shimesu (*is shown*).

F   The main verb is している shite iru, used here idiomatically with the intentional/volitional form 見つけ出そうと mitsuke-dasoo + to *tries to identify.*

G   加速する kasoku suru means to go faster; sareru is the causative which is translated as *to make go faster or accelerate* (transitive).

H   Here, as noted several times, the conjunction が **ga** represents something intermediate between "and" (in English) and "but"; "however" would be too strong. In English it can be left out.

I   The Japanese uses the convenient phrase によって **ni yotte** which means *depending on, based on, by means of...*

J   説明されていない **setsumei sarete inai**; as often happens the present tense in Japanese corresponds to the English perfect* tense, ie *has not been explained.*

◇ ◇ English into Japanese ◇ ◇

Sentences and Themes

1. It will take (kakaru) long/years before (made ni) the so-called standard model of the atom can be verified. (Use 実証する JISSHOO suru= *to prove.*)

2. A lot of the research (takusan no kenkyuu) into the atom is done by mathematicians, who use only pencil and paper.

3. However, to do research into the structure of the atomic nucleus becomes more and more expensive, so that (dakara) even (sae mo) the rich countries have to cooperate (協力する KYOORYOKU suru).

4. In your opinion (anata no iken de wa) how important is it to understand the universe?*

*universe is a quite easy kanji 宇宙 U CHUU (U = heaven, CHUU = heaven, space (phonetic: 由 YUU as in JIYUU = freedom).

Transformation

1. [The] so-called standard model が verification to-be-done until, what years も it takes (かかります).

2. Much of research は, pencil と paper を use mathematicians owing-to (によって) is-done.

3. However, [the] atom's nucleus' structure を research to do (dictionary form + のは) more and more (ますます) expensive becomes, therefore rich countries even mutually have-to-cooperate.

4. In your opinion [the] universe を to understand (dictionary form + 事は) how much (どのぐらい) important do-you-think?

Unit **8**
JAPANESE POLITICS
日本の政治

◇ ◇ Introductory Note ◇ ◇

There are necessarily specialised kanji compounds in this political text, but few of their components are outside the primary school list. This shows that the cumulative effect of building up the knowledge of the kanji is starting to pay off. The Japanese for "proportional representation", for example, may at first look formidable, but its five kanji will respond to closer scrutiny.

It will also be seen what a rich vocabulary Japanese possesses; there are a number of concepts like system, power, vote and even change, which are rendered by different words according to the context, as indeed such concepts are in English.

There are few new points of grammar or construction in this unit: more …koto clauses with (i) 意味した imi shita (meant), and (ii) 事が約束された …koto ga yakusoku sareta (promises were made to…); the idioms ni naru and to naru, meaning to come to some result (as in the English "Did it come to that?"); a fraction (three-fifths); examples of the usage requiring two postpositions, of which the first states the relation between two nouns and the second is the no which links the two nouns.

Above all there are long Japanese sentences. Literary Japanese, as we know, uses participles or the -masu stem instead of the first of two English main verbs roughly in parallel. This means that the Japanese sentence tends to be longer than the English because, as it were, it joins several English sentences together. A further complication can be the use of several wa and ga tags, giving the reader an apparent choice of grammatical subject.

The real difficulty of this text, therefore, lies in the syndrome which afflicted the man who said of the dictionary that he understood all the words but could not make head or tail of the story. The only remedy is a painstaking process of first identifying the main verb, then the subject, if any, then the main clause, and finally sorting out the inter-relationship of main clause and subordinate clauses and phrases. The Grammar Notes offer examples of analysis to this end.

We commented in Unit 7 that the physics could change; here it is the politics which are in transition…

を獲得し、政権交代となった。

（三）　新しい国会では、野党の自民党と、選挙制度の改革が協議され合意に至った。要するに、衆議院総定数の五分の三が、小選挙区制の単純多数方式で選ばれ、残りは、十一区に分かれた全国から、比例代表制で選ばれる事になった。又、企業や団体からの政治献金の制限と政府補助金の導入でも同意した。

（四）　一九九四年前半に、政府は二回交代し、三番目の内閣は主に社会党と自民党から成って、思いも寄らない連立だった。

（五）　今後、連立政権は習慣化するだろうか。そうなら、どんな組み合わせだろうか。それとも、新しい党が出現するだろうか。又、内閣に対する官僚の力は、前より強まるだろうか、弱まるだろうか。

日本の政治

（一）　一九九三年まで、日本の民主主義の主な特色は、一選挙区から何名かの国会議員が選ばれる、比例代表制だった。この制度は、第二の要点—自由民主党の三八年間に渡る与党の座—と結び付いて、本当の競争は、同じ政党の候補者の間にある事を意味した。各候補者には寄付を集める地元の後援会が付き、地元には便宜を図る事が約束されたが、これには、互恵関係による、汚職の可能性があった。政党中央への政治献金も、同じ危険性を伴っていた。

（二）　ところが、一九九三年、事態は急変し、何名かの自民党国会議員が離党した。自民党は今や過半数を割り、続く選挙では、非自民連立七党が、自民党以上の票

Unit 8

NIHON NO SEIJI

1 1993 nen made, Nihon-no minshu shugi no omona tokushoku wa, ichi senkyoku kara nan-mei[a] ka no kokkai giin ga erabareru[b], hirei-daihyoo-sei datta[c]. Kono seido wa, dai ni no yooten, Jiyuu-Minshu-Too no sanjuu-hachi nenkan ni wataru yotoo no za, to musubi-tsuite, hontoo no kyoosoo wa, onaji seitoo no koohosha no aida ni aru koto o imi shita[d]. Kaku koohosha ni wa kifu o atsumeru jimoto no kooenkai ga tsuki[e], jimoto ni wa bengi o hakaru koto ga yakusoku sareta[f] ga, kore ni wa, gokei kankei ni yoru, oshoku no kanoosei ga atta. Seitoo chuuoo e no[g] seiji kenkin mo, onaji kikensei o tomonatte ita.

2 Tokoroga, 1993 nen, jitai[h] wa kyuuhen shi, nan-mei ka no jimintoo kokkai giin ga ritoo shita. Jimintoo[i] wa imaya kahansuu o wari, tsuzuku senkyo de wa, hi-jimin-renritsu nana-too/shichi-too ga, Jimintoo ijoo no hyoo o kaku-toku shi, seiken kootai to natta[j].

JAPANESE POLITICS

The main feature of Japanese democracy until 1993 was the system of proportional represen-tation by which several members of the Diet were elected for each constituency. This sys-tem, allied to the second key point–the 38 years in power of the Liberal Democratic Party–meant that the real competition took place between candidates of the same party. Since each candidate had a local association to collect (campaign) contributions this led to promises (by the candidate) to look after local interests. This, via a relationship of reciprocal benefits, meant the possibility of corruption. Central political donations to party funds car-ried the same risk.

However a sudden change took place in 1993, when a number of LDP members of the Diet defected from the Party. The latter no longer had a majority, and in the ensuing general elec-tion a non-LDP coalition of 7 parties gained more votes than the LDP, which led to a change of government.

3 Atarashii kokkai de wa, yatoo no[k] jimintoo to, senkyo seido no kaikaku ga kyoogi sare gooi ni itatta. Yoo suru ni, shuugi-in soo-teisuu no 5 bun no 3[l] ga, shoo-senkyoku-sei no tanjun tasuu hooshiki de erabare, nokori wa, 11-ku ni wakareta zenkoku kara, hirei-daihyoo-sei de erabareru koto ni natta[j]. Mata, kigyoo ya dantai kara no[g] seiji kenkin no seigen to seifu hojokin no doonyuu de[m] mo dooi shita.

4 1994 nen zenhan ni, seifu wa nikai kootai shi, sanbanme no naikaku wa omoni Shakaitoo to Jimintoo kara natte, omoi mo yoranai[n] renritsu datta.

5 Kongo, renritsu seiken wa shuukan ka suru daroo ka? Soo nara, donna kumi-awase daroo ka? Soretomo, atarashii too ga shutsugen suru daroo ka. Mata, naikaku ni taisuru kanryoo no chikara wa, mae yori tsuyomaru daroo ka, yowamaru daroo ka.

In the new Diet, a change in the electoral system was negotiated with the opposition LDP. In effect, 3/5 of the Diet would be elected to small constituency seats by straight majority. The rest of the seats would be subject to proportional representation, but on the basis of the whole country divided into 11 regions. It was also agreed to limit donations to party funds from firms and groups, and to introduce state subsidies for the parties.

The government changed twice in the first half of 1994, and the third cabinet was an unlikely coalition, mainly of Socialists and LDP.

From now will coalitions now become the rule? And, if so, what will their composition be? Will new parties emerge? And will the bureaucracy be more or less powerful in relation to Ministers?

◇◇ Notes on Kanji ◇◇

KANJI character	RADICAL no	shape	KANJI / COMPOUND reading	derivation and meaning
政	66	攵	SEI	See Unit 6: with "action" radical 66; *administration*.
治	85	氵	JI/nao-su/ osa-meru	RHS phonetic as in 始 SHI/hajimeru; not clear why, with water radical means *to govern* (and to heal). (Note that several different kanji have readings naosu and osameru.) ◆政治 SEIJI *politics*.
民	(1)	一	MIN/tami	Same word in Chinese: said to be shortened form of a symbol for a proliferating plant; bio<u>mass</u> > the mass > *the people*.
主	8	丶	SHU/omo	Unit 4—*master, main* (cf omona and SHUGI below). ◆民主 MINSHU *democracy*–"people the master".
義	123	羊	GI	An important kanji, but one of the more difficult of the school list–even though it is not required until the fifth year. It is based on two radicals: top is the sheep (radical 123). Base is the kanji 我 GA/ware meaning I, myself; this in turn was two spears (radical 62). Message could be the change of conflict into peace? Anyway, it means *justice*. (See also below 議 GI discussion.) ◆主義 SHUGI *a principle* ("justice rules OK?"). ◆民主主義 MINSHU-SHUGI *democracy*.
特	93	牛	TOKU	See Unit 6; *special*.
色	139	色	SHOKU/iro	See Unit 3. ◆特色 TOKUSHOKU *feature*.
選	162	辶	SEN/era-bu	RHS two hands below and, two bows, above, originally radical 57. With radical 162, *choose, elect*.

KANJI character	RADICAL no	shape	KANJI / COMPOUND reading	derivation and meaning
挙	64	手	KYO	Top is simplified form of hands meshing; with the hand radical below indicates *arrest, give, act*. ◆選挙 SENKYO *election*. ◆選挙区 SENKYOKU (KU in KUBETSU (distinguish) in Unit 4) *constituency*. <u>Not</u> the same as局 KYOKU office/bureau!
何	9	亻	KA/nani/nan	See Unit 6.
名	36	名	MEI/na	See Unit 6. ◆何名 nanMEI (like 何人 nanNIN how many people? – counter for number of people; with the interrogative KA, (how many people?) *several*.
				◇国会 KOKKAI (Unit 6) *the Diet*.
議	149	言	GI	Same sign as in SHUGI above, but with speech radical; *discuss*
員	30	口	IN	Bottom half looks like shell radical 154 but is said to represent a kettle. ?Mnemonic: shell means payment of subscription and mouth means speaking > *member*. (Cf also Unit 10–社員 SHAIN.) ◆議員 GI IN *member* (of an assembly). ◆国会議員 KOKKAI GIIN *Member of the Diet*.
比	81	比	HI/kura-beru	See Unit 5; *compare*.
例	9	亻	REI/tato-eru	See Unit 4; *example, compare*. ◆比例 HIREI *proportion*.

KANJI character	RADICAL no	shape	reading	KANJI / COMPOUND derivation and meaning
代	9	亻	DAI/ka-eru	See 代わりに kawari ni in Unit 2; as verb means *to replace*.
表	(2)	丨	HYOO/ arawa-su	See Unit 4; *surface*. ◆代表 DAIHYOO *representation*.
制	18	刂	SEI	LHS said to be felled tree with roots and all; RHS blade used to trim it, suggests *regulate* and *control*. ◆比例代表制 HIREIDAIHYOOSEI *(System of) proportional representation*.
度	53	广	DO/tabi	See Unit 7; *degree, times*. ◆制度 SEIDO *system*.
要	146	西	YOO/i-ru	Chinese *yao* wish to–strictly nothing to do with radical 146: bird on nest suggesting west (Unit 4). Originally two hands round a waist (not west!); borrowed for word with the same sound (see also note on HYOO below) *necessary, to need*.
点	25	灬	TEN	Basic kanji (like a buoy with a flag) is 占 SEN; here used phonetically with four dots for black (radical 203); *a point*. ◆要点 YOOTEN *main point*.
党	42	⺌	TOO	Same radical (small) and sound as 当 TOO/ateru; said to have been a clan name (hence the legs) but borrowed to mean *group* or *party*.
				◇自由 JIYUU JI (self) + YUU (cause) *freedom*. ◇自由民主党 JIYUU-MINSHU-TOO (abbr 自民党 JIMIN-TOO) *Liberal Democratic Party* (LDP).
渡	85	氵	DO/wata-ru	See 度 DO/tabi in 制度 SEIDO above. With water radical, means *to cross over* or *extend*.

KANJI character	RADICAL no	RADICAL shape	reading	KANJI / COMPOUND derivation and meaning
与	(1)	一	YO/ata-eru	For once the simple form seems to be the original, showing a spoon with something on it, meaning to give. Later, hands were added (not in this version). <u>Not</u> the same verb as 当 TOO/a-taru below!) Another kun reading kumi suru means to take part, and this may explain the following compound. ◆与党 YOTOO *party in power.*
座	53	广	ZA/suwa-ru	Two persons sitting on the floor under a roof; *seat.* ◆与党の座 YOTOO no ZA *occupying the seat of power.*
結	120	糸	KETSU/ musubu	See Unit 7; *join, bind.* ◆結び付く musubi-tsuku *to combine with.* (Cf 結び付ける musubi-tsukeru in Unit 7.)
当	42	⺌	TOO/a-taru	See Unit 6; *hit, be right.* ◆本当 HONTOO *truth.*
競	117	立	KYOO/kiso-u	Originally = 2 x radical 149, but two little men is more picturesque, perhaps also reflecting the reading KYOO (as in 兄弟 KYOODAI) for 兄 ani elder brother: *compete.*
争	(4)	ノ	SOO/araso-u	See Unit 5; *fight, struggle.* ◆競争 KYOOSOO *competition.*
				◇政党 SEITOO *political party.*
候	9	亻	KOO	Original phonetic, also with person radical LHS, may have meant a target; with the arrow (radical 111) at the bottom indicates nobleman. Here, with an additional radical 9, the sign recalls subsidiary meaning of "awaiting" (ie election).

KANJI character	RADICAL no	shape	reading	KANJI / COMPOUND
				derivation and meaning
補	145	衤	HO/ogina-u	LHS is fairly unusual radical 145 for clothes (almost the same shape as radical 113 = altar). RHS is phonetic for several other words pronounced **HO**. Basic meaning of this sign is *to supplement*. ◆候補 KOOHO (not clear why) *candidacy*. ◆候補者 KOOHOSHA *candidate*.
間	169	門	KAN/aida	Cf **kono aida** in Unit 1: basic meaning is interval; …**no aida ni** *between*.
意	180	音	I	See Unit 4; *thought, feeling*.
味	30	口	MI/aji	See Unit 4; *taste*. ◆意味 IMI *meaning*. 意味する IMI suru *to mean*.
各	34	夂	KAKU/ono'ono	Radical 34/35 (walking slowly, dragging a robe or your feet): extended, fancifully, to going ahead without taking notice of people calling to you implying going your own way or individual and *each*! Not the same as 名 MEI/na name.
寄	40	宀	KI/yo-ru	In addition to the kanji in the **KA** family, there is another small branch with a man above the **KA** sign, having the sound **KI** and the meaning "strange". Here, with the roof radical added, there is a range of meanings, including *gather, accumulate, go to one side*. (The idiomatic meaning of 寄らない **yoranai** is explained below.) ◆寄付 KIFU *contribution*. (FU as in **tsuku** above; see also Unit 3.)
集	172	隹	SHUU/ atsu-meru	Radical, on top, is "short-tailed bird": thus mnemonic, if not origin, is that birds collect in a tree (lower half); *collect*.

KANJI character	RADICAL no	RADICAL shape	KANJI / COMPOUND reading	KANJI / COMPOUND derivation and meaning
				◇地元 JImoto *locality*. (See CHI/JI in Unit 5 and GEN/GAN/ moto in Unit 1.)
後	60	彳	GO/nochi/KOO/ ushi-ro/ato	See Unit 4: RHS has on top radical 52 (thin thread) + feet-dragging radical below. With LHS step radical extended to *after* (in time), *behind* (in place).
援	64	扌	EN	RHS said to be two hands pulling at an object extended to pull out implying rescue or *help*. ◆後援 KOOEN (help from behind) *support*. ◆後援会 KOOENKAI *support association*.
便	9	亻	BEN/BIN/ tayo-ri	No credible derivation for this kanji with several meanings: for example 便り tayori a letter, 郵便 YUUBIN the post, and 便所 BENJO a toilet. Here, the sign means *convenience, advantage*. <u>Not</u> the same as in 勉強 BENKYOO study.
宜	40	宀	GI/yoro-shii	Most of the kanji containing the sign 且 have the sound SO and the sense of piling up. Several have reading GI. Here, with the roof radical and possibly a dish full to overflowing means *right, OK*. (Cf (minasan ni) 宜しく yoroshiku regards to everyone.) ◆便宜 BENGI *benefit*.
図	31	囗	haka-ru	In Unit 2, 地図 CHIZU map: the reading TO/haka-ru, however, as here, means *plan*.
約	120	糸	YAKU	RHS said to be a ladle; LHS is the thread radical: one suggestion is that food and gifts of cloth were used to seal an *agreement*. Often means "approximately". ◆約束 YAKUSOKU (SOKU bundle in Unit 7) *promise*.

KANJI	RADICAL		KANJI / COMPOUND	
character	no	shape	reading	derivation and meaning
互	(1)	一	GO/taga-i	See Unit 5: *mutual, reciprocal*.
恵	61	心	KEI/E	Spool, or a heart in tow; means *bless* or *give alms*. ◆互恵 GOKEI *mutual advantage*.
汚	85	氵	O/yogo-su/ kitana-i	For meaning with LHS water radical see Unit 2 (kitana-i): concavity + water suggests a puddle which is extended to mean *dirty*. Not the same as 与 YOO/ataeru.
職	128	耳	SHOKU	There is a risk of making as complicated as this kanji any explanation of why an ear (radical) + the sign for sound (ON/oto: see Unit 4) + radical 62 (spear) should mean *office* or *job*. ◆汚職 OSHOKU *corruption* ("dirty work").
可	(1)	一	KA	Mouth + corner: ?sound of approval implies *agreement*. (?Mnemonic: "<u>ca</u>n do".)
能	28	厶	NOO	Simplified: RHS said to have been the tracks of a bear and LHS, with the radical, its head and growl. Transferred from alleged qualities of bear to mean *ability, talent*. ◆可能な KANOO (na) *possible*.
性	61	忄	SEI/SHOO	RHS is birth, be born (umareru): with heart radical means *sex, nature*; often used, as here, to form an abstract noun. (See Unit 7.) ◆可能性 KANOOSEI *possibility*.
央	(2)	丨	OO	The base of the sign for 英語 EIGO English (Unit 3); Large person (OOKII) either in the middle of somewhere or with something round his middle; *centre*. (This sign, with the plant radical above, is used both in Chinese and Japanese as the

KANJI character	RADICAL no	shape	reading	KANJI / COMPOUND derivation and meaning
				phonetic for the first syllable of England–*ying* in Chinese and in Japanese (Unit 3) EI; *ying* means "brave" and EI means "brilliant". Different explanations of the sign are offered accordingly: for Chinese the rationale is that you have to be brave in the middle of a jungle (Plant radical): for Japanese the centre of a flower is beautiful. So much for the derivation of kanji…) ◆中央 CHUUOO *centre*.
献	94	犬	KEN	LHS, now sign for south, said to have been a kettle + tripod for cooking offerings to the gods. With dog radical RHS (unclear why, unless the offerings were that kind of meat) means *offer*. Probably a phonetic, but mnemonic, coincidence that dog is KEN/inu. ◆献金 KENKIN *donation*.
危	(4)	ノ	KI/abu-nai	Picturesquely, a man looking over a cliff, or kneeling under one, means *danger*.
険	170	阝	KEN/kewa-shii	Phonetic RHS simplified; with mound radical LHS means *steep, harsh*. ◆危険 KIKEN *danger*. (Cf also 保険 HOKEN *insurance*.) ◆危険性 KIKENSEI *risk*. (Cf 可能性 KANOOSEI above for the use of 性 SEI as an abstract.)
伴	9	亻	HAN/tomona-u	RHS is HAN (half) in Unit 1: with person radical means *accompany, involve*.
態	61	心	TAI	See above (可能 KANOO) for derivation of top (qualities of the bear); indeed this top sign, with the fire radical underneath [熊] had a reading of kuma bear. Here, with the heart radical, *condition, state*.

KANJI	RADICAL			KANJI / COMPOUND
character	no	shape	reading	derivation and meaning
				◆ 事態 JITAI *situation* . (See JI/koto in Units 1 and 6.)
急	61	心	KYUU/iso-gu	Top (simplified) is phonetic; with heart radical means *urgent, sudden.*
変	8	亠	HEN/ ka-eru/ka-waru	Simplified phonetic; base said to be action radical 66, though it looks like 34 (slow walk). Means *alter, change.* ◆ 急変 KYUUHEN *sudden change.*
離	172	隹	RI/hana-reru	Phonetic LHS based on the insect motif in radical 142 [虫]: the story behind it may help to recall a difficult kanji. With a head and tail added the sign means monkey; and with additional horns (now the roof radical 40) becomes a yak, the name for which was *li*–the Chinese equivalent of RI. Tradition then explains the connection between this sound and the current meaning. With the "short-tailed bird" radical RHS the sign stood for a bird, the song of which was the signal for girls to leave their parents' home and marry. Hence the basic meaning of *to leave, forsake.* ◆ 離党 RITOO suru *leave a political party.*
過	162	辶	KA/su-giru	Inside is phonetic (skull or a wry mouth): whole sign means *to go past*; also kun reading su-giru as suffix means *too* (ie too much; cf 高すぎます takasugimasu (too dear) Unit 3, but in hiragana).
半	(3)	丶	HAN/naka-ba	See Unit 1 (hantoshi); *half.*
数	66	攵	SUU/ kazu/kazo-eru	See Unit 4 (tasuu no kanji); *number, to count.* ◆ 過半数 KAHANSUU (number exeeding a half) *majority.*

KANJI	RADICAL			KANJI / COMPOUND
character	no	shape	reading	derivation and meaning
割	18	刂	KATSU/wa-ru	LHS is **GAI**: with cutting edge RHS means to break, extended to *dividing*, *diluting* (eg 水割り mizuwari=whisky with water); and, as here *reducing* a number.
非	175	非	HI	Primitive showing two sides in mirror image implying opposed and as a prefix extended to mean *negative*: here 非自民 **HIJIMIN** *non-LDP*.
連	162	辶	REN/tsu-reru/ tsura-neru	Go forward radical + wheel or car carries meaning of movement or being put in a row or group. (Cf 国連 **KOKUREN** United Nations.) ◆連立 RENRITSU *coalition*. (RITSU/tatsu in Unit 1.)
以	(9)	亻	I	Derived from a primitive written variously; Japanese meaning, as a prefix, *more than and including*. ◆以上 IJOO *above, more*. (Cf 以下 IKA *below, less than and including*; 以外 IGAI *besides, excluding*.)
票	146	西	HYOO	As noted above (要 YOO) top is said to be a waist, classified anomalously, but mnemonically, to radical 146, west. Here the base is an altar (radical 113). Somehow extended to mean a ticket (as in Chinese) and, as here, *a vote*. Same sign provides the phonetic for a number of kanji pronounced HYOO, but also as seen above YOO/i-ru meaning need.
獲	94	犭	KAKU/e-ru	RHS shows a hand (base), and a (short-tailed) bird: this is partly phonetic but with the plant radical (top) is said to mean catching a bird. With the dog/animal radical also means to *obtain*.
得	60	彳	TOKU/e-ru	This time RHS top said to show vestigial radical 154, wealth, with a variant of a hand below, extended to mean *acquisition*.

KANJI character	RADICAL no	RADICAL shape	reading	KANJI / COMPOUND derivation and meaning
				Alternatively, if the shape is an eye, then, get one's hand on what one sees. With walk radical, the sign means go and get, and hence, *obtain*. (See also 納得 NATTOKU in Unit 10.) ◆獲得する KAKUTOKU suru *obtain*. (This is an example of a compound of two kanji with such identical meanings that both have a kun reading e-ru which also means to obtain.)
権	75	木	KEN	Phonetic RHS said to derive from birds cawing: with tree radical, extended to mean a balance implying *authority*. ◆政権 SEIKEN *political power*.
交	8	亠	KOO/ma-jiru/ maji-waru/ kawa-su	Looks like the sign 父 for father, with a lid: however, the legs crossed motif extends meaning to *exchange*. Cf KOO in 学校 GAKKOO (with tree radical) school (Unit 3).
代	9	亻	DAI/TAI/ ka-eru/ka-waru	See kawari in Unit 2: the basic meaning is *to change* or *take turns* to speak or whatever. ◆交代 KOOTAI *change-round*.
新	69	斤	SHIN/atara-shii	See Unit 6: *new*.
野	166	里	YA/no	RHS is the phonetic YO (eg in 予定 YOTEI plan) and LHS is RI/sato, village/field, (as in 古里 furusato in Unit 3); *an (uncultivated) field*. (Cf 上野 UENO part of Tokyo and the company 野村 Nomura). For some reason, it means the political opposition–out in the wilds? ◆野党 YATOO *the parties in opposition*.
改	49	己	KAI/arata-meru	See Unit 6 (改造 KAIZOO) *to change, renew*.

KANJI	RADICAL		KANJI / COMPOUND	
character	no	shape	reading	derivation and meaning
革	177	艹	KAKU/kawa	A radical and primitive of an animal skin stretched out which gives kun reading kawa and means leather. Unclear why ON reading means *change*. ◆改革 KAIKAKU *reform*.
協	24	十	KYOO	An easy sign: the combined strength (RHS) of ten (LHS) gives *cooperation*.
議	149	言	GI	See GI above: with words radical 149, meaning extends to *discussion*. ◆協議する KYOOGI suru *negotiate, discuss*.
合	9	人	GOO/a-u	See Unit 4; *come together*.
意	180	音	I	See Unit 4; "the sounds (top) in your heart" gives us *feelings*. ◆合意 GOOI *agreement*.
至	133	至	SHI/ita-ru	Variously, a bird or an arrow coming down to earth shows the extreme, *to reach* .
				◇要するに YOO-suru ni *in brief, in effect.* (By itself 要する YOO suru, with an object, means to need, require.)
衆	143	血	SHUU	The current radical (on top) is, quite irrelevantly, a phial of blood; used to be an eye (radical 109) or the sun: below are several persons suggesting a *meeting, mass* as in 民衆 MINSHUU "the people".
院	170	阝	IN	Three characters with phonetics originally similar: we have seen 元 GEN; 完 KAN, as in 完全 KANZEN, complete. Here, with the mound radical, IN is a walled building, as in 病院

KANJI character	RADICAL no	shape	reading	KANJI / COMPOUND derivation and meaning
				BYOOIN hospital. ◆衆議院 SHUUGIIN *House of Representatives.*
総	120	糸	SOO	Perhaps this kanji takes phonetic derivation to its limits. Top RHS is 公 KOO/ooyake public (公式 KOOSHIKI *formula* in Unit 7). However, another branch of the same family has the reading SHOO−as (with tree radical) becomes SHOO/matsu a pine (cf 小松 Komatsu, the name of a maker of construction machinery). With the heart radical added below RHS (a kanji not used in Japanese) and, the thread radical on LHS makes SOO meaning *total, general.* (The RHS with a roof on top makes SOO/mado *window.*) ◆定数 TEISUU *a (fixed) number.* ◆総定数 SOOTEISUU *the total number.*
				◇小選挙区制 SHOOSENKYOKUSEI *small constituency.*
単	(3)	丶	TAN	Phonetic original had two mouths (radical 30) on top: the sound was used for several kanji, of which this is the "simplest"; *simple.*
純	120	糸	JUN	Phonetic RHS said to have shown a plant sprouting, but with LHS thread radical implying undyed thread means *pure.* ◆単純 TANJUN *simple.*
				◇多数 TASUU *(large) number* equivalent to *majority.* ◇方式 HOOSHIKI *method.*
残	78	歹	ZAN/noko-ru	Phonetic made of LHS bones radical + RHS a spear and hand holding it(?) Here, it means *to be left over* . (Cf 残念 ZAN-NEN pity, nuisance.)

KANJI character	RADICAL no	shape	reading	KANJI / COMPOUND derivation and meaning
区	22	⊏	KU	See Unit 4 *quarter, ward* (of a town). Cf 文京区 BUNKY-OOKU in Tokyo and 選挙区 SENKYOKU above.
分	12	八	wa-kareru	A kun reading of 分 BUN meaning *to be divided*.
全	9	人	ZEN/matta-ku	A lid over a jewel? (top assimilated to the person radical) said to show *completeness*. ◆全国 ZENKOKU *the whole country*. (Cf 全部 ZENBU everything, and 全然 ZENZEN completely or (with negative) = not at all.
企	9	人	KI/kuwada-teru	With foot radical 77 at the base and the person radical above said to represent a man on tip-toe wanting something or looking into the future.
業	(3)	丶	GYOO/waza	Some derive the top from a primitive of a tree-trunk with foliage extended to activities of man. Or a rack to hold instruments. An important kanji meaning *profession*; cf 工業 KOOGYOO manfacturing industry, 産業 SANGYOO (productive) industry. ◆企業 KIGYOO *a firm, enterprise*.
団	31	囗	DAN/TON	Very much simplified inside, but enclosure radical gives clue to meaning of set or group; much used as a suffix defining *a group of people*. ◆団体 DANTAI *body, group*.
限	170	阝	GEN/kagi-ru	Two primitives, now radicals, are written rather like a Greek beta: one, on the LHS of the kanji, means a hill (thus yin and yang, referred to in Unit 7, mean the shady and sunny side of a hill); the other radical, written on the right, is a smaller

Unit 8

KANJI character	RADICAL no	shape	reading	KANJI / COMPOUND derivation and meaning
				mound, as in 都 TO/miyako (capital, as in 京都 KYOO-TO). The RHS is also used as a phonetic for KON, and for GIN in silver. Here means *frontier, limit*. ◆制限 SEIGEN *limitation*. (SEI as in 制度 SEIDO above.)
府	53	广	FU	Phonetic (cf FU/tsuku in Unit 3): with sloping roof radical shows a store, and now means *government office*. ◆政府 SEIFU *government*.
補	145	ネ	HO/ogina-u	Phonetic RHS, of uncertain meaning, serves several kanji: with LHS clothes radical means *patch, add to*. ◆補助 HOJO *help, support* . (助 JO/tasu-keru in Unit 3.) ◆補助金 HOJOKIN *subsidy*.
導	41	寸	DOO/michibi-ku	Phonetic from 道 DOO/michi: with hand radical means *lead, guide*. ◆導入 DOONYUU *introduction*. (NYUU is ON reading of the familiar kanji for hairu, iru, ireru.)
				◇同意 DOOI ("same meaning") *agreement*. ◇前半 ZENHAN *first half year*.
番	165	釆	BAN	Radical means to sort or separate: this gives little clue to why the meaning here is a *sentry* and, notably, as here, a counter for ordinal* numbers. (See Alphabetical Reference Grammar.)
				◇社会党 SHAKAITOO *Socialist Party*
寄	40	宀	KI/yo-ru	See above 寄付 KIFU contribution: the same verb, in the negative in this idiom, can, as explained in the grammar notes, be translated as *not approaching*. ◇今後 KONGO *from now on*.

KANJI character	RADICAL no	shape	KANJI / COMPOUND reading	derivation and meaning
習	124	羽	SHUU/nara-u	Top is radical 124–feathers: pleasant to believe that this sign comes from a bird learning to fly; *learn*.
慣	61	忄	KAN/na-reru	RHS is phonetic–meant pierce (strings of money): with heart radical, *get used to*. ◆習慣 SHUUKAN *habit, custom*.
化	9	亻	KA/ba-keru	Convincingly, shows two people but in different positions and thus means change. Often used, as here, for the suffix corresponding to "…isation" in English. ◆習慣化 SHUUKAN KA *habituation*.
				◇出現する SHUTSUGEN suru *make an appearance*. (SHUTSU is ON reading of deru/dasu (Unit 1); for GEN/arawareru see Unit 7.)
官	40	宀	KAN	The base is an old sign for the buildings of a city: several characters are derived from it; this one means the authorities who, presumably, operate from an office block with a roof.
僚	9	亻	RYOO	RHS phonetic: with person radical means *a companion* or *an official*. ◆官僚 KANRYOO *bureaucrat*.

◇ ◇ **Grammar Notes** ◇ ◇

A   As explained in the kanji notes, 名 mei is a counter for persons, like 人 nin; 何名か nan-mei ka means a number of (people), just as 何か nanika means something.

B   選ぶ erabu (elect): 選ばれる erabareru is the passive plain form; *are elected.*

C   A sandwich with thick bread, but a single filling: symbolically A…[B…B]…A. The main clause A…A is:
日本の民主主義の主な特色は[B…B]比例代表制だった
Nihon no minshushugi no omona tokushoku wa [B…B] hirei-daihyoo-sei datta
The main feature of Japanese democracy was the proportional representation system…

[B…B] is a adjectival clause (in English a relative clause* beginning "by which…")
一選挙区から何名かの国会議員が選ばれる
ichi senkyoku kara nan-mei ka no kokkai giin ga erabareru *from one constituency several members of parliament are elected.* This adjectival clause comes in front of and refers to "proportional representation system".

D   A rather more complicated sentence: symbolically,

A…B–C…C–B…[D…D]…A

The difficulty is that the reader has to choose between two apparent possible subjects/topics: この制度（は） kono seido (wa) (this system); and 本当の競争 hontoo no kyoosoo (wa) (the real competition).

To resolve this dilemma, first, the main verb must be identified as 意味した imi shita (meant). Thereafter, trial and error (and, later, cumulative experience) will reveal that the statement makes sense only if the first topic/subject この制度（は） kono seido (wa) is the true grammatical subject of the main verb: thus, A…A is, この制度は…意味した Kono seido wa…imi shita *This system… meant…*

The next question is <u>what</u> it meant; this has to be the clause D…D, because this ends with …koto o, showing that it is the object of 意味した imi shita:
本当の競争は同じ政党の候補者の間にある事（を） hontoo no kyoosoo wa onaji seitoo no koohosha no aida ni aru koto (o) *"the fact that"* (事を koto o) *the real competition takes place between candidates of the same party.*

The sentence is complicated by the phrase B…B which, in English, runs parallel to the main clause:
第二の要点…と結び付いて dai ni no yooten…to musubi-tsuite *in combination with the second important point.*

C...C is a parenthesis which explains the second important point:
自由民主党の三十八年間にわたる与党の座 Jiyuu-Minshu-Too no sanjuu hachi nenkan ni wataru yotoo no za *the LDP's span of 38 years as ruling party.*

E   This sentence uses a variant of the construction A は B が... A wa B ga... as in Unit 1 = A has B.
各候補者には［寄付を集める］地元の後援会が付き kaku koohosha ni wa [kifu o atsumeru] jimoto no kooenkai ga tsuki *each candidate having (attached) a local society [which collects contributions].*

F ．便宜を図る事が約束された bengi o hakaru koto ga yakusoku sareta *promises were made "to look after benefits"* ie that each side, the voters and the candidate, would provide benefits to the other.

G   政党中央への政治献金 Seitoo chuuoo e no seiji kenkin uses two postpositions together. This is standard: the first–へ e–indicates the relationship between two nouns or noun phrases, here, *(donations) to the central party;* the の no provides the link between the prepositional phrase "to the central party" and the noun phrase to which it refers, "political donations".

企業や団体からの政治献金 kigyoo ya dantai kara no seiji kenkin is another example of the use of two postpositions: the first expresses the substantive relation *"from enterprises and groups"* while no links this phrase to seiji kenkin *political donations.*

H   事態 jitai is one of a number of words meaning "situation" which are added in Japanese to complete the meaning. (Rather like the English usage "a defeat situation" or "a winning position".) In this context, it is more natural Japanese to say "The situation changed suddenly" rather than "A sudden change occurred".

I   This sentence, like the one above, has two **wa** tags, and in addition one **ga** tag. Thus, there are three potential subjects/topics; which of them can be the subject of the main verb? On inspection, it becomes clear that 自民党（は）jimintoo (wa) is the subject of the verb 割り wari (-masu stem of 割る waru meaning "to have reduced" or "to lose"), while 連立七党（が）renritsu nana-too/shichi-too (ga) *a seven-party coalition,* is the subject of the -masu stem verb 獲得し kakutoku shi meaning *obtained.* This phrase bears the **ga** tag; the second **wa** is attached to the phrase, 続く選挙で tsuzuku senkyo de *in the ensuing election,* since this, semantically though not grammatically, introduces the main point. The main verb, in this case なった natta, has no grammatical subject in Japanese: *(It) came to a change of government.*

J   となる to naru is an idiom like になる ni naru in para 3 below, and in general refers to a condition which was decided or was somehow due to happen. If there is a distinction between the two, it is that になる ni naru is more usual, and that となる to naru is more decisive and final.

K   In 野党の自民党 yatoo no Jimintoo, we have the usual no used to link two nouns in apposition*. Once again, the main verb 至った itatta has no stated subject: "*they*" *reached agreement with…the LPD.*

L   五分の三 5 bun no 3 is the usual formula for a fraction–"of 5 parts 3" *three-fifths.*

M   …制限と政府補助金の導入でも同意した …seigen to seifu hojokin no doonyuu de mo dooi shita *(they) made agreement on a limitation of party funding…and on the introduction of state subsidies…* Note that it has become more usual to use phrases like 政府補助金 seifu hojokin *state subsidies* (as in English) rather than 政府の補助金 seifu no hojokin. This is why newspapers in particular seem to use what look like new compounds (kango) which the reader does not always find in the dictionary.

N   思いも寄らない omoi mo yoranai is an idiom, based on the verb 寄る yoru (to approach). In the negative, it means "not approaching thought" or *not easily thought of.* (The same verb occurs in 年寄り toshiyori (elderly), where, however, the meaning is "gathering in the years".)

A further point here is that the Japanese do not always use a kanji even when one is available. Thus, for によって ni yotte (depending on), it is usual to use hiragana. (There are, incidentally, several verbs with kun reading yoru: ni yotte would use the kanji 因 with ON reading IN meaning cause, as in 原因 GEN'IN cause.)

◇ ◇ **English into Japanese** ◇ ◇

Sentences and Themes

1. What is democracy? Is it in your opinion truly democratic (use suffix -TEKI) if one party obtains power without a majority of the votes in the country?

2. Which is more important, democracy or good government? Do we have to choose?

3. What is the role (任務 ninmu) of officials—only to do what they are told? Or to make policies (政策 SEISAKU)?

Transformation

1. Democracy は what is? One party が majority not acquiring, in the political seat-of-power to exist (dictionary form + 事は) in-truth democratic is (plain form) だと do-you-think?

2. Democracy と good government は, which が [more] important would-be? If-we-were-not-to-choose is it no go?

3. Officials' role は what is [it]? As-[they]-are-told to do would-be? or (それとも) policy を to make (dictionary form) would-be?

Unit **9**
THE JAPANESE ECONOMY(1)
日本の経済(1)

Frontispiece character : 経 KEI *path*.

◇ ◇ **Introductory Note** ◇ ◇

Because, for so many countries, Japan is an important trading and manufacturing partner, economics is an important field in relation to Japan. Thus two units are devoted to the specialised vocabulary and expressions of economics. As noted in relation to Unit 8, more and more of the compounds contain kanji we have already met. But a significant effort of memory is still required to associate the given new combinations of two or more kanji with the English technical expressions which they map on to.

One feature of this text is the use, in verb form, of kanji which are often more familiar in their **ON** readings. (Verbs proper are, of course, in the kun reading because they are native Japanese words.) Examples include, 抜きん出る nu(kin-deru) excel **BATSU** extract, 基づ く moto-zuku be based on **KI** foundation, 優れる sugu-reru excel **YUU** exceed, 甘んじる ama-njiru be content **KAN** sweet, 下がる sa-garu fall **KA** under, down, 招く mane-ku cause **SHOO** invite, and 危ぶむ aya-bumu **KI** danger.

There are few entirely new points of grammar, but there is reinforcement of difficult concepts, and the ever-present problem of unravelling the long Japanese sentences.

These economic themes are developed further in Unit 11.

日本の経済(1)

1) 日本は、1991年まで、経済において抜きん出た成功を収めていた。日本銀行（中央銀行）は、独立してはいながら、大蔵省と人脈に基づいた関係が深い。そのため、政府当局は、ある程度市場の調整ができ、実際、巧みに調整を行って来た。

2) 日本経済の成功と優れた競争力の主な理由の一つは、資本収益が低い事だった。ドイツと同様に、普通銀行は、長期貸し出しを積極的に進めている。投資家は、株価や不動産価格が着実に上昇すると見込んで、当座の利益は少ししか期待しなかった。同じ様に、労働者—働き中毒と呼ばれる事もある—も、高い貯蓄率を維持していても、ずっと、住宅と休暇に関しては、比較的低い報酬に甘んじて来た。

3) 長年、市場は常に上向きだった。ところが、1991年以降、世界不況の中で、大きな転換があり、日本の奇跡は終わってしまったか、と思われた。

4) 一度、株価の上昇が終わるや否や、売り手が買い手を上回った。日経（日本経済）株価指数は半値に下がり、不動産の価値も急落した。これは、消費者の将来と現在に対する不信を招き、耐久消費財の購入は減少した。延いては、製造業者は製品開発を縮小し、直接労働力—大企業の終身雇用は当然とされていた—を削減する事につながった。

5) 銀行の貸借対照表は、株価や土地価格の下落と不良貸し出しを負い、負債準備金の8パーセント率も危ぶまれた。

Unit 9

NIHON NO KEIZAI (1)

1 Nihon wa, 1991 nen made, keizai ni oite nukindeta seikoo o osamete ita. Nippon Ginkoo (Chuuoo ginkoo) wa, dokuritsu shite wa ina-gara[a], ookurashoo to jinmyaku ni motozuita kankei ga fukai. Sono tame, seifu tookyoku wa, aru teido shijoo no choosei ga deki, jissai, takumi ni choosei o okonatte kita[b].

2 Nihon keizai no seikoo to sugureta kyoosooryoku no omona riyuu no hitotsu[c] wa, shihon shuueki ga hikui koto[d] datta. Doitsu to dooyoo ni, futsuu ginkoo wa, chooki kashidashi o sekkyoku teki ni susumete iru. Tooshika wa, kabuka ya fudoosan kakaku ga chakujitsu ni jooshoo suru to mikonde, tooza no rieki wa sukoshi shika kitai shinakatta. Onaji yoo ni, roodoosha, hataraki chuudoku to yobareru koto mo aru[e], mo, takai chochikuritsu o iji shite ite mo[f], zutto, juutaku to kyuuka ni kanshite wa, hikakuteki hikui hooshuu ni amanjite kita.

3 Naganen, shijoo wa tsune ni uwamuki datta. Tokoroga, 1991 nen ikoo, sekaifukyoo no naka de, ookina tenkan ga ari, Nihon no kiseki wa owatte shimatta[g] ka to omowareta[h].

THE JAPANESE ECONOMY (1)

Until 1991 the Japanese economy had out-standing success. The Bank of Japan–the Central Bank–is independent, but keeps close contact, based on a personal network, with the Ministry of Finance. In this way the authorites can to some extent regulate the market, and this they had done skilfully.

A main reason for the success of the economy and Japan's superior competitive power was the low return on capital. The ordinary banks are positively willing, as in Germany, to advance long term credit. Investors, expecting prices of stocks and property and real estate to keep on rising steadily, looked for only a small imme-diate return. Similarly the workers, sometimes referred to as workaholic, had accepted a rela-tively low reward in terms of housing and leisure, while maintaining, all through, a high rate of saving.

For many years the direction of the market was always upward. However, after 1991, as part of a world recession, there was such a change that people wondered whether the Japanese mira-cle had ended.

4 Hitotabi, kabuka no jooshoo ga tomaru ya inaya[i], urite ga kaite o uwamawatta. Nikkei (Nihon keizai) kabuka shisuu wa hanne ni sagari, fudoosan no kachi mo kyuuraku shita. Kore wa, shoohisha no shoorai to genzai ni taisuru fushin o maneki, taikyuu-shoohizai no koonyuu wa genshoo shita. Hiite wa, seizoo gyoosha wa seihin kaihatsu o shukushoo shi, chokusetsu roodooryoku, daikigyoo no shu-ushin koyoo wa toozen to sarete ita, o sakugen suru koto ni[j] tsunagatta.

5 Ginkoo no taishaku-taishoo-hyoo wa, kabuka ya tochi kakaku no geraku to furyookashidashi o oi, fusai-junbi-kin no hachi paasento ritsu mo ayabumareta[k].

Once the market stopped rising, there were more sellers than buyers. The Nikkei share price index went down by half and property values also fell sharply. This meant that consumers lost confidence in the future–and the present; they reduced the buying of new hardware. This led manufacturing industry, furthermore, to cut down on product development and even to reduce their direct work force, who, in the major companies, had expected employment for life.

The banks' balance sheets now suffered from falling equity and property values and from bad debts. Their 8 per cent ratios were a matter of concern. (Ie the 8% of their liabilities which they have to keep in liquid form.)

◇◇ Notes on Kanji ◇◇

KANJI character	RADICAL no	shape	KANJI / COMPOUND reading	derivation and meaning
経	120	糸	KEI/he-ru	The phonetic RHS, found in several **KEI** kanji was an underground watercourse, but is simplified as a common-use kanji. With thread radical implies warp threads and thus *path* taken through time.
済	85	氵	SAI/ZAI/su-mu	Partly phonetic: RHS radical 210 simplified from two plants growing together to indicate order; with water radical means *regulate*. ◆経済 KEIZAI *economy* (regulated path?!)
抜	64	扌	BATSU/nu-ku	Looks like **YUU/tomo** with the hand radical; *take out, except*. ◆抜きん出る nukin deru *stand out*.
功	48	工	KOO	To the LHS construction radical supplying the sound **KOO** is added on RHS the sign for strength; *achievement*. ◆成功 SEIKOO *success*. (See SEI/ńaru in Unit 4.)
収	29	又	SHUU/ osa-meru	LHS primitive for tendrils but here phonetic, with hand RHS suggests *obtain, earn*. Cf 収支 SHUUSHI income and expenditure, 国際収支 KOKUSAISHUUSHI balance of payments.
銀	167	金	GIN	The metal radical + radical 138, probably phonetic; *silver*. ◆銀行 GINKOO *bank*.
央	(2)	|	OO	Large person (**ookii** in the middle of somewhere or with something round his middle); *centre*. (See Unit 8.) ◆中央 CHUUOO *central*. ◆中央銀行 CHUUOO GINKOO *central bank*.
独	94	犭	DOKU/hito-ri	LHS dog/animal radical + RHS insect radical 142: somehow means *alone*. (独身 DOKUSHIN unmarried; 独学 DOKU-GAKU selfstudy; also used phonetically for Germany, 独逸

KANJI character	RADICAL no	shape	KANJI / COMPOUND reading	derivation and meaning
				[Doitsu].) ◆独立 DOKURITSU (RITSU/tatsu Unit 1) *stand alone, independence.*
蔵	140	艹	ZOO/kura	Phonetic: bottom two-thirds is simplified form of an even more complicated kanji with vassal (see "minister" kanji–radical 131) and spear (radical 62); with plant radical on top means *to store away.* Cf 冷蔵庫 REIZOOKO fridge.
省	(4)	ノ	SHOO/ habu-ku	SHOO/sukoshii (top) and eye (base) imply to look carefully (or narrow vision?): usual word for *Ministry*; cf 文部省 MON-BUSHOO Ministry of Education; 外務省 GAIMUSHOO Ministry of Foreign Affairs. ◆大蔵省 ookuraSHOO *Finance Ministry.*
脈	130	月	MYAKU	With the meat radical LHS, = *a blood-vessel,* RHS said to show a liquid splitting into several streams: in compound with 人 JIN becomes JINMYAKU "personal connections" (probably on the analogy of veins and arteries). The other kanji with this sign on the RHS is HA (sect), as in HABATSU (political faction)—with the same implication of separation into streams.
基	32	土	KI/motoi/ moto-zuku	Top, the phonetic, said to have been a sieve or some square structure with a stand: with the earth radical, *a basis, foundation.* Verb 基づく moto-zuku *based on.*
関	169	門	KAN/seki	Gate + crossbar = *barrier, frontier.*
係	9	亻	KEI/kaka-ru	The thread radical with a line over it means tied together. ◆関係 KANKEI *connection.* (See also Units 6, 7, and 8.)

Unit 9

KANJI character	RADICAL no	shape	reading	KANJI / COMPOUND derivation and meaning
深	85	氵	SHIN/fuka-i	RHS is the phonetic; top is (almost) radical 116, showing a roof with an aperture, but without the ridge. The radical is 穴 KETSU/ana a hole or cave. (Cf KYUU in 研究 KENKYUU research, in Unit 7.) Here, the lower component was a hand tending a fire under a roof with a hole: with LHS water radical; *deep*.
				◇政府 SEIFU *government*. (See Unit 8.)
当	42	⺌	TOO/a-teru	Phonetic and simplified; hit the right place thus the [one] concerned (Unit 6). Cf 当時 TOOJI at that time; 当分 TOOBUN for the time being; idiom **atari** means right—"got it!"
局	44	尸	KYOKU	Origin murky: *authority, bureau*. ◆ 当局 TOOKYOKU *the relevant authority*.
程	115	禾	TEI/hodo	Fancifully RHS a man reporting (by mouth) about his crops (LHS); *standard or norm*.
度	53	广	DO/tabi	(See 速度 SOKUDO in Unit 7): origin obscure, but most useful concept is that of a hand holding a measure: *degree, time* (as in 今度 KONDO this time). ◆程度 TEIDO *to some degree*.
市	8	亠	SHI/ichi	Sound and kanji taken from Chinese; *market, town*. ◆市場 SHIJOO *market (place)* (JOO/ba in Unit 6). Cf市長 SHICHOO mayor.
調	149	言	CHOO	See **shiraberu** in Unit 6; *check on*.

KANJI character	RADICAL		KANJI / COMPOUND	
	no	shape	reading	derivation and meaning
整	77	止	SEI/totono-eru	Top LHS a bundle (taba in Unit 7) + top right what was a hand: radical below provides sound SEI (tadashii). ◆調整 CHOOSEI *regulation*.
際	170	阝	SAI/kiwa	RHS is the phonetic 祭る SAI/matsuru (with altar base) meaning worship: 祭り matsuri is a festival. With LHS hill/mound radical means *occasion*, and also shares meaning of the kun reading kiwa, *edge, side*. (Cf 国際 KOKUSAI international "touching the side of other lands".) ◆実際 JISSAI *fact, reality*. ("on the side of truth?")
巧	48	工	KOO/taku-mi	RHS a primitive also found at the base of 考 KOO/kangaeru; here the phonetic is probably the LHS working tool radical 48; *skill* . (み -mi is a suffix [like -sa] which in some cases can make a noun from an adjective or verb: thus 赤み aka-mi reddishness, 弱み yowa-mi a weakness, and 重み omo-mi weight.)
行	144	彳	okona-u oko-nau	A reading of 行 KOO/i-ku meaning *to carry out*.
優	9	亻	YUU/ sugure-ru/ yasa-shii	A difficult kanji: phonetic RHS alone YUU ure-eru is worry (head on top and radical 35–dragging feet–below); somewhat reminiscent of 夏 KA/natsu summer, but with a residual heart radical 61 in the middle). With person radical 9, *excel*. Adjective 優しい yasashii means *kind, gentle*.
競	117	立	KYOO/KEI	See Unit 8: was two speech radicals 言言 "words against words": easier mnemonic for present kanji is two elder brothers, with hats, quarrelling; *compete*. (Phonetic coincidence that elder brother 兄 is KYOO/ani.)

KANJI character	RADICAL		KANJI / COMPOUND	
	no	shape	reading	derivation and meaning
争	4	ノ	SOO/araso-u	See Unit 5: two hands grasping the same object; *strife*. ◆競争 KYOOSOO *competition* .
主	8	亠	SHU/omo	See Unit 4; 主な omona *main*. Cf idiom 主として SHU to shite mainly.
				◇理由 RIYUU see Unit 4; *reason*.
資	154	貝	SHI	Phonetic (but not to be confused with any of the 56 other SHI's): base is shell radical meaning money; top is phonetic 次 kanji for JI/tsugi (next); *resources*. ◆資本 SHIHON *capital*. Where HON means origin–Unit 2.
益	12	八	EKI	Base is radical 108, a dish: top is a form of the water sign 水. A full dish > abundance > *advantage, profit*. ◆収益 SHUUEKI (with SHUU/osameru above) *profit, return*.
低	9	亻	TEI/hiku-i	RHS is the clan radical 83, a floating plant with sound SHI, but with a line below suggesting roots reaching to the bottom and having sound TEI in several kanji, including this one; <u>*low, short in stature*</u>.
様	75	木	YOO/sama	RHS top is phonetic 羊 YOO/hitsuji sheep (cf 羊毛 YOOMOO and 羊肉 YOONIKU in Unit 5). ◆同様に DOOYOOni *in the same way*.
普	12	丷	FU	Top alone is 並 HEI/nara-bu, with two people standing (2 x radical 117 立) meaning lined up, together: here, with sun radical below, *general, universal*. Presumably the top is distantly phonetic and the base implies everything under the sun.

KANJI character	RADICAL		KANJI / COMPOUND	
	no	shape	reading	derivation and meaning
通	162	辶	TSUU/ too-ru/kayo-u	Reading **kayou** in Unit 2: middle said to be flower coming through giving meaning of "pierce"; thus with walk radical, *go through*. ◆普通 FUTSUU *ordinary*.
期	130	月	KI/GO	Phonetic sieve on a stand: LHS is a stand, regular, with reading **KI**; + the moon radical means *a set period*. ◆長期 CHOOKI *long term*.
貸	154	貝	TAI/ka-su	Top **DAI/kawari** is phonetic: base is shell/money radical; *lend* ◆貸し出し kashidashi *a loan*.
積	115	禾	SEKI/tsu-moru	RHS is the phonetic (cf 責任 SEKININ in Unit 6) and with the cereal radical LHS means *heap up/estimate*.
極	75	木	KYOKU/ kiwa-meru	Uncertain derivation but means the extreme (thus 北極 HOKKYOKU north pole). ◆積極的 SEKKYOKUTEKI *positive*.
進	162	辶	SHIN/ susu-meru	Go forward radical + short-tailed bird means *advance, promote*. (Cf 進歩 SHINPO progress.)
投	64	扌	TOO/na-geru	LHS is the hand radical 64; RHS is radical 79, a spear, and the hand throwing it: *to throw*. ◆投資 TOOSHI (throwing resources into a project) *investment* (<u>not</u>, we hope, throwing good money after bad).
家	40	宀	KA/ie	See Unit 1 for meaning of house/home: here, as often, -**KA**, a person practising a profession. Cf 投資家 TOOSHIKA *investor*.
株	75	木	kabu	RHS was phonetic (**ON** reading now dropped): with tree radical signifies stub/stump and thus stocks and shares (cf English

KANJI character	RADICAL no	RADICAL shape	reading	KANJI / COMPOUND derivation and meaning
				usage "coupon"). (株式会社 kabuSHIKIGAISHA joint stock company.)
価	9	亻	KA/atai	RHS simplified was cover over money, where base was shell radical: with person radical means *price, worth*. ◆株価 kabuKA *stock prices*.
不	(1)	一	FU/BU	The usual Chinese negative, bu, used in Japanese as negative prefix: seen as a bird flapping its wings or a flower opening. Usually pronounced F' as in 不可能 F'KANOO = impossible, and here in F'DOOSAN.
産	117	立	SAN/u-mu	Main component, at the base, is the SEI/umareru sign for life, birth: the rest is somewhat simplifed, but the presence of the shed radical and the standing radical above contribute to the meaning *produce* and *property* (umu give birth to). Cf the 日産 NISSAN Company , where the sun is short for NIHON. ◆不動産 FUDOOSAN "immoveable property" *real estate*.
格	75	木	KAKU	RHS phonetic **KAKU** each. With tree/wood radical, *standing, norm*. ◆価格 KAKAKU *price level*.
着	123	羊	CHAKU/ ki-ru/tsu-ku	Top is sheep radical, used in 様 YOO/sama, but here with a definite tail; base is radical 109, eye. The two main but disparate meanings are not easily explainable: *arrival* (tsuku) and *wear* (kiru–cf 着物 kimono). ◆着実に CHAKUJITSU ni *steadily*.
昇	72	日	SHOO/nobo-ru	Phonetic is the base, *sheng*, a Chinese measure; with sun radical; *promote, rise*. (One of several kanji that can be read noboru.) ◆上昇 JOOSHOO *rise*.

KANJI character	RADICAL no	shape	reading	KANJI / COMPOUND — derivation and meaning
				◇見込む miko-mu *be confident about*; the kanji 込む komu is Japanese, and by itself means be crowded: the many compounds of komu all have the notion of "into"–here, see into (the future). ◇当座 TOOZA *for the time being.* Cf 当座預金 TOOZA YOKIN *current account.*
利	115	刂	RI/ki-ku	LHS (radical) is a rice plant, RHS is a cut (variant of 刀 katana sword): reap one's corn, *profit*. ◆利益 RIEKI; we saw 収益 SHUUEKI above; RIEKI is not very different *profit*.
待	60	彳	TAI/ma-tsu	Oddly, belongs to the JI family, *wait*. (Unit 4.) ◆期待 KITAI *expectation* (KI in 長期 CHOOKI above).
				◇同じ様に onajiYOOni = DOOYOOni above.
労	19	力	ROO	Top, now simplified, represented lights: thus, with strength radical below, interpreted as working through the night or burning energy in light; in either case means *work, labour*.
働	9	亻	DOO	ON reading of hataraku (Unit 3). ◆労働者 ROODOOSHA *worker*.
毒	(80)	毋	DOKU	Origin ambiguous: top is variant of 生SEI growth, but base may be mother (Unit 1) or a prohibition, ie a plant to be avoided; *poison*. ◆中毒 CHUUDOKU *intoxication* (being poisoned).
貯	154	貝	CHO/ takuwa-eru	LHS is shell (money); RHS a form of the phonetic 丁 CHOO/CHO (T shape originally a nail) now used for block of buildings in addresses: cf also 貯金 CHOKIN savings.

Unit 9

KANJI	RADICAL		KANJI / COMPOUND	
character	no	shape	reading	derivation and meaning
蓄	140	艹	CHIKU/ takuwa-eru	Phonetic base CHIKU means to raise animals: with plant radical on top, *to save up*.
率	8	亠	RITSU	Origin unclear; this reading means *rate, ratio*–an important word in economic and scientific texts. ◆貯蓄率 CHOCHIKURITSU *rate of saving*.
維	120	糸	I	RHS (short-tailed bird radical) is the phonetic here: with thread radical LHS means *tie*. ◆維持 IJI *maintain, keep up*.
宅	40	宀	TAKU	Phonetic base is rooted plant: with roof radical means *residence, house*, esp. with honorific O = (your) house (TAKU with speech radical 託す TAKUsu entrust). ◆住宅 JUUTAKU *housing*.
休	9	亻	KYUU	ON reading of yasu-mi (Unit 2).
暇	72	日	KA/hima	Not an easy sign; the two RH components were a hand holding a mask: with sun radical, *leisure*. ◆休暇 KYUUKA *holiday, vacation*.
				◇...に関して ...ni KAN shite: *as regards...*
較	159	車	KAKU	RHS is the KOO of 学校 GAKKOO (Unit 3) but the same Chinese phoneme became KAKU at this borrowing, with the same basic meaning of *exchange*: what the vehicle radical is doing is anyone's guess, except as a mnemonic that one exchanges cars to compare them. ◆比較 HIKAKU *comparison*. (HI/kuraberu in Unit 5.) This an example of a typical Chinese compound (漢語 KANGO)

KANJI character	RADICAL no	RADICAL shape	reading	KANJI / COMPOUND derivation and meaning
				where the two components have similar meanings and reinforce one another. ◆ 比較的 HIKAKUTEKI *comparative(ly)*.
報	32	土	HOO/muku-iru	Mnemonically, LHS is the same as 幸い KOO/saiwai luck, though the two almost certainly have different origins: the present sign, on the contrary, has on its RHS a hand with a seal (or someone kneeling); giving *penalty* or "just deserts".
酬	164	酉	SHUU	RHS is phonetic SHUU (province) as in 本州 HONSHUU ; with wine-jar radical, *reward*. ◆ 報酬 HOOSHUU *reward*.
甘	99	甘	KAN/ama-i	A radical, but with few characters in tow; simple sign showing mouth with something in it and meaning sweet: verb amanjiru means *to be contented*.
常	42	⺌	JOO/tsune	Radical 42 (small) SHOO is really part of a larger phonetic (cf 堂 DOO a hall and 党 TOO party): *usual*.
				◇上向き uwamuki (uwa is a reading of 上 ue [Unit 1] and 向き muki direction [Unit 1]) *upwards*.
降	170	阝	KOO/ o-riru/fu-ru	RHS is the phonetic, and had the meaning of descend, emphasized by the LHS mound radical. 降る furu means *to fall*–particularly of snow and rain. ◆ 以降 IKOO *from* [of time] For 以 I see Units 4 and 8.
世	(2)	⎮	SE/SEI/yo	Originally three times ten = thirty years or a *generation* (as in 二世 NISEI), *era*.

KANJI	RADICAL			KANJI / COMPOUND	
character	no	shape	reading	derivation and meaning	
界	102	田	KAI	Bottom is the phonetic (see 媒介 BAIKAI in Unit 7). With paddy radical on top means *world*. ◆世界 SEKAI *the world*.	
況	85	氵	KYOO	Phonetic: RHS KYOO is ON reading of ani (cf KYOOSOO above): with water radical, for no obvious reason, *situation*. ◆不況 FUKYOO (with negative 不FU–see above)*recession*.	
転	159	車	TEN/koro-bu	RHS simplified is phonetic (専SEN/moppara); with vehicle radical means *tumble, roll*.	
換	64	扌	KAN/ka-eru	RHS phonetic, said to have shown something going from one hand to another: with hand radical LHS, *to exchange*. ◆転換 TENKAN *turning point*.	
奇	37	大	KI	Large man above + for some reason, the KA phoneme below, *strange*; (cf奇数 KISUU odd number).	
跡	157	𧾷	SEKI/ato	LHS is leg radical and RHS may be phonetic from 赤 SEKI/akai (red): *footprint, remains, trace*. ◆奇跡 KISEKI *miracle*.	
思	102	田	SHI/omo-u	Although the radical is a paddy the sign may be a head, or even the sign for IN below: + heart, *think*.	
				◇一度 hito tabi (DO/tabi above) *once*. (Kun reading as in hito-tsu.)	
否	(1)	一	HI/ina	Mouth with negative (FU/BU above) means *to say no*; used as negation in some compounds: here ina-ya *as soon as*.	
				◇上回る uwamawaru *exceed*. Cf *upwards* above.	

KANJI character	RADICAL no	RADICAL shape	KANJI / COMPOUND reading	KANJI / COMPOUND derivation and meaning
				◇指数 SHISUU (SHI/yubi = finger + SUU = number) *index* (which also meant a finger). ◇日経 NIKKEI = 日本経済 NIHON KEIZAI = Japanese economy: thus 日経指数 NIKKEI SHISUU = one of the stock exchange price indexes–particularly those carried by the 日本経済新聞 NIHON KEIZAI SHIMBUN (cf the British "Footsie" indexes [FTSE=Financial Times Stock Exchange]).
値	9	亻	CHI/ne/atai	RHS as in 直接 CHOKUSETSU direct (Unit 6); idea of sizing up by eye carried into *value, price*. ◆半値 hanne *half-price*.
				◇下がる sa-garu. Yet another reading for KA/shita (down); cf 下さい kudasai.
落	140	艹	RAKU/o-chiru	Why the plant radical on top is unclear–perhaps the image was of leaves falling… Phonetic 各 =KAKU/RAKU. ◆急落 KYUURAKU *a (sudden) sharp fall*.
消	85	氵	SHOO/ke-su	RHS is phonetic SHOO = alike (said, because of the "small" radical on top, to "chip off the old block"): with water radical means *extinguish*; see also 削減 SAKUGEN below.
費	154	貝	HI/tsui-yasu	Shell/money radical with on top, what is said to be a bundle of rods means brush off or negation (cf also 弟 DAI/otooto and 第 DAI as prefix for ordinals). Brushing off or negating money? Or the top can mnemonically be seen as a dollar, hence *to spend*. ◆消費 SHOOHI *consumption* + 者 SHA *consumer*.
将	90	爿	SHOO	Simplified RHS with fingers and a hand + matched board radical (see HEN in mokuhen in Unit 4) as phonetic gives the longest finger which belongs to the *leader*. (Cf 将軍 SHOO-

KANJI character	RADICAL no	RADICAL shape	reading	KANJI / COMPOUND derivation and meaning
				GUN where GUN is army) ◆将来 SHOORAI *future*. (See Unit 6.)
現	96	王	GEN/ arawa-reru	LHS gem radical, RHS KEN/miru (to see): together becomes the glister of a jewel which is *visible* and *actual*. The verbs mean *to appear* and *to show*.
在	32	土	ZAI/a-ru	(See SONZAI in Unit 7.) ◆現在 GENZAI *the present*.
対	67	文	TAI/TSUI	Simplified LHS: original radical was 41–RHS hand/inch: TSUI means a pair, and this offers a clue; basically TAI implies contrast; here 対する TAI suru means *towards, in relation to*.
				◇不信 FUSHIN *no confidence*.
招	64	扌	SHOO/ mane-ku	RHS is a common phonetic meaning to summon; with hand radical LHS implies beckon and, here, *cause*.
耐	126	而	TAI/ta-eru	LHS radical (hardly used) was a beard : with one of the hand radicals RHS means *to suffer, endure*. (That this sign has the same sound as 対 TAI just above [also with a hand] must be coincidental.)
久	(4)	ノ	KYUU/hisa-shii	A man held back, as if by a trailing coat, implies *a long time*: often heard in hisashiburi "long time no see". ◆耐久 TAIKYUU *durable*.
財	154	貝	ZAI	Phonetic RHS was counter for years of age in Unit 1: with shell radical, signifies *money* and *property*. ◆消費財 SHOOHIZAI *consumer goods*.

KANJI character	RADICAL		KANJI / COMPOUND	
	no	shape	reading	derivation and meaning
購	154	貝	KOO	See 構 KOO/kama-eru in Unit 7. Here RHS is still the phonetic and with shell radical, *money* or *buy*. ◆購入 KOONYUU *purchase* ("buy in").
減	85	氵	GEN/he-ru	With LHS water radical means *reduce*. ◆減少 GENSHOO *reduction*.
延	54	廴	EN/ no-basu/no-biru	LHS rare "stride" radical (not to be confused with the far more common radical 162), enclosing the SEI/tadashii sign has the sound EN meaning *extend, lengthen*. By "extension" all carries the sound hiite. ◇延いては hiite wa *furthermore*.
製	145	衣	SEI	Base is clothing radical in its full form; top is SEI system as in 制度 SEIDO (Unit 8.): *manufacture*.
造	162	辶	ZOO/tsuku-ru	RHS is KOKU/tsugeru tell, report; not clear why with movement radical means *produce*. ◆製造 SEIZOO *manufacture*.
業	(3)	丶	GYOO/waza	A difficult kanji to remember but harder to explain: one says a rack for instruments; another a tree crowned with foliage; *results, activity*. In compounds means *business occupation* thus here 製造業者 SEIZOOGYOOSHA *persons in manufacturing industry*.
				◇製品 SEIHIN *products*.
開	169	門	KAI/a-keru	Gate with two hands on a bolt; *open*. ◆開発 KAIHATSU *development*.

KANJI	RADICAL		KANJI / COMPOUND	
character	no	shape	reading	derivation and meaning
縮	120	糸	SHUKU/ chiji-meru	RHS is phonetic—下宿 GESHUKU is a lodging: with LHS thread radical means *shrink* or *reduce*. ◆縮小 SHUKUSHOO *reduction*.
				◇労働力 ROODOORYOKU *work force*. ◇大企業 DAIKIGYOO *large enterprises*. ◇終身 SHUUSHIN *for life*. (SHUU/owaru end thus until the body ends!—SHIN/mi in Unit 6.)
雇	63	戸	KO/yato-u	Door radical above with one of the bird radicals (172) below: unknown why this means *to hire labour* (verb yato-u). ◆雇用 KOYOO *employment*.
然	86	灬	ZEN/NEN	Complicated but picturesque: LHS a variant of what was radical 130 for meat (now in effect combined with the very similar radical 74 for moon) + RHS radical 94 for dog, all over radical 86 for fire> dog meat: borrowed to mean a *state* or *condition*. ◆当然 TOOZEN *naturally, as a matter of course*.
削	18	リ	SAKU/kezu-ru	Same LHS as SHOO in SHOOHI above: convenient to relate it to the three strokes on top which recall 小 SHOO/chiisa-i = a little: with the cutting tool RHS *to pare away, reduce*. ◆削減 SAKUGEN *reduction*.
借	9	亻	SHAKU/ka-riru	RHS is piling up of days (see mukashi in Unit 4) with person radical, *to borrow*. ◆貸借 TAISHAKU *debts and loans /assets and liabilities*.
照	86	灬	SHOO/teru	The original phonetic RHS is SHOO to summon (to cut [the air] with one's mouth ?) With the sun radical 昭 bright. (Cf the 昭和 SHOOWA era 1926-1989.) With the further addition of the fire radical underneath, *shine, illumine*.

KANJI	RADICAL		KANJI / COMPOUND	
character	no	shape	reading	derivation and meaning
				◆対照 TAISHOO *contrast, comparison*. ◆貸借対照表 TAISHAKU TAISHOO HYOO *balance sheet* (one meaning of 表 HYOO/omote, usually a surface, is a table or sheet, eg of figures).
				◇下落 GERAKU *fall*. ◇不良 FURYOO (not good) *bad*.
負	154	貝	FU/ ma-keru/o-u	We have seen this kanji in Unit 7 as defining negative electricity: here the reading o-u means *to bear* or *owe debts*. See also FUSAI just below.
債	9	亻	SAI	Same base as 責任 SEKININ (Unit 6) ie what is owed: here with person radical means *liabilities*. ◆負債 FUSAI *obligations, debt, liabilities*.
備	9	亻	BI/sona-eru	RHS best guess is a quiver of arrows: *equipped*. ◆準備 JUNBI *preparation* (JUN in 標準 HYOOJUN of Unit 7). ◆準備金 JUNBI KIN *reserves* ("ready cash" is 現金 GENKIN).
危	(4)	ノ	KI/abu-nai/ aya-bumu	Said to be a man kneeling on a cliff and afraid to fall; *danger*: abunai dangerous; ayabumu *to be apprehensive (about something)*. See grammar notes for the passive construction.

◇ ◇ Grammar Notes ◇ ◇

A いながら inagara is the simultaneous form of the verb iru, used here with the present participle of suru. As is often the case, this form can convey a nuance of "although". Here the implication is that though the Bank is independent it still keeps contact etc. English often uses "while…" in the same way.

B 行って来た okonatte kita, participle + kuru, is the equivalent of "they have or had been doing something" up to the point at which the comment is made. Cf Unit 1 出て来ました dete kimashita and 甘んじて来た amanjite kita below.

C English has "**a** main reason", but Japanese has no indefinite article and thus uses 主な理由の一つ omona riyuu no hitotsu *one of the main reasons*.

D Because 低い hikui, like all true Japanese adjectives, contains its own copula, だ da is not required; thus 事 koto alone makes this into a noun phrase.

E This is an example of nominalisation, using koto + aru. *The fact of their being called workaholic also occurs.* Cf …koto ga arimasu in Unit 6.

F The use of も mo indicates a touch of "though" or "while" (with the same sense); *the workers, while maintaining a high rate of saving, put up with…* etc.

G 終わってしまった owatte shimatta is the construction we saw in Unit 2, 吐いてしまいました haite shimaimashita "she ended up by being sick".

H One of the idioms corresponding to "…wonder whether, where etc" in English. In the first person, the word, かしら kashira is used, with の no as the linkage: 彼はどこにいるのかしら Kare wa doko ni iru no kashira "I wonder where he is". But in the third person, だろうかと思う daroo ka to omou is common: 彼は奥さんが次の日来るだろうかと思った Kare wa okusan ga tsugi-no hi kuru daroo ka to omotta "he wondered if his wife would arrive next day".

I や否や ya inaya (with the particle ya at both ends) is a convenient conjunction meaning "as soon as…"

J 削減する事につながった sakugen suru koto ni tsunagatta; here koto nominalises the phrase sakugen suru (to reduce), but the sense of the verb (was connected with, involved) requires the postposition ni and this is added to the koto.

K 危ぶむ ayabumu is a transitive verb, meaning "to be fearful (about something)"; the object of the verb is the thing which is feared. It is often used in the passive, as it is here; in which case the thing to be worried about is the subject of the verb. Thus in this sentence, 危ぶまれた ayabumareta is the past passive and means "was the subject of fear" or *was a reason for concern*.

◇◇ **English into Japanese** ◇◇

Sentences and Themes

1. To what extent does the success of Japan depend on economic factors?

2. What other reasons, like social reasons, in your opinion, are important?

3. Do economists (経済学者 KEIZAIGAKUSHA) really know how to control* economic forces?

4. The problem of the banks balance sheets is that there are companies who cannot even pay interest (利息 risoku).

Transformation

1. Japan's success は where until economic causes on dependent (による ni yoru) might-[it]-be?

2. Social reasons like, other which (どちら・どの dochira/dono) reasons, が important is/are と do-[you]-think?

3. Economists は, economic forces を really to control* are-able?

4. [The] banks' balance sheets' problem は, interest even not-able-to-pay companies が exist fact is (事が).

*調整できる CHOOSEI dekiru

Unit 10
PARADOX
逆説

◇ ◇ **Introductory Note** ◇ ◇

This unit offers some light relief as to content, but it also introduces a few colloquial phrases and adds to the repertoire of grammatical points and idioms, and at least one more opaque sentence.

手に、自分の父親の生まれた家が有る場所に行く様に言いました。運転手は、お客をそこへ連れて行きましたが、悪い事に、酒に酔っていたので、家から出てきた所の少年をひいてしまいました。

（四）人々が急いで介抱しましたが、少年は死んでしまいました。「可哀相なジム・ウィルビーちゃん！」と近所の人が言いました。それを聞いて、アメリカ人は、真っ青になりました。死んだ少年は、自分の祖父だったのです。

（五）最近まで、この逆説は、タイム・トラベルがそれ自体の持つ矛盾のために不可能だ、という証明とみなされて来ました。しかし、今、量子物理学者は、因果関係が直接的かつ決定的だと言う事を否定しています。つまり、いくつかの平行世界が可能で、ジム・ウィルビーにも子孫が存在する、と言うのです。

（六）さて、納得がいきましたか。あなた自身は、過去への旅人に会った事がありますか。

逆説

（一）　二千五十年のこと、ある研究会社が、時間を旅する方法を発見しました。沢山の大金持——大金持でなければいけません——が、この可能性を利用したくてたまりませんでした。ウィルビーというアメリカ人が、タイム・トラベルをする会社に行き、子孫がどうなっているか見たいので、未来への旅はいくらかかるか聞きました。

（二）　社員は、未来はまだ実現していないから、その旅行はだめだが、過去なら大丈夫だと説明しました。「いいですよ。」お客は言いました。「一九三七年への往復切符に決めましょう。　私は先祖を訪問してみたいので。　この町でお願いする。」

（三）　五十万ドル払い、トラベル・マシンに座った彼は、やがて、一九三七年の町の一角に現れました。　タクシーを止めると、運転

Unit 10

GYAKUSETSU

1 2050 nen no koto[a], aru kenkyuu-gaisha ga jikan o tabi suru hoohoo o hakken shimashita. Takusan no oo-ganemochi (oo-ganemochi de nakereba ikemasen) ga, kono kanoosei o riyoo shitakute[b] tamarimasen deshita. Uirubii to iu Amerika jin ga taimu toraberu o suru kaisha ni iki, shison ga doo natte iru ka mitai[b] node, mirai e no tabi wa ikura kakaru ka kikimashita

2 Sha-in wa, mirai wa mada jitsugen shite inai kara, sono ryokoo wa dame da ga, kako nara[c] daijoobu da [d] to setsumei shimashita. "Ii desu yo" okyaku wa iimashita. "1937 nen e no oofuku-kippu ni kimemashoo[e]. Watashi wa senzo o hoomon shite mitai[f] node. Kono machi de onegai suru".

3 50 man doru harai, toraberu-mashin ni suwatta kare wa, yagate 1937 nen no machi no ikkaku ni arawaremashita. Takushii o tomeru to, untenshu ni, jibun no chichi-oya no umareta uchi ga aru basho ni iku yoo ni iimashita. Untenshu wa, okyaku o soko e tsurete ikimashita ga, warui koto ni[g], sake ni yotte ita node, ie kara detekita tokoro no[h] shoo-nen o hiite shimaimashita[i].

PARADOX

In the year 2050, a research company discovered the way of travelling in time. A lot of rich people—you had to be rich—were keen to make use of this possibility. An American by the name of Willoughby went to the company offering time travel and asked how much a trip into the future would cost, since he wanted to see what would happen to his descendants.

The employee explained that this journey was not on, because the future had not yet taken place, but that the past would be all right. "OK" said the client, "I'll settle for a return ticket to 1937—and in this town, because I want to try and look up my ancestors".

He paid his half a million dollars, sat in the machine, and eventually found himself, in 1937, in some place/corner of the town. He hailed a cab and told the driver to go to the place with the house where his father was born. The driver took him there, but unfortunately, was drunk, and knocked over a boy who had just come out of the house.

4 Hitobito ga isoide kaihoo shimashita ga, shoonen wa shinde shimaimashita. |Kawaisoo na Jimu Uirubii chan[j]| to kinjo no hito ga iimashita. Sore o kiite, Amerikajin wa massao ni narimashita. Shinda shoonen wa jibun no sofu datta no desu.

5 Saikin made, kono gyakusetsu wa, taimu toraberu ga, sore jitai no motsu mujun no tame ni, fukanoo da to iu shoomei to minasarete kimashita[k]. Shikashi, ima, ryooshi-butsuri-gakusha wa, inga-kankei ga chokusetsu-teki, katsu kettei-teki da to iu koto o hitei shite imasu. Tsumari, ikutsuka no heikoo sekai ga kanoo de, Jimu Uirubii ni mo shison ga sonzai suru to iu no desu.

6 Sate[l], nattoku[m] ga ikimashita ka? Anata-jishin wa, kako e no tabi-bito ni, atta koto ga ari-masu[n] ka?

People rushed to help, but the boy was dead. "Poor little Jim Willoughby!" said a neighbour. On hearing this the American went white; the dead boy was his grandfather.

Until recently this paradox was regarded as proof that time travel was impossible because of the contradictions it would involve. Now, however, the quantum physicists deny that causation is direct and determined. In short, they say that several parallel universes are possible and Jim Willoughby's descendants would still exist.

Are you convinced? And have <u>you</u> yourself met travellers into the past?

◇ ◇ Notes on Kanji ◇ ◇

KANJI character	RADICAL no	shape	reading	KANJI / COMPOUND derivation and meaning
逆	162	辶	GYAKU/ saka/saka-rau	RHS said to be someone upside down: with radical means *contrary, wrong way up*. ◆逆説 GYAKUSETSU *paradox* .
旅	70	方	RYO/tabi	LHS radical indicates direction (cf **HOO** just below); RHS shows men camping under trees or two persons travelling? Sign means *journey.* Cf 旅人 tabibito "travel-people" below. ◆旅行 RYOKOO *travel, journey.*
法	85	氵	HOO	For RHS see **KYO/KO** below. Here, with LHS water radical means *law;* traditional mnemonic is that the sign represents the water level and by analogy the level of behaviour. ◆方法 HOOHOO *method.*
				◇大金持ち ooganemochi having (mochi) a large amount (oo) of money (kane) *very rich.* ◇可能性 KANOOSEI *possibility* (see Unit 8 and cf below 不可能 FUKANOO *impossible*).
利	115	禾	RI/ki-ku	See Unit 9; RIEKI *return* (ie on capital, investment). ◆利用 RIYOO use–with **suru** *make use of.*
孫	39	子	SON/mago	RHS is thread radical with extra line on top meaning connection cf 関係 KANKEI; with child radical extended to *grandchild.* ◆子孫 SHISON *descendant.*
未	(4)	ノ	MI	Short line over tree kanji said to mean not yet grown; *not yet.* ◆未来 MIRAI *future* .
員	30	口	IN	See Unit 8: bottom half looks like shell radical 154 but is said to represent a kettle. ?Mnemonic: shell means payment of subscription and mouth means speaking; *member.*

KANJI	RADICAL		KANJI / COMPOUND	
character	no	shape	reading	derivation and meaning
				◆社員 SHA-IN *company employee.*
実	40	宀	JITSU/mi	See Unit 7; *truth.*
現	96	王	GEN/ arawa-reru	See Unit 7; *the present.* ◆実現する JITSUGEN suru *bring about, realise.*
過	162	辶	KA/su-giru	See Unit 8; *to pass (eg of time).*
去	32	土	KYO/KO/sa-ru	Was (oddly) a pot with lid –top has nothing to do with radical 32 – but somehow came to mean go (still does in Chinese), perhaps because an empty pot implied *leaving* and so *time passing.* Cf 去年 KYONEN last year (and 法 HOO above). ◆過去 KAKO *the past.*
丈	(4)	ノ	JOO/take	Was a unit of length; *stature.* ◆丈夫 JOOBU *healthy* (BU from FU/otto Unit 1). ◆大丈夫 DAIJOOBU *fine.*
往	60	彳	OO	RHS is phonetic, but its origin is not clear: 主 = king? With LHS radical 60, *go away.*
復	60	彳	FUKU	RHS is phonetic, with dragging foot at the base; with radical 60, *do something again.* ◆往復 OOFUKU *going and returning.*
切	18	切	SETSU/ki-ru	LHS phonetic meant seven; RHS is the knife/sword radical; *cut* (Unit 3).

KANJI character	RADICAL no	RADICAL shape	KANJI / COMPOUND reading	KANJI / COMPOUND derivation and meaning
符	118	⺮	FU	Top is bamboo radical, bottom is phonetic **FU**, attach (man + hand); originally a tally with matching pieces. ◆切符 kippu *ticket*.
決	85	氵	KETSU/ ki-meru	See **KETTEI** in Unit 6; *decide*.
祖	113	礻	SO	RHS phonetic means pile up (cf **kumiawase** in Unit 4): with altar radical, *ancestor*. ◆先祖・祖先 **SENZO** or **SOSEN** (SEN = early–cf teacher 先生 SENSEI) *ancestor*.
訪	149	言	HOO/ tazu-neru	RHS is phonetic **HOO**; with speech radical, *visit*. ◆訪問する **HOOMON** (suru) *visit*.
願	(4)	ノ	GAN/nega-u	LHS phonetic (spring, source, as in 原因 GENIN, 原子 GEN-SHI) + RHS = head (and radical 181); *desire, beg for*. (Set phrase お願いします **onegai shimasu** please.)
万	1	一	MAN/BAN	See Unit 1, *ten thousand*.
払	64	扌	FUTSU/hara-u	See Unit 1, *pay*.
座	53	广	ZA/suwa-ru	See Unit 8, *sit*.
				◇一角 **IKKAKU** *one corner/place* equivalent of "someplace". (German *schönes Eck* and French *un joli coin* also use corner in this way.)

KANJI	RADICAL		KANJI / COMPOUND	
character	no	shape	reading	derivation and meaning
運	162	辶	UN/hako-bu	Phonetic RHS is GUN army–lid over a vehicle (kuruma in Unit 1); with radical 162 used for phonetic UN *luck*; and for kun reading hakobu *to transport*.
転	159	車	TEN/koro-bu	Vehicle is the radical and RHS is sound: (転換 TENNKAN in Unit 9) *revolve* . ◆運転 UNTEN *operation of a machine.* ◆運転手 UNTENSHU *driver* .
親	147	見	SHIN/oya	LHS phonetic; (Cf 新しい SHIN/atarashii new) with see radical; *parent.* ◆父親 chichi-oya *father.*
家	40	宀	KA/ie/(uchi)	See uchi in Unit 2; base is pig radical 152 under a roof; *house.*
有	130	月	YUU/a-ru	Hand holding what looks like the moon but, as often, is probably the meat radical; *be, have.*
				◇場所 BASHO *place, location.*
様	75	木	YOO/sama	See 同じ様に onaji YOO-ni in Unit 9. Here YOO-ni is used with verb iu to indicate an indirect* command–what you are told to do: iku YOO-ni iimashita "said so as to go…" *told him to go…* (See also Unit 2.)
連	162	辶	REN/tsu-reru	See Unit 8: same inner sign as GUN above, but different phonetic; kun reading is verb 連れる tsu-reru *to accompany.* ON reading REN includes meaning of group; thus 国連 KOKU-REN United Nations; in Unit 8 連立 RENRITSU coalition; in Unit 12 連続的 RENZOKUTEKI serial.

KANJI character	RADICAL		KANJI / COMPOUND	
	no	shape	reading	derivation and meaning
悪	(1)	一	AKU/waru-i	Top represented deformation: used alone = A but often indicates what is secondary or "sub…"; with heart radical, *bad*.
酒	85	氵	SHU/sake	RHS is radical 164, a wine-jar. With water radical means *alcoholic drink*.
酔	164	酉	SUI/yo-u	RHS phonetic; + LHS jar radical means *drunk*. (Mnemonic: not "one over the eight" but "nine over the ten".)
				◇少年 SHOONEN *boy*. ◇人々 hitobito (plural) *people*.
急	61	心	KYUU/iso-gu	Top (simplified) is phonetic (perhaps from 及 KYUU/oyobu); with heart radical means urgent, sudden; here, *hurry*.
介	9	人	KAI	Cf Unit 7; person kanji at the top, with two lines means getting between and thus *intervene*.
抱	64	扌	HOO/da-ku	RHS is phonetic, but also HOO/tsutsumu wrap (Unit 1); with hand radical, *take in one's arms*. ◆介抱する KAIHOO suru *look after, tend*.
死	78	歹	SHI/shi-nu	LHS is radical for bones; + RHS a person; *to die*. (Cf also in Unit 12 並列 HEIRETSU parallel, where this same radical implies lining things up.)
哀	8	亠	AI/awa-re	Though this kanji is classified to radical 8, the basis can be seen as the clothing radical 145 (see HYOO in Units 4, 7 and 8), with sleeves and all; the addition of a mouth is explained by the image of mourners crying AI-AI; *pity*. ◆可哀相 KAWAISOO *poor thing*: KA is the phonetic as in KANOOSEI above; SOO is the sign also used as SHOO in 首相 SHUSHOO (Unit 6) Prime Minister.

KANJI character	RADICAL no	shape	reading	KANJI / COMPOUND derivation and meaning
近	162	辶	KIN/chika-i	RHS (weight/axe) is phonetic; with walk radical; *near* (Unit 5). ◆近所 KINJO *neighbourhood*.
真	24	十	SHIN/ma	Base said to be kettle on a tripod; radical on top derived from shape of spoon; filled to brim extended to mean *truth* or *pure*.
青	174	青	SEI/ao-i	Top is grass; base was a well, thus growing things fed with water and so *blue/green* and young, unripe. (Cf 青年 SEINEN young man.) ◆真っ青 massao *completely white* (green); ma is used in such compounds to give emphasis; eg magokoro 真心 (pure heart) *sincerity*.
				◇祖父 SOFU *grandfather*.
最	72	日	SAI/motto-mo	Origin unclear: *most*. ◆最近 SAIKIN *recently*.
証	149	言	SHOO	RHS phonetic (SEI and SHOO) + speech radical; *proof*. See Unit 7. ◆証明 SHOOMEI *proof*.
体	9	亻	TAI/TEI/karada	RHS trunk of a tree thus cylinder and scroll so book but here borrowed to mean *body*. ◆自体 JITAI *itself*.
矛	110	矛	MU/hoko	A radical; *spear* or *halberd*.
盾	(4)	丿	JUN/tate	A shield (originally for the eye). ◆矛盾 MUJUN *contradiction* (spear v shield).

KANJI character	RADICAL no	shape	reading	KANJI / COMPOUND derivation and meaning
				◇不可能 FUKANOO *impossible.*
量	72	日	RYOO/haka-ru	See Unit 7: sun radical results from slight simplification; top was perhaps a container of grain; bottom either a deformation of 重い omoi heavy or, perhaps, 里 the sign for Chinese mile–li. Sign means *quantity, to measure.* ◆量子 RYOOSHI *quantum.* ◆量子物理学 RYOOSHIBUTSURIGAKU *quantum physics.*
				◇…学者 …GAKUSHA an academic here *quantum physicist.*
果	(2)	丨	KA/ha-teru	Pictorial: *fruit.* ◆因果 INGA *cause and effect.*
				◇直接的 CHOKUSETSU-TEKI *immediate, direct.* ◇決定的 KETTEI-TEKI *decided, determined.*
否	1	一	HI/ina	Cf Unit 9: negative 不 FU + mouth, *deny something.*
定	40	宀	TEI/JOO/ sada-meru	Cf Unit 1 (Masa): base like SHOO (above) + roof radical; *fix, settle.* ◆否定する HITEI suru *to deny.*
				◇平行 HEIKOO *parallel.* ◇世界 SEKAI *world.*
瞬	109	目	SHUN/ mabata-ku	RHS an original phonetic; with eye radical, *blink, flicker.* ◆瞬間 SHUNKAN *moment.*

KANJI	RADICAL			KANJI / COMPOUND
character	no	shape	reading	derivation and meaning
存	39	子	SON/ZON	LHS ?grass shoots + child radical; *to exist*.
在	32	土	ZAI/a-ru	LHS ?grass shoots + earth radical; *to exist* ("I think, therefore I am" is translated as 我思う故に我在り ware omou, yue-ni ware ari). ◆存在する SONZAI (suru) *exist* (another of these compounds of two kanji having the same meaning).
納	120	糸	NOO/NA/TOO/ osa-meru	RHS (NAI) phonetic; with thread radical, *render, remit*.
得	60	彳	TOKU/e-ru	RHS was money (radical 154) and below a hand; with go radical, *obtain* (eru), *profit*. ◆納得 NATTOKU *understanding, conviction*.
会	9		KAI/a-u	See Unit 3 and 6.

◇◇ **Grammar Notes** ◇◇

A   …のこと……no koto… is rather like "once upon a time"; or like a refrain *It was in the year 2050.* Aru means *a certain…*

B   したくて shitakute is the desiderative* participle* of suru: shi-tai becomes shi-taku-te; 利用する riyoo suru make use of, so this phrase means wanting to make use of… Mitai is, again, the desiderative of miru wants to see (how his descendants will fare). The tense used in Japanese is that of the speaker.

C   過去なら kako nara is a convenient way of saying *if it is the past…* Nara is in effect the hypothetical* (if/when) form of desu. (See Table 6.)

D   大丈夫だ daijoobu da is one way of saying "that's OK". Other expressions are 結構です kekkoo desu and, simplest of all, いいです ii desu, used below; よ yo is a particle used at the end of a sentence to give emphasis. The opposite to ii desu–"it's no good"–is seen above in だめです dame desu.

E   （往復切符）に決めましょう (oofuku kippu) ni kimemashoo is a usual way of saying "Let's decide" or "I will decide" <u>on</u> something; a colloquial alternative is …にしましょう …ni shimashoo.

F   訪問してみたい hoomon shite mitai uses the idiom* consisting of a participle + miru, with the sense of "try and see"; mitai is desiderative*, *I want to try to look up…*

G   悪い事に warui koto ni "for a bad thing" and corresponds to our "unfortunately"; another expression, written in hiragana, is あいにく ainiku. "Luckily" is translated as 幸いに／運のいいことに saiwai ni/un no ii koto ni.

H   所の tokoro no; such verbal expressions with tokoro correspond to "just leaving" or "just left". Dekakeru tokoro just leaving; here 出て来た所 detekita tokoro *just came out*, and the no links the adjectival phrase to the boy.

I   しまいました shimaimashita is the past of shimau, a verb often used as an auxiliary*, together with the participle of another verb, in a context where the implication is that you have ended up by doing the action referred to–usually something unfavourable. Here the meaning is something like *ended up by knocking over…* Similarly, below, in para 4, 死んでしまいました shinde shimaimashita implies "ended up by dying".

The converse auxiliary is おく oku to do something in advance or **with** an eye to the future.

J   Whereas the normal さん san can be used both after the surname and the personal name, ちゃん chan can be attached only to the first name, and is used as a term of endearment, especially for a child–Taro chan, Hanako chan. A bit like Jimmy or Manuelito or, in German, coincidentally, Hän<u>chen</u>.

K   The construction of this involved sentence is

     A…{B…[(D…D)C…C]…B}…A

     A   …この逆説は…という証明とみなされて来ました…kono gyakuset-su wa…to iu shoomei to minasarete kimashita *This paradox came to be seen as a proof…*

     B   (proof of what) タイムトラベルが…不可能だ taimu toraberu ga…fukanoo da *that time travel is impossible.*

     C   (embedded in B) is the adverbial phrase 矛盾のために mujun no tame ni *because of the contradiction.*

     D   qualifying mujun is the embedded adjectival phrase それ自体の持つ sore jitai no motsu *which these circumstances possess.*

L   さて sate is a continuity word, used classically when, in a letter, you have got over the salutation and the state of the weather, and at last come to the substance. Here, it implies *Well now…*

M   納得 nattoku is a noun meaning persuasion, conviction; the phrase means *has conviction come?* An alternative is nattoku suru (to be convinced); nattoku saseru (to convince).

N   Another instance of nominalisation* using 事がありますか koto ga arimasu ka "is it a fact that…?" Atta is the past of 会う au (meet). The expression is the equivalent of *The fact of having met people travelling into the past, have you experienced it?* Note also the use of no as the necessary link in Japanese between the two phrases "into the past" and "travel people".

Unit 10

◇ ◇ English into Japanese ◇ ◇

Sentences and Themes

1. If time travel really becomes possible would you want to try it? (やってみる yatte miru)

2. What about* travel to the stars (星 HOSHI)? At the moment energy for the return journey (往復の OOFUKU no), with the food for many years of travel, would be too he

3. Science fiction** is popular in most countries. The result is that many people cannot make the distinction between what is possible and what is not.

4. How important do you think it is to understand the universe (宇宙 UCHUU)? Or do you think the social sciences may be more important?

*How about X? = X wa, doo daroo ka?
**usually referred to as SF = E SU E FU in katakana.

Transformation

1. Time travel が, really possible were-to-become, yourself try it [you] want と do-you-think?

2. To-[the]-stars travel は , how would-it-be? At present, for [the] return journey's energy と of-many-year's food は too-heavy are.

3. Science fiction は in many countries popular being because (だから) many people は what possible is と what not-possible is を distinguish cannot-do.

4. [The] universe を to-understand のは how much important　do-you-think? Or than-universe [the] of-society sciences' direction [の方が] important may-be と do-you-think?

Unit II
THE JAPANESE ECONOMY (2)
日本の経済 (2)

Frontispiece character : 円 EN *Japanese yen*.

◇ ◇ **Introductory Note** ◇ ◇

As noted in Unit 9 the economic importance of Japan–not to speak of the intricacies of the measures taken in the recession which began in 1989–justifies a second bite at economics and trade policy. This unit aims to reinforce the acquisition of the specialised terms and of the kanji which go with them. Thus there is some repetition, and many new compounds are, as is desirable at this stage, made up of kanji already used in earlier units, or contain at least one familiar kanji.

There are a few finer points of grammar and one or two idioms.

There are also two verbs which are written in hiragana, ie without using kanji. There are several reasons for this: first, it is not thought to be good style in Japanese to write solely in kanji. Second, though each of the verbs concerned has a kanji associated with it, neither is among **JOOYOO** "the common use" kanji. One (繋がる **KEI/tsuna-garu**) is particularly complicated to write and remember, and no doubt for this reason is not among the common use kanji recognised as such–though it is in the better word-processing packages. It is not missed by the Japanese–nor by those learning the language.

日本の経済(2)

1) 不況に直面して、日本は、他のどの国よりも、ケインズ経済対策を打ち出したと言えるだろう。公定歩合は、非常に低い水準(1.75%)まで、下げられた。いくつかの総合経済対策で、公共投資拡大、民間投資促進、企業への租税特別措置が明示された。銀行は、共同債権買収機構を設立し、不動産担保付き不良債権の一部買収も行われた。

2) 対策の中でも、個人と企業の直接税引き下げは論争を呼んだ。大蔵省の政統派官僚は、赤字財政に同意せず、社会党は、減税相当額の消費税をすぐに引き上げる事に反対した。

3) 今後対外的には、能率的で、安い労働力の中国等アジアへの海外投資も伸びるだろう。一方、長引く貿易収支黒字がもたらした、米ドルに対する円高は、輸出を妨げ、結果

的に、需要主導の景気回復を阻止する。円高に成れば成る程、輸出に頼る日本経済は落ち込み、延いては、貿易相手国の経済活動に反映する。

4) 貿易相手国は、貿易黒字削減を目的とした内需拡大を求め、それと同時に、外国企業の日本進出に不利な談合その他の非関税障壁の廃止、規制緩和、流通機構の単純化などを要求している。

5) 不況対策と貿易の自由化は、日本の政界、財界、官界の伝統的バランスを崩すかもしれない。しかし、長い目で見ると、米等農産物を含めた市場開放は、世界経済の中の日本にとって避けられないだけでなく、日本人消費者の選択拡大にもつながる事は、言うまでもない。

Unit II

NiHON NO KEIZAI (2)	THE JAPANESE ECONOMY (2)

1 Fukyoo ni chokumen shite, Nihon wa, tano dono kuni yori mo, Keinzu keizai taisaku o uchidashita to ieru daroo[a]. Kootei-buai wa, hijoo ni hikui suijun (1.75%) made sagerareta. Ikutsuka no[b] soogoo keizai taisaku de, kookyoo-tooshi-kakudai, minkan-tooshi-sokushin, kigyoo e no sozei-tokubetsu-sochi ga meiji sareta. Ginkoo wa, kyoodoo-saiken-baishuu-kikoo o setsuritsu shi, fudoosan tanpo tsuki furyoo-saiken no ichi bu baishuu mo okonawareta.

2 Taisaku no naka demo, kojin to kigyoo no chokusetsu-zei hikisage wa ronsoo o yonda. Ookura-shoo no seitoo-ha kanryoo wa, akaji zaisei ni dooi sezu[c], shakai-too wa, genzei sootoo-gaku no shoohi-zei o suguni hikiageru koto ni hantai shita.

3 Kongo taigaiteki ni wa, nooritsu-teki de, yasui roodoo-ryoku no Chuugoku nado Ajia e no kaigai-tooshi mo nobiru daroo. Ippoo[d], nagabiku booeki-shuushi-kuroji ga motarashita, bei-doru ni taisuru en-daka wa, yushutsu o samatage, kekka-teki ni, juyoo-shudoo no keiki kaifuku o soshi suru[e]. En-daka ni nareba naru hodo,[f] yushutsu ni tayoru nihon-keizai wa ochikomi, hiite wa, booeki-aite-koku no keizai-katsudoo ni han'ei suru.

Confronted by the recession Japan can be said to have taken more Keynesian measures than those of any other country. Official interest rates were reduced to very low levels (1.75%). In several economic packages public investment was expanded, private sector investment promoted and tax credits enacted in favour of corporations. A cooperative credit purchasing corporation was set up by the banks and arranged the purchase from them of some part of the loans backed by real estate collateral.

But, among these measures, the reduction of direct taxes on individuals and corporations was contentious. The orthodox officials of the Finance Ministry were against deficit financing, while the Socialists were opposed to a corresponding immediate increase in the consumption tax.

Internationally, from now on overseas investment will increase in China and Asia which are efficient and have cheap labour. At the same time the appreciation of the yen in relation to the US dollar, caused by the long-standing trade surplus, would be an obstacle to exports and thus in the result would inhibit a demand-led economic recovery. The stronger the yen the more the Japanese economy, which relies on exports, would turn down and this in turn would reflect back on the economic activity of her trading partners.

4 Booeki-aite-koku wa, booeki-kuroji sakugen o mokuteki to shita naijukakudai o motome, sore to dooji ni, gaikoku kigyoo no Nihon shin-shutsu ni furi-na dangoo sono ta no hi-kanzei-shooheki no haishi, kisei kanwa, ryuutsuu-kikoo no tanjun-ka nado o yookyuu shite iru.

5 Fukyoo taisaku to booeki no jiyuu-ka wa, Nihon no seikai, zaikai, kankai no dentoo-teki baransu o kuzusu kamo shirenai. Shikashi, nagai me de miru to, kome nado noo-sanbutsu o fukumeta shijoo-kaihoo wa, sekai-keizai no naka no Nihon ni totte[g] sakerarenai dake de naku[h], Nihon-jin shoohisha no sentaku kakudai ni mo tsunagaru koto wa, iu made mo nai[i].

Japan's trading partners, aiming at the reduction of the trade surplus, sought domestic expansion and at the same time called for the abolition of non-tariff barriers, such as collusion which disadvantaged foreign firms entering Japan, the relaxation of regulation, and the simplification of the apparatus of distribution.

The measures taken in the recession and the liberalisation of trade may break down the traditional balance in Japan between politicians, finance and officialdom. However, taking a long view, the opening-up of the market–including rice and other agricultural products–is not only unavoidable for Japan in the world economy but it goes without saying that it is also linked with expansion of consumer choice for the Japanese.

◇◇ Notes on Kanji ◇◇

KANJI character	RADICAL no	shape	reading	KANJI / COMPOUND derivation and meaning
				◇不況 FUKYOO *recession*. (See Unit 9.)
直	24	十	CHOKU/nao-su	See Unit 6; *direct/repair*.
面	176	面	MEN/omote	See Unit 4; *face, surface*. ◆直面する ·CHOKUMEN suru *face, confront*.
対	67	文	TAI/TSUI	See Units 7,8, & 9; *against*.
策	118	竹	SAKU	See Unit 6; *a policy, measure*. ◆対策 TAISAKU *(counter) measure*.
打	64	扌	DA/u-tsu	Phonetic (just) from RHS CHOO, originally a nail (now most used for a block of houses): with LHS hand radical; *to hit*. ◆打ち出す uchi-da-su *"hammer out"* a policy.
公	12	八	KOO/ookake	See Unit 7; (公式 KOOSHIKI *formula*) *public, official*.
定	40	宀	TEI/JOO/ sada-meru	See Units 6 & 10; *set, determine*. ◆公定 KOOTEI *officially set*.
歩	77	止	HO/BU/aru-ku	See Units 2 & 7; *walk*; BU *rate, percentage*.
合	9	人	GOO/a-u	See Units 4, 6, & 8; *fit, match*. ◆歩合 BUAI *a rate*. ◆公定歩合 KOOTEI BUAI *official (discount) rate*.
				◇非常に HIJOO-ni *unusually, very*. (Cf <u>JOO</u> YOO kanji.)

KANJI character	RADICAL		KANJI / COMPOUND	
	no	shape	reading	derivation and meaning
低	9	亻	TEI/hiku-i	See Unit 9; *low.*
準	24	氵	JUN	See Unit 7; (標準 HYOOJUN *standard*). ◆水準 SUIJUN *level.*
下	(1)	一	sa-geru	Sa-geru is the transitive verb *to reduce*, corresponding to the transitive **sa-garu** *to fall*: sa- is among the kun readings of this sign.
総	120	糸	SOO/su-beru	See Unit 8; *general, all.* ◆総合 SOOGOO *total, overall.*
共	12	八	KYOO/tomo	See Units 4 & 5; *together.* ◆公共 KOOKYOO *public* . ◇投資 TOOSHI *investment.*
拡	64	扌	KAKU	RHS is KOO/hiro-i wide, used here as phonetic for KAKU *expansion.* ◆拡大 KAKUDAI *expansion.*
民	(1)	一	MIN/tami	See Unit 8; *the people.* ◆民間 MINKAN ("among the people") *private.*
促	9	亻	SOKU/ unaga-su	RHS is the pictorial SOKU/ashi foot,leg: with person radical LHS, *urge.*
進	162	辶	SHIN/susu-mu	See Unit 9; *promote.* ◆促進 SOKUSHIN *promotion, encouragement.* ◇企業 KIGYOO *enterprise, firm* (Unit 8).

KANJI character	RADICAL no	RADICAL shape	reading	KANJI / COMPOUND derivation and meaning
租	115	禾	SO	Here the cereal radical LHS is the stored grain given up as *tax*.
税	115	禾	ZEI	RHS is alternative reading ZEI of the SETSU in 説明SET-SUMEI; the basic meaning may have been to get rid of (eg words or, in this case) grain (LHS) taken by the taxman (who can be seen as Big Brother or the devil) *tax* (cf税金 ZEIKIN tax as money and 関税 KANZEI customs duty). ◆租税 SOZEI *taxes, taxation*.
				◇特別な TOKUBETSUna *special*.
措	64	扌	SO	RHS SEKI/mukashi (Unit 4) but, as with KAKU and KOO above (KAKUDAI) SO here corresponds to the sound SEKI with other radicals: *put aside*.
置	122	罒	CHI/o-ku	We have seen the base in Unit 6 直接 CHOKUSETSU direct and in Unit 9 値 CHI/atai price: here the reading CHI, with the net radical on top (as in 買 BAI/ka-u buy) *to put*. ◆措置 SOCHI *measures* (what one lays down).
				◇明示する MEIJI suru *state clearly, enact*. ◇共同 KYOODOO *cooperative*.
債	9	亻	SAI	See Unit 9; *liabilities*.
権	75	木	KEN	See Unit 8; *authority*. ◆債権 SAIKEN *credits* (as obverse of debts–see below).
買	122	罒	BAI/ka-u	See Unit 1; *buy*.

KANJI character	RADICAL		KANJI / COMPOUND	
	no	shape	reading	derivation and meaning
収	29	又	SHUU/ osa-meru	See Unit 9; *earn*. ◆買収 BAISHUU *purchase*.
機	75	木	KI/hata	RHS phonetic is a complicated combination of two cocoons (radical 52) on top and a man with a lance underneath: meaning, for obscure reasons, several/how many (幾つ ikutsu). With LHS wood radical hata *a loom*; ON reading refers to *machines* in general and a *chance*; hence 機会 KIKAI *opportunity*. Cf 危機 KIKI *crisis*.
構	75	木	KOO/kama-eru	See Units 7 & 8; *build up*. ◆機構 KIKOO *mechanism, organisation*.
設	149	言	SETSU/ moo-keru	RHS is radical 79; this may look like a chair under a table but is said to represent a hand (below) grasping the shaft of a spear or something to hit with. With speech radical means *set up, establish* . (?Mnemonic: when something new is set up people sit on chairs at a table and speeches are made.) ◆設立する SETSURITSU suru *establish*.
担	64	扌	TAN/nina-u	See Unit 7; *bear, support*.
保	9	亻	HO/tamo-tsu	Phonetic RHS can be seen as a baby or helpless creature 呆 HOO stupid or as a bird spreading its wings over the nest; either provides a clue to the meaning, *keep, protect*. ◆担保 TANPO *security, collateral*.
付	9	亻	FU/tsu-ku	See Units 3, 7, and 8 *to be or have attached*.
				◇不良債権 FURYOOSAIKEN *bad debts*. (bad "credits")

KANJI character	RADICAL no	shape	reading	KANJI / COMPOUND derivation and meaning
				◇個人 KOJIN *individual*. ◇直接税 CHOKUSETSUZEI *direct taxes*.
引	57	弓	IN/hi-ku/hi-keru	Bow radical gives *pull, reduce*: much used in compounds with other verbs and verbal nouns; thus 取り引き torihiki dealings, 引き出し hikidashi a drawer; –引き–biki a discount; here, 引き下げる hiki-sa-geru *to reduce* ("hike downwards"!–but see 引き上げる hiki-a-geru below).
				◇論争 RONSOO *controversy*. (RON Unit 7, SOO Unit 8)
呼	30	口	KO/yo-bu	See Unit 6; *call, invite*.
統	120	糸	TOO/su-beru	統合 TOOGOO in Unit 7; *control*. ◆正統 SEITOO ("correct control") *orthodox*.
派	85	氵	HA	RHS said to show branching; with water radical becomes a sect or *faction* (often used of groups inside political parties). Cf 脈 MYAKU in Unit 9.
				◇官僚 KANRYOO *officials* (Unit 8).
赤	155	赤	SEKI/aka-i	The radical meaning *red*; large man on top, fire below. ◆赤字 akaJI "red figures" *deficit*.
				◇財政 ZAISEI *finance*. (ZAI Unit 9, SEI Unit 6 and 8) ◇同意 DOOI *agreement*. ◇社会党 SHAKAI-TOO *Socialist Party* (Unit 8). ◇減税 GENZEI *reduction of taxation*. (GEN/heru Unit 8) ◇相当 SOOTOO *correspond*.

KANJI character	RADICAL no	shape	reading	KANJI / COMPOUND derivation and meaning
額	181	頁	GAKU/hitai	Yet another of the **KAKU/GAKU** group: here, with head radical RHS original meaning was forehead, carried through into the **kun** reading hitai; **ON** reading is framed picture and a *sum* or *amount*. ◆相当額 SOOTOOGAKU *corresponding amount*.
				◇消費 SHOOHI (Unit 9) *consumption*. ◇消費税 SHOOHI-ZEI *consumption tax* (corresponds to sales tax / tax on value added). ◇引き上げる hiki-a-geru *increase*.
反	27	厂	HAN	Outside is the radical and phonetic **HAN**, cliff. The hand inside somehow gives the meaning *is against* or *anti–*. ◆反対する HANTAI suru *oppose*.
				◇対外的に TAIGAI-TEKI ni *internationally*. ◇能率的 NOORITSU-TEKI *efficient*.
安	40	宀	AN/yasu-i	See Unit 1; *cheap*.
				◇労働力 ROODOORYOKU *work-force*.
等	118	竹	TOO/nado	Bamboo radical, with equal spacing, may be the clue; *and the like*.
				◇海外 KAIGAI *overseas*. (KAI/umi in Unit 5) ◇海外投資 KAIGAI-TOOSHI *overseas investment*.
伸	9	亻	SHIN/no-biru	RHS by itself is the phonetic, **SHIN/moo-su** meaning to say (deferential*); Origin variously hands on a rope, a ribcage, or lightning, and thus deity. With the person radical; *expand*.

KANJI character	RADICAL no	RADICAL shape	reading	KANJI / COMPOUND derivation and meaning
				◇長引く nagabiku "long-drawn-out" *long-standing, continuous.* ◇貿易 BOOEKI *trade.*
支	65	支	SHI/sasa-eru	This radical shows a hand carrying the branch of a tree: it thus now means both a bough and to support. However, there is another implication–that of paying out, and this is interpreted on the analogy of pulling the bough from the tree. ◆収支 SHUUSHI *a balance.* ◆貿易収支 BOOEKI-SHUUSHI *trade balance.*
黒	203	黒	KOKU/kuro-i	A radical, showing a window or chimney with the fire radical below; *black.* ◆黒字 kuroJI (cf akaJI earlier) *in the black; surplus.*
				◇米ドル BEI-DORU *US dollar.* (See Unit 5.) ◇対する TAI-suru *in relation to.* ◇円高 EN-daka *a strong yen.*
輸	159	車	YU	RHS is the phonetic for this and other kanji; may have meant a boat, with a river sign as part of the base instead of the present knife. With the vehicle radical LHS fittingly; *transport.* ◆輸出 YUSHUTSU *export.* ◆輸入 YUNYUU *import.*
妨	38	女	BOO/ samata-geru	Sound from RHS HOO/kata (radical 70): not at all clear why addition of woman radical 38 LHS should mean *obstruct.*
				◇結果的に KEKKA-TEKI ni *as a result.*
需	173	雫	JU	The unmistakeable rain radical above, and radical 126 –a beard–below somehow means need (need a wet shave?) *demand.*

KANJI character	RADICAL no	shape	reading	KANJI / COMPOUND derivation and meaning
要	146	西	YOO/i-ru	The now familiar kanji; *need* (Units 7 & 8). ◆需要 JUYOO *demand* (供給 KYOOKYUU supply). ◆…需要主導 …JUYOO-SHUDOO no *demand-led.*
景	72	日	KEI	Phonetic is base KYOO/KEI capital: sun makes it into a *spectacle, view.* Cf 景色 KESHIKI scenery. ◆景気 KEIKI *business conditions* (not necessarily good).
復	60	彳	FUKU	RHS, including foot at the base, is phonetic in several kanji; for complicated reasons said to mean return to base: with radical 60 means *do something again.* ◆回復 KAIFUKU *recovery.*
阻	170	阝	SO/haba-mu	RHS phonetic **SO**: with hill radical; *to obstruct.* ◆阻止する SOSHI suru *block, obstruct.*
程	115	禾	TEI/hodo	See 程度 TEIDO degree, extent, in Unit 9: here the kun reading hodo is used, in the idiom "the more…the…" (See grammar notes.)
頼	181	頁	RAI/ tayo-ru/tano-mu	LHS is SOKU/taba a bundle (Unit 7) and RHS is now the head radical: this at least provides the mnemonic of a bundle relying on the head to support it; tayo-ru *rely.* (Reading tano-mu request.)
				◇落ち込む ochi-ko-mu *to drop, fall.* ◇延いては hiite-wa *furthermore, in addition.* ◇活動 KATSUDOO *activity.*
映	72	日	EI/utsu-ru	Phonetic RHS recognisable as the base of 英 EI as in 英国 EIKOKU England: with sun radical LHS; *reflect, project* (Cf 映画 EIGA film).

KANJI character	RADICAL no	RADICAL shape	reading	KANJI / COMPOUND derivation and meaning
				◇内需 NAIJU (*internal*) *domestic demand.*
求	3	丶	KYUU/ moto-meru	See Unit 7; *request.*
進	163	辶	SHIN/susu-mu	As in Unit 8; *go forward, promote.* ◆進出 SHINSHUTSU "setting out in order to" <u>*enter (a market).*</u>
				◇不利な FURI na *disadvantageous.* ◇談合 DANGOO talking together, *collusion* (eg in bidding). ◇関税 KANZEI *a tariff/customs duty.*
障	170	阝	SHOO/sawa-ru	Phonetic RHS (SHOO section of text) ingeniously derived from ON=sound, with the idea that the sign for ten underneath means ten notes, after which there is a break in the music! Here, with hill radical, *obstacle.*
壁	32	土	HEKI/kabe	With the earth radical below the rest must represent a phonetic, but of uncertain origin–and hard to remember: *wall.* ◆非関税障壁 HI-KANZEI-SHOOHEKI *non-tariff barriers.*
廃	53	广	HAI/suta-reru	Base, no doubt phonetic, is HATSU–simplified version. Here means *fall into disuse, discontinue.* ◆廃止 HAISHI *abolition.*
規	147	見	KI	LHS could represent an arrow (矢) used, with a good look (RHS), as a measure or standard. Basis of a number of terms signifying *regulation.* ◆規制 KISEI *regulation.*
緩	120	糸	KAN/ yuru-mu/yuru-i	RHS here and in other kanji has sound kan (in other cases en): shape almost (but not quite) identical to 受YU/u-keru receive

KANJI	RADICAL			KANJI / COMPOUND
character	no	shape	reading	derivation and meaning
				(Unit 6) where two hands figure. Here basic meaning is *slack, loose.*
和	115	禾	WA/ yawa-/nago-	Radical is the phonetic here, but in addition cereal + mouth = ease thus *peace, harmony*. This sign figures in the names of several Japanese eras: 昭和 SHOOWA was the name given to that which ended in 1989–昭 SHOO brightness. WA also means Japan/Japanese in such phrases as 英和 EI-WA English-Japanese, 和風 WAFUU Japanese style. ◆緩和 KANWA *relaxation, loosening.*
流	85	氵	RYUU/ naga-reru	Possibly the birth of a baby with long hair, or just water flowing, the sign means *flow*, and also *style*. 流行る haya-ru to be in fashion. ◆流通 RYUUTSUU *distribution.* (TSUU/toosu in Unit 6.)
				◇単純化 TANJUN-KA *simplification.* (Unit 8) ◇要求する YOOKYUU suru *demand.* (See KYUU above.) ◇自由化 JIYUU-KA (JIYUU freedom) *liberalisation.*
界	102	田	KAI	Phonetic base meaning go-between (see 媒介 BAIKAI in Unit 7); with paddy radical on top said to imply boundaries: easier to see it as a globe on a stand; *world.* ◆政界 SEIKAI, 財界 ZAIKAI, and 官界 KANKAI all use this world kanji with the kanji SEI (politics, government) ZAI (economy) and KAN (officials) to denote their respective spheres.
伝	9	亻	DEN/tsuta-eru	RHS is a phonetic, now simplified: means *hand down.* ◆伝統的 DENTOOTEKI *traditional.* (See SEITOO above.)

KANJI	RADICAL		KANJI / COMPOUND	
character	no	shape	reading	derivation and meaning
崩	46	山	HOO/kuzu-su	Graphic sign indicating two objects 朋 merging into one geologically (the mountain): means *collapse, break down*.
農	161	辰	NOO	Not an easy kanji, but figures in the school list; the radical is rare, and is presented as a dragon, a shell, or something to be ashamed of. Even the top is seen as a paddy or a wood (no-one has related it to the kanji 曲げる KYOKU/ma-geru a tune and to bend). Has to be learnt; *agriculture*.
産	117	立	SAN/u-mu	The inner sign is life, birth and gives the meaning *produce*. ◆産物 SANBUTSU *a product*.
含	9	人	GAN/fuku-meru	Though the radical is treated as the person radical, it is better seen as a lid with something under it, or a mouth: *include*.
				◇市場 SHIJOO *market-place*.
放	70	方	HOO/hana-tsu	Phonetic and radical is LHS, with action radical RHS (hand holding a stick); *loosen*. ◆開放 KAIHOO *opening-up*.
避	162	辶	HI/sa-keru	Same original sound as HEKI/kabe above, but just as difficult to explain the meaning–here, *avoid*–or rather, not avoid.
択	64	扌	TAKU	RHS phonetic; with hand radical means (pick and) choose. ◆選択 SENTAKU *choice*.

◇ ◇ Grammar Notes ◇ ◇

A   言える ieru is the passive of the potential of 言う iu to say and thus means "can be said". The addition of だろう daroo carries both a hint of uncertainty–"may be said" and a tinge of the future tense that the Japanese do not have.

B   In phrases of number and quantity it is not always easy to get the Japanese order right. Here, in いくつか...の対策 ikutsuka no...taisaku, the order is the same as in English: *a certain number of measures*. However, below in 不良債権の一部買収 ...furyoo-saiken no ichi bu baishuu the order appears to be reversed, but this is because this ichi-bu qualifies baishuu meaning *(of bad debts) a part-purchase*.

C   せず sezu is an old negative form, in this instance of the verb suru. We have also seen にもかかわらず ni mo kakawarazu in spite of or not taking heed of.

D   The conjunctions of Japanese do not coincide with those of English, though Japanese is as keen as English to establish the logical connection between statements. We have seen that が ga can mean "and" or "but". A number of words mean "however"–でも demo, しかし shikashi. "Moreover" has among its equivalents 又 mata, 延いては hiite wa (below). 一方 ippoo usually means one-sided, and "on the one hand", but it is also used for "on the other hand." Here the two statements reinforce rather than stand in contrast; thus English can say "at the same time". (Below, in para 4, "at the same time" really implies that the actions are contemporaneous, and the Japanese too says 同時に dooji ni.)

E   By now the syntax of sentences like this will be familiar. The subject of the main verb in this case nests inside the subordinate clauses. The main clause is ...円高 は...景気回復を阻止する ...endaka wa...keiki-kaifuku o soshi suru *the strong yen will inhibit recovery.*

F   The comparison conveyed in English by "the more...the..." uses the -eba form of the verb or adjective followed by a repetition of the basic form of the verb or adjective in question + hodo. Hodo is perhaps best seen as a noun meaning that amount, degree: thus in 早ければ早いほどいいです hayakereba hayai hodo ii desu *the sooner the better*, and in 多ければ多いほどいいです ookereba ooi hodo ii desu *the more the better*, we can think in terms of "If it were early <u>that amount</u> of early is good" and "If it were many <u>that degree</u> of many would be good".

Here 円高になればなる程、...日本経済は落ち込み en-daka ni nareba naru

hodo,…nihon-keizai wa ochi-komi *if the yen becomes strong, <u>by that amount</u> of becoming the Japanese economy drops.*

G　…にとって …*ni totte* is a very useful phrase meaning as for, as regards…Thus 私にとって watashi ni totte (as for me…) is often heard. 私にとって、英語は難しいです Watashi ni totte, eigo wa muzukashii desu *For me, English is difficult.* (Incidentally, totte looks like a participle but is always written in hiragana.)

H　Another favourite tournure in many languages "not only…but…" In Japanese, the first part of the comparison is followed by だけでなく dake de naku, where naku is the adverbial form of nai (is not)–strictly an adjective; でない de nai is the negative of de aru and means "does not exist". なく naku is the equivalent of なくて nakute–the suspensive form used when another verb is still to come. Thus the first part of the idiom means XXX not only exists, but…The second part contains the particle も mo also.

I　言うまでもない iu made mo nai "to say even it is not" *it goes without saying.* The subject (what goes without saying) is the clause ending …事は …koto wa.

◇ ◇ English into Japanese ◇ ◇

Sentences and Themes

1. Why have the rich countries not wanted to adopt Keynesian measures? Was the reason that they were more worried about inflation* than about unemployment/recession?

2. All goverments are convinced that free trade and the opening of markets is a good thing, but they think differently about imports.

3. What devices (工夫 kufuu) can governments use against recession? Interest rates, tariffs, subsidies, how effective are they?

*インフレ

Transformation

1. Why (なぜ naze) [the] rich countries は of-Keynes measures did-not-want-to-take? That は, recession と unemployment than inflation を worry because was-it?

2. Of-all governments は freedom trade と market opening が good thing と conviction-making are, but about imports so is-not.

3. Recession-against (に対して ni taishite) governments は, what-sort-of (どんな donna) devices (工夫 kufu) can-do (できる dekiru) may-be? Interest rates (利子 rishi) tariffs (関税 kanzei), subsidies (補助金 hojokin) は, to what extent (どの程度 dono teido) effective may-be?

Unit 12
THE FIFTH GENERATION
第五世代

Frontispiece character : 機 KI *machine*.

◇ ◇ Introductory Note ◇ ◇

This text is notable for the number of foreign (ie European/American) words it contains; in fields like computing they are a necessary part of the language, and their difficulty is only that they are not always immediately recognisable either in transliteration into katakana or, indeed, when heard for the first time.

There are not many grammar notes; this reflects the fact that by now we have traversed the main points–both the inflections of the verbs and adjectives and the ways in which sentences are put together. However, this text still provides typical examples of relatively complicated sentences which require dissection and clarification.

Let there be no mistake, however; there is some way to go before an ordinary Japanese text becomes accessible: first, because we have covered only some 600 kanji out of the 2,000 used in normal writing; second, because learning Japanese means coping with the numerous combinations of these kanji and third, because it is not easy, even with the use of symbols, to make Japanese syntax transparent–either to the foreign reader or, as noted earlier, to translating machines.

第五世代

1) 通常のコンピューターは決して賢くない。ただ指示された通りに作動するだけだ。命令のプログラムに頼りながら、極めて短い時間に、本質的に算術の演算を連続的に実行するのだ。

2) コンピューター業界は、長年、人間の脳の様に機能させる事ができるコンピューターを追求して来た。人工知能（AI）の研究は、実際に考える能力は無くても、推論する能力は有り、数字を処理する代わりに、思考を扱い、自然言語に対応できるコンピューターを目指している。

3) その研究開発（R & D）を目的として、1982年、通産省（通商産業省―MITI）は研究機関 ICOTを設立した。コンピューターの会社は100人の社員を提供し、政府援助金は500億円に上った。最終的目標は、10年間でPIM（並列推論マシン）のハードウェアとソフトウェア（PIMOSと言うオペ

レーティング・システム）のプロトタイプを作る事だった。

4）しかしながら、1992年6月、この開発計画最後の会議で、1024パラレル・プロセッサーの付いたプロトタイプ・マシンは、まだ完成されていないと発表された。通産省は、もう2年、その完成を目指す研究に資金を払う事になった。

5）結果は、成功だろうか、失敗だろうか。いずれにしても、このプロジェクトは、他の国が同じ様な企画に着手する事への刺激となった。コンピューター業界は満足し、会社は、論理型プログラミングの原則を学んだと言っている。しかし、局外者には、根本的戦略が正しかったかどうか、定かでない。恐らく、例えばニューラル・ネットワーク等、特定の応用に適したAI技術の研究に焦点を当てた方がよいのではないだろうか。

DAI GO SEDAI

THE FIFTH GENERATION

1 Tsuujoo no konpyuutaa wa kesshite kashikoku nai. Tada shiji sareta toori ni[a] sadoo suru dake da[b]. Meirei no puroguramu ni tayori nagara, kiwamete mijikai jikan ni, honshitsu-teki ni sanjutsu no enzan o renzoku-teki ni jikkoo suru no da.

Conventional computers are not at all clever; they do only what they are told. Relying on their programme of instructions they perform serially a large number of essentially numerical operations in a very short time.

2 Konpyuutaa-gyoo-kai wa, naganen, ningen no noo no yoo ni kinoo saseru koto ga dekiru[c] konpyuutaa o tsuikyuu shite kita. Jinkoochinoo (AI) no kenkyuu wa, jissai ni kangaeru nooryoku wa nakute mo, suiron suru nooryoku wa ari, suuji o shori suru kawari ni, shikoo o atsukai, shizen-gengo ni taioo dekiru kon-pyuutaa o mezashite iru[d].

The computing community has for a long time sought a computer which can be made to work more in the way the human brain does. The research into Artificial Intelligence aims at a computer which, though it would not really be capable of thinking, would be able to reason and, instead of handling numbers, would be able to handle ideas and react to ordinary language.

3 Sono kenkyuu kaihatsu (R&D) o mokuteki to shite, 1982 nen, Tsuusanshoo [Tsuu Shoo San Gyoo Shoo] (MITI) wa kenkyuu kikan ICOT o setsuritsu shita. Konpyuutaa no kaisha wa hyaku-nin no shain o teikyoo shi, seifu-enjokin wa 500 oku en ni nobotta. Saishuu-teki mokuhyoo wa, juu nen kan de PIM (heiretsu suiron mashin = Parallel Inference Machine) no haadouea to sofutouea (PIMOS to iu opereetingu.shisutemu) no purototaipu o tsukuru koto datta[e].

With R&D in this field as the objective, in 1982 MITI established ICOT as a research institu-tion. The computer companies lent one hun-dred staff, and the government contribution would be 50 billion yen. The ultimate objec-tive was to produce over ten years the prototype hardware and software–ie an operating system called PIMOS–of a PIM (Parallel Inference Machine).

4 Shikashi nagara[f], 1992-nen 6-gatsu, kono kaihatsu keikaku saigo no kaigi de, 1024 parareru.purosessaa no tsuita puroto-taipu.mashin wa, mada kansei sarete inai to happyoo sareta[g]. Tsuusanshoo wa, moo 2-nen, sono kansei o mezasu kenkyuu ni shikin o harau koto ni natta[h].

5 Kekka wa, seikoo daroo ka, shippai daroo ka? Izure ni[i] shite mo, kono purojekuto wa, ta no kuni ga onaji-yoo na kikaku ni chakushu suru koto e no shigeki to natta[j]. Konpyuutaa gyookai wa manzoku shi, kaisha wa, ronriga-ta puroguramingu no gensoku o mananda to itte iru. Shikashi, kyokugai-sha ni wa, konpon-teki senryaku ga, tadashikatta ka doo ka[k], sadaka de nai. Osoraku, tatoeba nyuuraru-nettowaaku nado, tokutei no ooyoo ni tekishi-ta AI gijutsu no kenkyuu ni shooten o ateta hoo ga yoi[l] no dewa nai daroo ka?

However, at the final meeting on the development project in June 1992 it was announced that the prototype machine with 1024 parallel processors was not yet ready. MITI would pay for another two years research for it to be completed.

Is this outcome success or failure? In either case this Project stimulated other countries to launch similar schemes. Computer circles are satisfied; the companies say they have learnt the principles of logic programming, but outsiders are not sure that the basic strategy has been right. Better perhaps to focus on AI techniques, like neural networks, for example, suitable for specific applications?

Unit 12

◇◇ Notes on Kanji ◇◇

KANJI character	RADICAL no	RADICAL shape	reading	KANJI / COMPOUND derivation and meaning
常	42	⺌	JOO/tsune	See Units 9 & 11: *normal*. ◆通常 TSUUJOO *usual*.
				◇決して Kesshite (from KETSU/ki-meru in Unit 6 decide) *never, not at all* (with negative verb).
賢	154	貝	KEN/kashiko-i	Top is vassal (cf DAIJIN) + a hand; base is shell radical ie money. ?Mnemonic "good and faithful servant; unto him that hath shall be given…"; *smart*.
指	64	扌	SHI/yubi/sa-su	Original phonetic was the RHS top (7 SHICHI): same sound used for various kanji. Here, with hand radical, *finger, point to*. ◆指示 SHIJI *indicate*. (JI/shime-su)
				◇通りに too-ri ni a way of doing something: cf その通りです sono toori desu that is right. Here as conjunction *as* (it is indicated that they should do). ◇作動 SADOO start, get going (eg an engine) + saseru *make it work*.
命	9	人	MEI/inochi	Similar to next kanji, but with a mouth added; *life*.
令	9	人	REI	Base could be someone kneeling; under a cover or roof, expecting a sign from above: or as a meeting (top) with a document on which a seal (underneath) is affixed; *order*. ◆命令 MEIREI *order, instruction*.
頼	181	頁	RAI/ tano-mu/ tayo-ru	See Unit 11. Tayoru means *to rely on*.

KANJI character	RADICAL no	shape	KANJI / COMPOUND reading	derivation and meaning
極	75	木	KYOKU/GOKU/ kiwa-meru	Difficult kanji for the primary school list: origin obscure, but in Chinese too meant *limit*; here *extremely*. (Cf 北極 HOKKYOKU North Pole.)
短	111	矢	TAN/mijika-i	LHS radical is an arrow; RHS (TOO/ZU/mame beans): borrowed to mean *small, short*.
				◇本質的 HONSHITSUTEKI *essential*.
算	118	竹	SAN	Top is radical for bamboo: thus perhaps an abacus, because made of bamboos; bottom is eye + the rare radical 55 meaning two hands (used to work the device) *calculate*.
術	60	彳	JUTSU	Middle sign, representing millet, is phonetic (as also in 述 JUTSU/no-beru in Unit 6) The outer signs are iku to go. Whole sign means *way, technique*. ◆算術 SANJUTSU (counting technique) *arithmetic*.
演	85	氵	EN	Water radical, but not obvious why; RHS phonetic, means *perform* (eg a play). ◆演算 ENZAN (mathematical) *operation*.
				◇連続的 RENZOKUTEKI (REN/tsureru in Unit 8 and ZOKU/tsuzuku in Unit 5.)*serial* (one after another). ◇実行する JIKKOO suru *carry out, put into operation*.
業	(3)	丶	GYOO/waza	See Unit 8: An important kanji; *profession*; cf 工業 KOOGYOO manufacturing industry, and 産業 SANGYOO (productive) industry. ◆業界 GYOOKAI *industry circle*.
				◇人間 NINGEN *a human being*.

Unit 12

KANJI character	RADICAL no	RADICAL shape	KANJI / COMPOUND reading	KANJI / COMPOUND derivation and meaning
脳	130	月	NOO	Base 凶 KYOO means bad luck, perhaps of someone falling into a pit: with three lines on top seems to acquire sound NOO; with LHS meat/flesh radical; *brain*.
機	75	木	KI/hata	See Unit 11. ◆機能する KINOO suru *to function*.
追	162	辶	TSUI/o-u	Go forward radical with the phonetic meaning ramparts; *to follow, chase*. ◆追求する TSUIKYUU suru *to pursue*–figuratively; eg an objective.
				◇人工 JINKOO *artificial*. ◇知能 CHINOO *intelligence*. (Cf kaNOOSEI) ◇能力 NOORYOKU *ability* (power of functioning).
際	170	阝	SAI/kiwa	See Unit 9. ◆実際に JISSAI NI *actually*.
無	86	灬	MU/BU/na-i	Inexplicable! The dots underneath–a form of the fire radical–seem to be a mistake: mnemonic could be bundle of wood burnt to nothing? Basic meaning: *is/are not*.
推	64	扌	SUI/o-su	LHS hand radical but on RHS the "short-tailed bird radical (172) carries the phonetic; *infer* (?little bird told me). ◆推論 SUIRON *reason*.
				◇数字 SUUJI *numbers*. (Cf 数学 SUUGAKU *mathematics*.)
処	34	夂	SHO	Not clear why LHS radical for dragging feet + RHS seat or table (cf tsukue Unit 3) > *decide, take care of*. ◆処理する SHORI suru *manage*.

KANJI character	RADICAL no	shape	reading	KANJI / COMPOUND derivation and meaning
				◇思考 SHIKOO *thought*.
扱	64	扌	atsuka-u	Somewhat anomalous in that reform has left this kanji with only the **kun** reading. The original **ON** reading was KYUU, and this persists in 及ぶ KYUU/oyobu *to reach*; here with LHS hand radical *manage* (the English word too is derived from Latin for hand).
然	86	灬	ZEN/NEN	See 当然 TOOZEN in Unit 9 Originally dog (RHS) meat (LHS) over a fire (bottom): borrowed to mean a *state* or *condition*. ◆自然 SHIZEN *nature*.
				◇言語 GENGO *language*.
応	53	广	OO	Mercifully simplified from complicated inside which was phonetic, and contained the heart radical among other signs; now *react, respond*. ◆対応 TAIOO *respond*. Cf 応用 OOYOO below.
				◇目指す mezasu *aim at*. ◇開発 KAIHATSU *development*. ◇研究開発 KENKYUU-KAIHATSU *R and D (Research and Development)*. ◇目的 MOKUTEKI *aim, objective*.
省	(4)	ノ	SEI/SHOO/ habu-ku	Probably phonetic from top component, which is 少 SHOO/sukoshi; *Ministry*. **Kun** reading habu-ku means *omit, curtail*. ◆通産省（通商産業省）TSUUSANSHOO *MITI (Ministry of International Trade and Industry)*.
				◇機関 KIKAN *a mechanism* or, as here, an *agency, organisation*.

KANJI character	RADICAL no	RADICAL shape	KANJI / COMPOUND reading	KANJI / COMPOUND derivation and meaning
設	149	言	SETSU/ moo-keru	See Unit 11. ◆設立する SETSURITSU suru *establish*.
提	64	扌	TEI/sa-geru	RHS is original phonetic, also found as 是 ZE right, correct as in 是非 ZEHI right or wrong: the base is sign for stop; with a line has meaning right (where to stop); with the sun at the right place, right, proper. With hand radical LHS, *offer*. ◆提供 TEIKYOO *offer, provide*.
援	64	扌	EN	RHS said to be two hands pulling at an object thus pull out, rescue, *help*. Cf 後援会 KOOENKAI support association in Unit 8. ◆援助する ENJO suru *assistance, support*.
				◇資金 SHIKIN *funds*. (TOOSHI in Unit 9.) ◇最終 SAISHUU *final*. Cf 最初 SAISHO first, and 最後 SAIGO usual word for last (see below). ◇目標 MOKUHYOO *aim*.
並	12	`	HEI/ nara-bu/nami	Originally 2 x radical 117 two persons standing side by side giving meaning *put in a row*. See also 平行 HEIKOO parallel.
列	78	歹	RETSU	LHS is radical 78: originally bones thus what falls apart. (Cf 死ぬ shi-nu to die in Unit 10.) With knife radical RHS, *row* (Cf 列車 RESSHA train.) ◆並列 HEIRETSU *in parallel rows*.
計	149	言	KEI/haka-ru	RHS could be phonetic variant of 十 JUU ten: with radical, *count, sum, plan*. (Cf 時計 TOKEI a watch, clock.)
画	(1)	一	GA/KAKU	Simplified from original with, on top (no longer there), a brush for writing, as in kaku write, and below a field with a line

KANJI	RADICAL		KANJI / COMPOUND	
character	no	shape	reading	derivation and meaning
				underneath: GA is a picture–of a rustic scene? KAKU is a stroke when writing kanji. (Cf 映画 EIGA a film and 画家 GAKA a painter.) ◆計画 KEIKAKU *plan, project.*
				◇最後 SAIGO *last* (see above). ◇会議 KAIGI *conference.* (See SHUUGIIN in Unit 8.)
完	40	宀	KAN	Base is 元 GEN as in 元気 GENKI: here, with a lid put on it, *complete.* ◆完成 KANSEI *completion.*
				◇発表 HAPPYOO *announcement.* (See HATSU in Unit 7 and HYOO in Unit 4.) ◇結果 KEKKA *result.* ◇失敗 SHIPPAI *failure.* See Unit 6: with 失 SHITSU/ushi-nau lose.
様	75	木	YOO/sama	See Unit 9: phonetic from YOO/hitsuji sheep (radical 123). Kun reading sama Mr/Mrs (in addresses). ◆同じ様な onajiYOOna *the same kind of.*
企	9	人	KI/kuwada-teru	See Unit 8: base radical 77 SHI/tomaru to stop (Unit 2) [the connection with this kanji is probably phonetic (SHI/KI) but the sign is also said to be a man on tiptoe] > desiring something > *planning.* ◆企画 KIKAKU *scheme, plan.*
着	123	羊	CHAKU/ ki-ru/tsu-ku	See 着実 CHAKUJITSU in Unit 9. ◆着手 CHAKUSHU *start-up.*

KANJI character	RADICAL no	shape	KANJI / COMPOUND reading	derivation and meaning
刺	18	刂	SHI/sa-su	LHS phonetic and semantic thorn: whole sign means *to stab*. Cf 刺身 sashimi and 名刺 meishi (card).
激	85	氵	GEKI/hage-shii	As three element kanji looks forbidding: the two RHS elements originally meant to emit light (white on top, direction below and on the far right the action radical 66): with LHS water radical > violent water, excite: > *impetuous*. ◆刺激 SHIGEKI *incentive, stimulus*.
満	85	氵	MAN/mi-tasu	Simplified: RHS could be scales in balance; with water radical; *full, complete*. Phonetic for Manchuria in Japanese MANSHUU as in Chinese 満州.
足	157	足	SOKU/ ashi/ta-riru	Radical for leg/foot–main meaning: kun reading tariru *suffice*. ◆満足する MANZOKU suru *be satisfied*.
				◇論理 RONRI *logic*.
型	32	土	KEI/kata	Original phonetic, LHS top, was two scales, also was seen as a variant of the frame round a well (井 SEI/i) used in names like 井上 Inoue (over the well). With knife RHS becomes 刑 KEI punishment: here, with earth radical underneath gives *shape, form* (also blood-*group*). ◆論理型 RONRIgata *logic type* (論理的 RONRITEKI logical, in most other contexts).
則	154	刂	SOKU	Gruesome but memorable explanation of this sign for a *rule* is that the penalty for breaking it could be a fine (LHS shell) or mutilation (RHS knife). Provides the phonetic for several other kanji with this sign. ◆原則 GENSOKU *principle*.

KANJI character	RADICAL no	RADICAL shape	reading	KANJI / COMPOUND derivation and meaning
学	39	子	GAKU/mana-bu	Manabu is kun reading of GAKU in Unit 3; *learn*.
				◇局外者 KYOKUGAISHA *observer, outsider* (one outside the office).
根	75	木	KON/ne	RHS is radical 138 but here it is phonetic and carries the sound KON, as in other kanji. With the tree radical it means *root*. ◆根本的 KONPONTEKI *fundamental* ("root origin").
戦	62	戈	SEN/ ikusa/tataka-u	Phonetic: LHS alone has sound TAN meaning simple: with RHS spear radical means *war*. (Cf 戦争 SENSOO *war*.)
略	102	田	RYAKU	RHS phonetic KAKU/RYAKU; with paddy radical; *shorten*. ◆戦略 SENRYAKU *strategy*.
正	(1)	一	SEI/tada-shii	Tadashii is kun reading of SHOO/SEI: *correct*. Also woman's first name Masa-ko (Unit 1).
定	40	宀	TEI/sada-meru	Sada-ka is kun reading of TEI in Unit 6; *sure, certain*.
恐	61	心	KYOO/ oso-reru/ oso-roshii	Base is heart radical: on top a hand with a tool or weapon; *fearful*, with a notion of feeling small or embarrassment. Here 恐らく osoraku *perhaps* (? "If I may be so bold as to say...")
				◇特定の TOKUTEI no *specific*. ◇応用 OOYOO *an application*.
適	162	辶	TEKI	Origin opaque: RHS is phonetic for several kanji pronounced TEKI: this one means *be suitable*.

KANJI character	RADICAL		KANJI / COMPOUND	
	no	shape	reading	derivation and meaning
技	64	扌	GI/waza	RHS phonetic **SHI** (cf 収支 **SHUUSHI** income and exprenditure in Unit 11): with hand radical LHS, *skill, technique*.
術	60	彳	JUTSU	See **SANJUTSU** above. ◆技術 **GIJUTSU** *technique*.
焦	172	隹	SHOO	Phonetic from "short-tailed bird"; with fire radical below > *set alight*. Not the same as 無 **nai** above.
点	25	卜	TEN	See Unit 8; *a point*. ◆焦点 **SHOOTEN** *focus*. Cf German *Brennpunkt* ("burn-point") focus.

◇ ◇ Grammar Notes ◇ ◇

A   Here 通りに toori ni is used to mean "in the way that" *as*.

B   We have met だけだ dake da before (Unit 2) as the idiom meaning *…only does this or that*.

C   The whole phrase 人間の脳のように機能させる事ができる ningen no noo no yoo ni kinoo saseru koto ga dekiru qualifies コンピューター konpyuutaa. The subject is understood as 人が hito ga "one", or "people". It is omitted because to the Japanese it is obvious. In させる事ができる saseru koto ga dekiru, saseru is the causative of suru *a computer which people can make to work like a human brain*.

D   In this long sentence the main clause is 人工知能の研究は…コンピューターを目指している Jinkoo chinoo no kenkyuu wa…konpyuutaa o mezashite iru *AI research is aiming at a computer…* The plentiful filling in the middle consists of no less than five phrases, all qualifying konpyuutaa:

実際に考える能力は無くても jissai ni kangaeru nooryoku wa nakute mo *though there not really being (not having) the brainpower to think*. (The construction using the -kute form of the adjective or participle + mo often means though…)

推論する能力は有り suiron suru nooryoku wa ari *there being (having) the brainpower to reason.*

数字を処理する代わりに suuji o shori suru kawari ni *instead of dealing with numbers.*

思考を扱い shikoo o atsukai *handling thought.*

自然言語に対応できる shizen-gengo ni taioo dekiru *being able to react to natural language.*

E   The main clause is …目標は…事だった …mokuhyoo wa …koto datta *the…aim was…* What the aim was is expressed in the noun phrase ending in …tsukuru koto.

F   しかしながら shikashi nagara… is a somewhat literary or formal way of saying しかし shikashi *however*.

G   The main verb is 発表された happyoo sareta *it was announced*. The subject (what was announced) is the long noun clause 1024 パラレル・プロセッサ・マシンはまだ完成されていないと 1024 parareru.purosessaa no tsuita purototaipu.mashin wa mada kansei sarete inai to… *that the prototype machine with 1024 parallel processors was not yet completed.*

H   The expression 事になる koto ni naru basically expresses a committment; thus it corresponds sometimes to "was due to…" and sometimes to the notion of an action to take place in the future. (Cf to natta below and, in Unit 8, 政権交代となった seiken kootai to nattta.)

I   いずれに izure ni is an idiomatic phrase, one key to its meaning being that it can be written 何れ, ie with the character for KA/nani what, which one. Thus the phrase means *in any case.*

J   The main clause is このプロジェクトは…刺激となった kono purojekuto wa… shigeki to natta *this project became an incentive…* What it was an incentive for is in the noun phrase 他の国が同じ様な企画に着手する事への ta no kuni ga onaji-yoo na kikaku ni chakushu suru koto e no *towards (e) [the fact of] other countries originating similar plans.* The verb in dictionary form (suru) is made into a verbal noun as usual by the use of koto. This phrase is then followed by two particles; the first is e meaning towards an incentive to. However, in order to link this with shigeki the particle no is also required.

K   正しかったかどうか tadashikatta ka doo ka shows the usual way of saying whether or not. Literally, *was it correct or how?*

L   This is a regular way of expressing a comparison. The preferred subject of the comparison–ie the thing which is better or bigger or whatever–is tagged with 方が hoo ga in the direction of. Here the thing being compared is a long clause …ニューラル・ネットワークなど、特定の応用に適したAI技術の研究に焦点を当てた …nyuu-raru-nettowaaku nado, tokutei no ooyoo ni tekishita AI gijutsu no kenkyuu ni shooten o ateta *focussing the research effort on AI suitable for specific applications, such as neural networks etc.*

The verb in this construction using 方が hoo ga is nearly always in the past tense, as 当てた ateta is here, even though the comparison relates to the present, or even to the future. (Typically, タバコをやめた方がいい tabako o yameta hoo ga ii desu it would be better to give up smoking, where yameta is in the past, though タバコを吸わない方がいいです tabako o suwanai hoo ga ii desu, where suwanai is in the present tense, is just as current).

Note also that the Japanese politely puts the question into the negative–would it not have been better to…Rather in the same way, in a restaurant: "Could I please have some water" would be translated as お水をくれませんか O-mizu o kuremasen ka can you favour me with (give me) some water?

◇ ◇ English into Japanese ◇ ◇

Sentences and Themes

1. Because computers are comparatively new they change fast. One of the last big changes–the PC*–has embarrassed the main-frame** manufacturers.

2. The fact that the PC is ubiquitous (至る所 itarutokoro) has supported (helped) the enormous (see Unit 7) development of networks.

3. Many of the users of this book are likely to be connected to the Internet*** or the World Wide Web. Their development depends on the speed of internal and external telecommunications (電気通信 DENKITSUUSHIN) and on more efficient and easy-to-use software with the possibilty of hypertext (ハイパーテキスト haipaateki-suto) and browsing (読み取り yomi-tori).

4. The so-called multimedia (マルチメディア maruchimedia) using sound and video have also been developing. If it were you, would you prefer multimedia to this book?

*PC is パソコン PASOKON
**メインフレームメーカー Mein fureemu meekaa
***インターネット Intaanetto ワールドワイドウェブ waarudo waido uibu

Transformation

1. Computers new being because, rapidly change. Of-recent of-big changes of-one [the] PC [the] main-frame manufacturers caused-embarrassment (困る komaru).

2. [The] PC everywhere to-exist fact of-networks [the] enormous development を helped.

3. Of-this-book of-users many, Internet や to-World Wide Web connected (つながって) are-likely-to-be. Of-these [the] development は, of in-country and abroad of-telecommunications [the] speed and hypertext と browsing possible being, efficient and easy-to-use on-software is-depending (かかっている).

4. [The] so-called mulltimedia (マルチメディア maruchimedia) also sound and video using, have-been-developing (participle + past of kuru). If-[it]-were-you, this book than, of-multimedia [the] direction (方が hoo ga) good is?

Appendices

付録

◇ ◇ **Alphabetical Reference Grammar** ◇ ◇

The objectives of this reference grammar are: (a) to define essential grammatical terms for the learner to whom they may be unfamiliar, and (b) to explain in greater detail the main points of Japanese grammar referred to in the grammar notes to each unit.

Tables 1-7, which follow the reference grammar, set out the ways Japanese verbs and adjectives change their endings.

active   Verbs are in the active form (or voice) when their subject is the doer of the action. They are passive when the subject suffers the action. "The dog (subject) chases (active form) the cat. The cat (subject) is chased (passive)". Japanese clearly distinguishes the active and passive forms of verbs, as will be seen from the tables.

adjectival nouns   See next entry

adjective   A word which describes ("qualifies") a noun. A *heavy* bag. An adjectival phrase is a combination of several words which together describe a noun. "The *pipe-smoking* Mr Smith." See also relative.

There are two types of adjective in Japanese: the true adjectives, which have endings in い -i (eg 新しい atarashii) and those "pseudo-adjectives" which can be regarded as adjectival nouns–ie nouns which become adjectives when followed by the suffix な -na, rather as in English "-ful" makes peace (noun) into the adjective *peaceful*. In the same way 静か shizuka is the adjectival noun meaning *quietness*; 静かな shizuka-na is the adjective meaning *quiet*. A few adjectives–大きい ookii (big), 小さい chiisai (small) and おかしい okashii (odd, strange)–are used both with and without -na.

adverb   Just as the adjective describes ("qualifies") a noun, so the adverb describes ("modifies") a verb, an adjective or another adverb: thus he writes *well/badly*, she sings *divinely*; he is *supremely* confident; he speaks *very* well... *less* well... *too* well. English often makes adverbs from adjectives by the use of the suffix "-ly"; Japanese makes adverbs from adjectives by the use of the suffix く -ku added to the stem of true Japanese adjectives, and by the use of the suffix に -ni instead of na (see adjective above) for the pseudo-adjectives: 静かに shizuka-ni *quietly*.

In both English and Japanese, apart from the adverbs which are derived from adjectives there are many which are not: adverbs of place–*here, there*; adverbs of time–*then, now, soon*; adverbs of manner or degree like *so, thus, very, too, more*.

The Japanese regard as nouns some of their equivalents of our adverbs. For example koko (here), ima (now) are treated as nouns and as such can be combined with other nouns: ここの家 koko-no ie the "here" house; 後の会話 ato-no kaiwa the "afterwards conversation". Thus, the Japanese adverb proper has a post-position particle added, eg ここに koko-ni, ここで koko-de, 後で ato-de…

affirmative   The affirmative form of the verb states the action in positive form, as opposed to the negative form which says what does not happen. He *smokes*–affirmative; he *does not smoke*–negative. In Japanese the two forms of the verb are very different; thus the affirmative and negative are shown separately in our tables.

agent   The person by whom some action is performed; with a verb in the passive "by" is expressed in Japanese by the post-position particle -ni: "he was taught Japanese by a friend" 彼は日本語を友達に教えてもらいました kare wa Nihongo o tomodachi ni oshiete moraimashita (using morau "he was done the favour of being taught…"). The same construction can be used with narau to learn: 日本語を友達に習いました Nihongo o tomodachi-ni naraimashita He learnt Japanese "from a friend". (See instrument.)

apposition   Two nouns are said to be in apposition in such phrases as Mr Brown, the doctor; Einstein, the mathematician. In Japanese the two nouns are linked by the particle no as in Unit 1, otto no Tanaka Kazuo san and Unit 2, Nihonjin no Tanaka san. The order is determined by the logical rule that the noun which is specific in the context–ie the one you are talking about–comes second, and the noun which serves to qualify it precedes it. For example "Einstein the mathematician" 数学者のアインシュタイン suugakusha no Ainshutain, where Einstein is the specific, and mathematician is the qualifier; イギリス人のスミス igirisu-jin no Sumisu *Mr Smith the Englishman*. The same construction can be used to qualify a pronoun: イギリス人の私を覚えていますか

igirisujin no watashi o oboete imasu ka? *do you remember me, the Englishman?*

attributive   Adjectives which are directly attached to a noun, as contrasted with adjectives in the "predicative" position. In Japanese this distinction is significant for the pseudo-adjectives: when used attributively they require the -na suffix, as in 静かな shizuka-na quiet; 静かな町 shizuka-na machi *a quiet town*, but "the town is quiet" (predicative) 町は静かです machi wa shizuka desu.

auxiliary   An auxiliary verb is one which "helps" the meaning of another verb. Thus, in English, he *may* sing, he *will* die, he *might* recover. The Japanese tend to regard as auxiliary verbs what we see as the verb endings -masu, -tai, -mashita, -seru, -saseru, -nai, -rashii etc. We can also consider as auxiliary verbs in Japanese, those verbs which, used together with the present participle (-te/de form), have special meanings: participle + iku it will [gradually]; participle + miru try (find out by trying); participle + oku to do something in advance (Unit 5); participle + *shimau* to end up by doing something (Unit 10)

causative   The two forms of the Japanese verb (shown in our tables) which mean to make, cause, or let, someone do something (active) or have something done to them (passive). Both forms conjugate as Group II (-eru) verbs. The endings (shown in the tables) are: active Group I (kaka)-seru and Group II (mi)saseru; passive Group I (kaka)sareru/se-rareru and Group II (mi)serareru/sase-rareru.

clause   By convention, a unit of speech which contains a finite verb, as opposed to a phrase, which does not. Thus "when he arrived" is a clause; "on arrival" is a phrase.

colloquial   Three levels of discourse are grammatically distinguished in Japanese: plain, formal and honorific. It would be going too far to open a colloquial level as yet another, but as in all countries Japan has usages which are special to the spoken language. For example, のです no desu becomes んです 'n desu. じゃ ja is used instead of では de wa (as shown in our verb tables). んじゃないでしょうか -'n ja nai deshoo ka similarly means *isn't it?* じゃありません ja arimasen is an alternative to de wa arimasen as the negative of desu. Again, しなくては shinakute wa becomes しなきゃ shinakya or しなくちゃ shinakucha–for example in a sentence ending with ikenai/naranai–often omitted in colloquial speech. わらっちゃいけない waratcha ikenai (laughing no go) *not a laughing matter*.

Other examples are the use, by male persons only, of ぼく boku for *I*–and 君 kimi, used by males to mean *you*, but only when talking to a male or female of similar or lesser status.

The continuous form of the verb is often contracted in speaking, eg, using kaku to write:
書いています kaite imasu > 書いてます kaitemasu
書いているとき kaite iru toki > 書いてるとき kaiteru toki.

Some pronouns are shortened, eg:
こちら kochira > こっち kotchi
そちら sochira > そっち sotchi
どちら dochira > どっち dotchi.

comparison The grammatical construction by which things are compared: "he is bigger than me", when two persons or things are being compared, uses the form called the comparative: "she runs the fastest", when there are more than two, uses the superlative.

In Japanese there is no equivalent of the English suffixes *-er* and *-est*, but to express the comparative motto (more) can be added in front of the adjective or adverb. Yori can be regarded as the equivalent of "than", but comes not before, as in English, but after the noun with which the comparison is being made.

Thus AはBよりもっと大きいです A wa B yori motto ookii desu *A is bigger than B*. Alternatively motto is left out–without affecting the comparison: AはBより大きいです A wa B yori ookii desu. Motto is omitted particularly when words like zutto, sukoshi "much (more), a little (more)" are added.

An important difference between the two languages is that in English, if A is bigger than B, A has to be mentioned first, but in Japanese either A or B can come first: thus BよりAが大きいです B yori A ga ookii desu still means *A is bigger than B*.

An alternative formula is to use の方が …no hoo ga with the noun you wish to qualify as the cheaper or better of two. Aの方が大きい A no hoo ga ookii *A is bigger*. (Literally, "A's side/direction is bigger".)

To express the superlative—"the most…" "the best…" Japanese adds 一番 ichiban *first* (see ordinal) before an adjective: 一番よい ichiban yoi *best* (adjective); 一番よく ichiban yoku (adverb) or, as alternative, もっともよい,もっともよく mottomo yoi, mottomo yoku. "The most beautiful of the daughters" in Japanese would be 娘の中で一番きれいな娘 musume-no naka de ichiban kirei-na musume.

conditional Used in some grammars for what we call here the hypothetical forms—ie the parts of the Japanese verb ending in **-eba** or **-tara/dara** and bearing the meaning *if* or *when*… The term conditional is more usually applied in European languages to the form taken by the verb in that part of a hypothetical expression which in English states the result of the hypothesis: "He *would be happy* (if he were rich)". The conditional in this sense does not exist in Japanese, which simply uses the normal present or past in such expressions. See also conjunctive

conjugate
conjugation Term used for the process of putting a verb—and, in Japanese, one group of adjectives—through all its forms, as in our tables. When verbs follow several different regular patterns (as with Group I and Group II in Japanese) these can be distinguished as two "conjugations". (See also inflections.)

conjunction A word which, in English, introduces—and precedes—a new clause: examples are: *and, but, when, if, after, because* etc. In Japanese, only a few words with this function come in front of the clause—thus ga (and/but); shi (and). (NB when ga begins a new sentence it can only mean but; shi cannot begin a sentence, but is put at the end of the preceding sentence.) In Japanese, most conjunctions come after their clause and not before. Thus toki (when); kara (after/because); node (because).

conjunctive Another term, like conditional, used in some grammars to refer to what we call in this book the hypothetical form of the verb meaning *if/when*

Appendix I

continuous

Just as English has a continuous form of the verb using the verb "to be" as the auxiliary with the participle of the verb–he *is singing*, he *was smoking*, she *has been drinking*–so in Japanese the verb iru (to be) with the participle (-te form) usually translates the English continuous present: thus, 書いています kaite imasu *he/she/we/they are writing*.

However, there are two catches: sometimes Japanese uses what looks like the continuous form where we should use the simple form: the three commonest cases are 知っています shitte imasu *we know*; 持っています motte imasu *we have*; and 住んでいます sunde imasu = *we live/are living* (residing). (See too, oboete imasu above under apposition.)

Again, sometimes the Japanese continuous form corresponds more to the English perfect tense: 入っています haitte imasu means *he/she/etc has/have entered* and not "are entering"; 出ています dete imasu *he/she has gone out*. The rationale is that with such verbs the act of entering or leaving is regarded as starting with the original act and remaining valid into the future.

copula

The verbs in Japanese which correspond to those meanings of "to be" in English which link two nouns or a noun and an adjective: he *was* my father, I *am* Smith, we *have been* ill. The Japanese verbs concerned–desu and aru–are set out in Table 6. ("To be or not to be" however, in Japanese, is 生きるか死ぬか、それが問題だ ikiru ka shinu ka, sore ga mondai da to live or to die; that is the question.)

De aru/de arimasu are more formal variants of desu–used in written Japanese–letters, newspapers, etc.

counter

The words which have to be used with numbers in Japanese and Chinese in such phrases as ten dogs, a hundred poems. English has a similar usage in "sheets of paper, head of cattle, cloves of garlic, loaves of bread, rounds of ammunition". There are dozens of counters in Japanese, each used with a specific noun or group of nouns. Examples are: 冊 SATSU books, notebooks, 枚 MAI sheets of paper, flat things, 本 HON cylindrical things like pencils, logs, 個 KO small objects, 台 DAI large objects (cars, pianos), 軒 KEN houses. For more about the use of counters see numbers.

demonstrative	Words which point something out: this, that, these those… They can be adjectives–as in *this* man, *that* woman: or they can be pronouns–*this* is mine, *that* is yours: or they can be adverbs–*here*, thus. (Though, as noted under adverbs, some of these are seen as nouns in Japanese.) Whereas English has only two sets of these words–this and that, here and there–Japanese has three, with distinctive forms beginning with ko-, so-, a-, corresponding to near, middle and distant, or "this one near me" (the speaker) "that one near you", and "that one not near to either of us". Examples of these sets follow. Adjectives: この ko-no, その so-no, and あの a-no (this…, that…); こんな ko-nna, そんな so-nna, and あんな a-nna (kind of). Pronouns: これ ko-re, それ so-re, and あれ a-re (this [thing], that [thing]). Adverbs: ここ ko-ko, そこ so-ko, and あそこ a-soko (here, there); こちら ko-chira, そちら so-chira, and あちら a-chira (this direction, that direction, but often also used as polite forms for kore, sore, and are and for persons. Thus in very polite conversation, kochira means *I*, the speaker; kochira sama, however, or sochira means *you*, the other party. See also honorific); こう koo, そう soo, and ああ aa (in this way, in that way).
desiderative	Refers to that form of the verb, ending in -tai which means *I/you want to…* -Tai is added to that stem of the verb which is also its suspensive form–called in our tables the -masu stem. When the person who wants the action is not I or you (the first or second person), but he/she/they (third person) it is not -tai which is used but the suffix verb -tagaru. -Tai is an adjective, and thus has for its negative -taku nai *I do not want to…* What we would call the object of -tai–the thing that is wanted–sometimes takes the tag ga, but it can also take the tag o, as does the thing which is the object of -tagaru.
dictionary form	The form of the Japanese verb which ends in -u and which is given in the Japanese dictionary. It corresponds in some ways to the European infinitive. The potential, passive, and causative forms, ending in -eru as we show them in our tables are in their own dictionary form–and have all the other endings typical of the -ru conjugation.
direct speech	What someone says, as contrasted with indirect speech which reports what was said or ordered. The rules about how to report speech in Japanese are summarised under indirect speech. Quotation marks for

direct speech in Japanese are 「 and 」 . The particle to is used when quoting direct speech just as it is for indirect: 「こんにちは」と言いました。 「Konnichiwa!」 to iimashita *"Hello" he said.*

embedded A computing term conveniently applied to the way in which a Japanese sentence often contains clauses and phrases which come between the subject and the main verb. Some of these will modify the main verb; others will qualify other parts of the sentence. This often leads to a dependency, between one phrase and a succeeding phrase, which has to be unravelled by the reader. (See also nested.) Examples in our texts are explained in the grammar notes by enclosing the various phrases in brackets and parentheses and representing them by symbols.

exhortation Can be used to indicate the usage "Let us…!" translated in Japanese polite style by the form 始めましょう hajimemashoo *let us start!* or 始めましょうか hajimemashoo ka? *shall we start?* The informal/plain equivalent would be 始めよう hajimeyoo. See intentional.

finite Applied to those forms of a European verb which are defined–by person, number, tense–as contrasted for example, with the participle, or the infinitive, which are not so defined. Japanese recognises this distinction, and the forms ending in -u or -masu are regarded as "final", as contrasted with the -masu stem, which, when used by itself has no tense of its own but borrows that of the finite verb with which it is in parallel.

formal Those forms of the Japanese verb, incorporating the endings (or, as the Japanese see it) the auxiliary: -masu, -masen, -mashita, (-mashite), which are used in polite speech–as contrasted with the plain forms. Our verb tables distinguish the polite and plain forms.

frequentative See iterative; the form of the verb or adjective ending in -tari (accent on the syllable before the -tari) which indicates an action which is frequent or repeated.

future Japanese has no future tense of the verb as such like the English "I shall go". The forms of the verb ending in -u and in -masu indicate a tense which is both present and future.

Group I/ **Group II**	See conjugation and verb: Japanese verbs (except for suru and kuru) are classified to two Groups: Group I stems end in a consonant or a vowel followed by the ending u; Group II stems end in e or i followed by the ending -ru.
honorific	That third style of Japanese which lies above plain and polite/formal discourse. It has four main components: prefixes, specific verbs to elevate the person spoken to, verbs to humble the speaker, and other special constructions.

1 In conversation with a superior, the speaker may use prefixes o–in front of some words of Japanese origin–and go in front of a "Chinese" word: for example, お電話 o-denwa (your honourable) *telephone call*; お手紙 o-tegami (your honourable) *letter*; ご両親 go-ryooshin (your honourable) *parents*. Some usages of this kind have become the rule even in ordinary speech–eg お金 o-kane (money), お茶 o-cha (tea), お菓子 o-kashi (cakes). These prefixes are also used to make a polite form of the verb (see below).

2 Specific verbs are used deferentially in referring to someone to whom you wish to show extra respect: examples are いらっしゃる irassharu > いらっしゃいます irasshaimasu which are used instead of iru (to be), iku (to go) and kuru (to come); おっしゃる ossharu (to say), when speaking to or referring to a superior being such as a customer or an office chief; めしあがる meshi-agaru for taberu (to eat).

The frequently used verb ございます gozaimasu is a somewhat special case; it is very formal, without necessarily being honorific. In practice gozaimasu means arimasu, while de gozaimasu means desu. Thus the chairman of a meeting with colleagues may ask, ご質問ございますか go-shitsumon gozaimasu ka *are there any questions?* This is formal but not honorific.

ありがとうございます arigatoo gozaimasu is a normally polite way of saying thank you.

3 Yet other specific verbs are used by the speaker in order to lower his own status in relation to that of his interlocutor. For example instead of 言う iu (to say) the speaker uses 申す/申し上げる moosu/mooshi-ageru (cf, perhaps, moshi, moshi when answering the telephone). Another

example is いただきます itadakimasu used instead of もらいます moraimasu receive (as a favour) from someone. These are sometimes called humble forms.

Illustrations of the above features are found in the following question and answer: お名前は何とおっしゃいますか O-namae wa nan to osshaimasu ka *What do you say is your honourable name?* (using ossharu–the verb used in referring to the utterances of a superior). スミスと申します Sumisu to mooshimasu *I say it is Smith*–using the humble verb moosu referring to the speaker's own words.

The inferior may use to describe his own actions the humble form which uses the -masu stem preceded by the deferential o. Thus a shop assistant may say to the customer, お待ちください o-machi kuda-sai *please wait*, but also, お待ちします o-machi shimasu *we shall wait* (for you).

Sometimes, instead of watashi, anata respectful periphrases are used like kochira, sochira–literally "this side, that side".

4 Special verb constructions can be used when referring to the superior: 先生はお教えになります sensei wa o-oshie ni narimasu *The professor teaches* (where oshie is the -masu stem of oshieru (Group II). おいでになる oide ni naru is used honorifically for come, go, and be present.

Alternatively the passive form can be used respectfully with the meaning of an active verb: 先生は教えられる sensei wa oshierareru *the professor teaches*.

humble forms   See honorific.

hypothetical   The term we use for the two parts of the Japanese verb or adjective which express "if/when": these are the forms ending in -eba and -tara. These, together with the use of to with the dictionary form of the verb, largely overlap but there are cases where one form or the other is to be preferred.

to and -eba are more general, and refer to a condition which has a natural, almost inevitable, consequence. Thus, 右に曲がると/曲がれば駅があります Migi ni magaru to/magareba eki ga arimasu *If/*

when you turn right, there is the station. Similarly, 冬になると、寒くなり
ますFuyu ni naru to, samu-ku narimasu *when winter comes, it gets cold.*

The idiom, …なければいけない/いけない …-nakereba ike-
nai/naranai *I/we/he etc must… has to…* use the kereba form (in its negative form).

-Tara is likely to be used when there is a judgement being made by a person concerned. Thus 雨が降ったら行きたくないです ame ga
futtara (accent on fu) ikitaku nai desu *if it rains I do not want to go.* Or 田
中さんが来たら、教えてください Tanaka-san ga kitara, oshi-
ete kudasai *if Mr Tanaka comes please let me know.*

The -tara form is also most likely to be used when the the result of the
condition includes a verb in the past tense. Thus, *if it had rained during
my holiday I would have studied Japanese* is best translated as 休みに
雨が降ったら、日本語を勉強しました/したでしょう yasu-
mi ni ame ga futtara, Nihongo o benkyoo shimashita/shita deshoo.

The third–and simplest–way of expressing a hypothesis is via the dictionary form + to; as noted above this is usually more general: 雨が降
ると ame ga furu to *if/when there is rain.*

idiom

Refers to the expressions in all languages which pack more meaning
than is implied merely by the words used–as with -nakereba ikenai in
the preceding entry. In Japanese 仕方がない Shikata ga nai literally,
there is no way, but it means the same as the English idiom "It can't be
helped". (Unit 1) …にする ….ni suru has the idiomatic meaning *to
decide on…*

imperative

That part of the verb which embodies an order like "write this!" or "go
away!". There are several ways of expressing such commands in Japanese:
the short imperative forms of the verb, like 来い koi (come!) and 食べ
ろ tabero (eat!) are used in direct commands only by males, and then in
quasi-military situations. These forms are, however, acceptable when
used in indirect commands: 食べろと言いました tabero to iimashita
he told me to eat up.

Less rude, and used, for example, in the family, are the forms which
combine a stem with the suffix -nasai as in 朝ご飯を食べなさい

asagohan o tabenasai *eat your breakfast!* Politer still, of course, is 食べ
てください tabete kudasai. Nasai is the short form of o…nasaimase;
this latter form is used by women in polite speech.

The negative imperatives "Don't come! don't eat! etc" have the abrupt
forms 来るな kuru na, 食べるな taberu na, but these too are not
used except by men in a quasi-military way. More usual, eg in the family, would be the colloquial usage with dame (desu) *it's no good*…: かん
じゃだめ kan-ja dame < かんではだめ kande wa dame *don't bite!*
More polite, of course, are the forms using the negative participle +
kudasai as in 来ないでください konaide kudasai (please don't
come) and 食べないでください tabenaide kudasai (please don't
eat).

indefinite
Identifies adjectives like *some, any*, and the pronouns like *someone,
something, anyone, anything*. In Japanese, *someone* is dareka, where dare
is *who?* (see interrogative) and nanika *something*, where nani is *what?*

Where, in English, "anyone" or "anything" comes after a negative,
Japanese uses だれでも daredemo and なんでも nandemo. See also
Unit 5, grammar note L.

indirect commands See under indirect speech.

indirect questions See under indirect speech.

indirect speech
The report of a statement or of a command or of a question originally
expressed in direct speech. Thus "It is a fine day" is direct speech; "he said
it was a fine day" is indirect speech. "Be careful"–direct command; "she
told me to be careful"–indirect command. "Are you well?" is a direct
question; "she asked if I was well"–indirect question.

The usual way of converting statements to indirect speech in Japanese is to
add to at the end of the sentence or phrase. Thus 天気が好い Tenki ga
ii–direct speech–*it's a fine day*; 天気が好いと言いました Tenki ga ii to
iimashita–indirect speech–*he said it was a fine day.* The tense of the indirect
speech changes in English when quoting a statement made in the past;
thus "is" in direct speech becomes "was" when the statement is reported. In
Japanese, the tense stays what it was in the original, but the verb of the

noun clause goes into the plain form. However, if the verb of the original statement refers to the past the Japanese noun clause would also have the past tense. *He said it had been a fine day* 天気が好かったと言いました Tenki ga yokatta to iimashita.

To is also used when quoting direct speech: 「天気が好い」と言いました 「Tenki ga ii」 to iimashita *"It is a fine day", he said.*

Indirect commands are translated by adding yoo ni to the dictionary form of the verb. Thus *The mother told the child to go to sleep* would be 母は子供に眠るように（と）言いました Haha wa kodomo ni nemuru yooni (to) iimashita.

Indirect questions (see also interrogative) are transposed from the direct form without change of tense, but with the substitution of the plain verb for the formal; the interrogative particle ka is retained. The verb 聞きました kikimashita *asked,* or an equivalent, comes at the end. 「元気ですか」 「Genki desu ka?」 (Present tense, direct question) *"Are you in good health?"* 元気か[どうか]（と）聞きました genki ka [doo ka] (to) kikimashita *he asked if I was well [or not].* (Past tense (was) in English; by implication present tense in Japanese.)

infinitive   In European languages indicates that part of the verb which is not defined by number or person and which is the form usually found in dictionaries; eg *to read, to go, to say.* There is no one-to-one equivalent in Japanese; the dictionary form ending in -u is the one shown in Japanese dictionaries. Operationally, it is the present tense of the plain form of the verb and also shares some of the functions of the European infinitive (eg in the example given above *...told the child to go to sleep*).

inflection   The endings of a verb or adjective. In Japanese, they are added, in hiragana, to the kanji which carries the basic meaning. These additions are called 送りがな okurigana.

instrument   The thing with which an action is performed. With a verb in the passive, Japanese uses the post-particle, ni, as for persons. (See agent.) Otherwise–that is, with a verb in the active form–the post-particle used is de; thus to write *with* a brush, to say it *in* Japanese, to make it *out of* wood–all these use de.

Appendix I

intentional The name we use in our tables for that part of the verb of which the polite form ends in -mashoo (as in 見ましょう mimashoo) and the plain form in -oo (as in 来よう koyoo). This form is called the intentional because it is used, normally with omoimasu, to mean *I intend to...* Thus, 行こうと思います ikoo to omoimasu *I intend to go.*

There are corresponding negative forms: 始めまい hajimemai (plain) and 始めますまい hajimemasumai (formal) *let us not start/don't let us start.* Although these are shown in our tables, they are now somewhat old-fashioned. One would be more likely to say 始めないでおきましょう hajimenaide okimashoo (let us decide in advance not to begin) *let us leave it to next time.*

No one label is entirely descriptive of these forms (see also exhortation and presumptive), because they have several applications. The term volitional is used in some grammars. Thus, 信じていようと、信じていまいと shinjite iyoo to, shijite imai to *believe it or not.*

With the plain form of the intentional, suru as auxiliary and the particle to the meaning is *I was going to...* or *I tried to...* 電話をかけよう としました Denwa o kakeyoo to shimashita *I tried to phone.*

interrogative Those forms of the adjective, adverb, or pronoun which help to ask a question: typically they begin with the syllable do. Adjective: どの dono which? and どんな donna what kind of? Adverb: どこ doko where? いつ itsu when? いくら ikura how much? and どのくらい donokurai how much? Pronoun: だれ dare who? なに nani what? and どれ dore which one?

The Japanese sentence asking a question, even if it contains an interrogative word, must end with the particle ka; this ka is carried over into an indirect question.

intransitive A verb which is self-contained and does not take an object is intransitive–as contrasted with the transitive verb which has an object and, incidentally, is capable of being used in the passive. Thus in "the dog barks" barks is an intransitive verb. Both in English and in Japanese some verbs can be both transitive and intransitive: "she sings" (intransitive); "she sings a song" (transitive). Para 5(d) of the introduction to our tables lists pairs of common Japanese verbs of which one is transitive and the other intransitive.

In Japanese some intransitive verbs can have a passive form with a specific meaning; typical examples are: 雨に降られた ame ni furareta *I was caught by the rain/ rained on;* 先生に死なれた sensei ni shinareta (I was died (on) by my teacher) *my teacher died on me.* 忙しいのに、お客に来られた Isogashii noni, okyaku ni korareta *though I was busy, I suffered the visitation (of a guest).* This is sometimes, picturesquely, called the passive of disadvantage or suffering. The passive in this usage can even have an object: 彼はお金をとられた/盗まれた Kare wa o-kane o torareta/nusumareta *He was stolen from (as to) his money/he was robbed of his money.*

iterative
The form of the verb or adjective, ending in -tari, which, with verbs, refers to a repeated action, often when a number of such actions are listed. 手紙を読んだり、手紙を書いたり、考え事をしたりします tegami o yondari, ...tegami o kaitari...kangae-goto o shitari...shimasu. The enumeration usually ends with the verb suru.

In the case of adjectives, it is the list aspect which dominates: 暑かったり、寒かったり atsukattari, samukattari *sometimes hot, sometimes cold.* An alternative name is frequentative.

main clause
By convention, the clause which makes the main statement of a sentence, it may indeed itself be the sentence. In "He will eat when he arrives" the main clause is "he will eat".

main verb
The verb of the main clause. (In the above example "will eat" is the main verb) It is important in Japanese to recognise the main verb, because when polite language is being used it is the main verb which is in the -masu form–the others normally being in plain form. The main verb is very often right at the end of the sentence and will thus be modified by clauses and phrases that precede it.

-masu stem
Shown as such in our verb tables, this is the English term for that form of the verb to which the masu ending, and the desiderative -tai, are attached. However, it also has other uses. For example, it can be used as it stands in parallel with another–usually main verb. This is similar to the use of the participle in parallel with a main verb, except that the action

Appendix I

of the participle often precedes that of the main verb.

The -masu stem is also used with verbs meaning to begin to do something, or to finish doing something, or to continue to do something. Thus in Unit 2 忘れ始めました wasure hajimemashita *began to forget* (his routine). We also see in Unit 4, the use of the -masu stem in such phrases as 読み方 yomi-kata (where yomi is the -masu stem of yomu to read), and in verb-adjective constructions like 分かりやすい wakari-yasui *easy to understand*, where wakari is the -masu stem of wakaru. This stem + ni also indicates purpose eg …飲みに行く…nomi-ni iku *to go (somewhere) to drink*.

modify   By convention, adverbs "modify" verbs and other adverbs, while adjectives "qualify" nouns.

negative   As pointed out under affirmative, the negative of the Japanese verb has a conjugation of its own which is shown separately in our tables.

nested   Like "embedded" a term shared with computing to describe the process whereby in Japanese one functional phrase is contained within another, rather as a computer program will go to a short software routine and after completing it return to the main program. These routines often "nest" one inside the other, and so do phrases in a Japanese sentence. The reason for this is the overriding Japanese rule that what modifies or qualifies something has to precede it.

This characteristic of the language can be illustrated if we put into Japanese the operative verb phrases of the final verse of the nursery rhyme "The house that Jack built":

This is the cock that crowed [in the morn] that wakened the priest [all shaven and shorn] that married the man, [all tattered and torn,] that kissed the maiden [all forlorn]
that milked the cow [with the crumpled horn] that tossed the dog that worried the cat that killed the rat that ate the malt
that lay in the house that Jack built.

The Japanese order would be reversed into

"This is Jack built house-in lay malt ate rat killed cat worried dog tossed

cow milked maiden kissed man married priest wakened cock crowed."
("malt ate" qualifies rat; "rat killed" qualifies cat; "cat worried" qualifies
dog, etc)

これは、ジャックが建てた家にあった麦芽を食べたネズミ
を殺した猫をからかった犬を飛ばした雌牛乳をしぼった乙
女にキスした男の結婚式を行った牧師を起こした雄鳥です。
Kore wa, Jakku ga tateta ie ni atta bakuga (malt) o tabeta nezumi o
koroshita neko o karakatta inu o tobashita me-ushi no chichi o shibotta
otome ni kisushita otoko no kekkon shiki o okonatta bokushi o okoshi-
ta ondori desu.

nominalisation The process by which Japanese puts certain expressions into a form in
which they are used as though they were nouns or noun clauses. For
example in Unit 6, there is the statement that *the Minister gives Press con-
ferences.* In Japanese, this is 会見する事があります kaiken suru koto
ga arimasu, where kaiken suru means *to give a Press conference,* koto
implies "the fact" (ie of giving a Press conference) and ga arimasu
means "exists" or "is so".

A similar construction is used with dekiru (to be able to…):
英語を話す事ができるので Eigo o hanasu koto ga dekiru node in
Unit 3 means *because he can speak English…*

The usual particle used to nominalise a phrase is koto but an alternative
is to iu koto.

Verbal nouns, which make a noun out of an action, as in "skiing is a
thrill" are a special case. Verbal nouns can be rendered in Japanese by the
use of the dictionary form + koto/no + wa/ga or + o according to whether
the verbal noun so formed is an object or a subject. *Seeing is believing*
would be 見る事は信じる事である Miru koto wa shinjiru koto de
aru. For *It is interesting to live abroad,* you can say 外国に住むのはお
もしろいです gaikoku ni sumu no wa omoshiroi desu or 外国に住む
と言う事はおもしろいです gaikoku ni sumu to iu koto wa omoshiroi
desu.

The main difference is that the constructions with koto are rather more
formal than those with no wa/no ga.
If the verbal noun is not just a concept (as in "seeing is believing"), but

an actual event–after a verb like "see" or "hear"–the appropriate tense is used in the noun clause, followed by koto/no + ga/o. Thus, *I remember meeting Churchill* would be チャーチルに会った事を覚えています Chaachiru ni atta koto o oboete imasu. *I heard him playing the flute* would be 彼がフルートを吹いているのを聞きました Kare ga furuuto o fuite iru no o kikimashita.

noun	A word which means a thing or a concept or a person–as distinguished from a verb which refers to an action.
noun clauses phrases	Putting the various English noun clauses and phrases into Japanese can best be seen as an extension of nominalisation. Examples in English are "Thank you *for helping me*; I was pleased *to receive your letter*; I was sorry that *you failed the exam*; it is useful for you *to hear the truth*; sorry *to be late*; I don't mind *your smoking*."

Japanese has two main ways of expressing these phrases and clauses: first, with the participle (-te/de form of the verb) or the -masu stem, and second, by nominalisation using …koto/no. Typical idiomatic expressions leading into these usages are かまう/かまわない kamau/kamawanai *I mind/I don't mind…* and 困る komaru *I am embarrassed about…* There is considerable overlap in practice between the two construction

1) Examples with the participle

Thank you for helping me
手伝ってくださって／くださりありがとうございます
tetsudatte kudasatte/kudasari arigatoo gozaimasu

He was pleased to receive your letter
彼はお手紙をいただいて喜んでいました
kare wa o-tegami o itadaite yorokonde imashita
彼はお手紙をいただいた事を喜んでいました
kare wa o-tegami o itadaita koto o yorokonde imashita

I am sorry I could not come
来られなくてすみません
Korarenakute (negative potential) sumimasen

It is no good eating this kind of food
こんなものを食べてはだめだ／いけない

konna mono o tabete wa dame da/ikenai

I was embarrassed at running out of money
お金が足りなくなって困りました／まごつきました
o-kane ga tarinaku natte komarimashita/magotsukimashita

I do not mind the children playing in this room
子供がこの部屋で遊んでもかまいません
kodomo ga kono heya de asonde mo kamaimasen

Many of the phrases listed could also be rendered with the koto construction exemplified below–and vice versa. Thus in the following list the alternatives are also shown.

2) Examples with nominalisation

Speaking Japanese is my weak point
日本語を話すのは苦手です
Nihongo o hanasu no wa nigate desu

I was sorry that you failed the exam
あなたが試験に落ちた事は／落ちて残念です
anata ga shiken ni ochita koto wa/ochite zannen desu

It is good that you should know the truth
事実を知る事（の）はいいです
jijitsu o shiru koto (no) wa ii desu

It is a good thing you came
あなたが来て下さった事は／下さってよかったです
anata ga kite kudasatta koto wa/kudasatte yokatta desu

I was glad you passed the exam
試験に受かった事は／受かってとても嬉しいです
shiken ni ukatta koto wa/ukatte totemo ureshii desu

numbers
numerals

There are two counting systems in Japanese: the one, with numbers from one to ten, based on the native numbers; and the other, derived from Chinese, covering the whole range, from one upwards, and including signs for powers of ten in steps of four (not three, as in the English thousand, million, billion, trillion): 10^4 10,000 万 MAN, 10^8 100,000,000 億 OKU, 10^{12} 1,000,000,000,000 兆 CHOO, and 10^{16}

10,000,000,000,000,000 京 KEI.

As pointed out in Unit 1, for the Japanese numerals one and two there are different forms for things and for people: one person is 一人 hitori and two people are 二人 futari. For other numbers of people the counter 人 nin (a special reading of jin) must be used, eg: 三人 san nin, 十三人 juusan nin.

Otherwise, for one to ten, the Japanese forms can be used for things, but not animals, without any other counter than the resident つ -tsu:

1	ひとつ	hito-tsu
2	ふたつ	futa-tsu
3	みっつ	mittsu
4	よっつ	yot-tsu
5	いつつ	itsu-tsu
6	むっつ	mut-tsu
7	ななつ	nana-tsu
8	やっつ	yat-tsu
9	ここのつ	kokono-tsu
10	とお	too (see below).

(There is a residual binary element in these forms: mittsu (3) corresponds to muttsu (6), yottsu (4) to yattsu (8); less obviously hitotsu and futatsu also have the same root)

Japanese numbers, but mainly without the -tsu counter, are also used as the basis for the dates in the month up to and including the tenth, and for the 14th, 20th and 24th, with the sign for day 日 pronounced ka. Thus the 1st–10th days of the month are: 1 一日 tsuitachi, 2 二日 futsuka, 3 三日 mikka, 4 四日 yokka, 5 五日 itsuka, 6 六日 muika, 7 七日 nanoka, 8 八日 yooka, 9 九日 kokonoka, 10 十日 tooka. The 11th, 12th, and 13th are juuichinichi, juuninichi, juusannichi but the 14th is juuyokka, the 20th hatsuka, and the 24th nijuuyokka.

Otherwise the Chinese numbers are used with counters proper (not -tsu); sometimes there are phonetic changes in the consonants where the number meets the counter.

Examples: one dog 一匹の犬 ippiki no inu (匹 hiki is the counter for small animals), one eraser 一個の消しゴム ikko no keshigomu, two lamp bulbs 二個の電球 niko no denkyuu (個 ko is the counter for small objects), two books 二冊の本 nisatsu no hon (冊 satsu is the counter for books etc).

There is sometimes, but not always, a choice of counting system; for example for fruit either hitotsu/futatsu or a "Chinese" number with the counter ko can be used. However, there is no choice when counting people, animals, sheets of paper, books, etc, when the appropriate counters (including -ri for one or two people) have to be used.

There is a often a choice of order: *There are two birds* is either 二羽の鳥がいます ni wa no tori ga imasu, or 鳥が二羽います tori ga niwa imasu; the counter 羽 wa for birds is radical 124, presenting two wings. It is the basis of a tongue-twister: 鶏が二羽庭にいます niwatori ga niwa niwa ni imasu *there are two chickens in the garden*.

object

As explained in other entries (active, intransitive, transitive) the object of a verb is the person or thing suffering the action of the verb. Thus "the dog chases the cat (object)", "the child eats its food (object)". In Japanese the object is usually tagged with the particle を o. However, what English sees as the object may be regarded differently in Japanese: for example, with the desiderative form of the verb, ending in -tai, which is, strictly, an adjective, the noun can have the tag ga, indicating the true translation as is *wanted* or *desired*; similarly with ほしいです hoshii desu *is wanted*, and 好きです suki desu *is liked*, the thing which is wanted or liked has the ga tag. However, o is now often found with -tai as well as with -tagaru. (See also desiderative).

obligation

The constructions by which Japanese renders such concepts as "ought to", "has to", "must" are explained briefly in the grammar notes to Unit 6. The strongest–"must"–corresponds to the negative stem of the verb (eg kaka in kaka-nai) + nakereba ikenai (potential) or naranai–ie, "if you were not to (do this) it can be no go (potential)", or "does not become (any good)". Colloquially, *I must do this* would be これをしなければ／しなくて Kore o shinakereba/shinakute wa (shinak(u)cha) ikenai. (See colloquial.)

Moral obligation is often rendered by the dictionary form + べきです beki desu ought to.
A further usage, apart from those in Unit 6, is the "must" which relates

to a logical inference–*He is eating a lot, so he must be hungry*. The best translation of this is にちがいない／ありません ni chigai nai/arimasen "there is no doubt about..." after the substantive phrase: 日本に五十年住んでいるから、日本語を上手に話すにちがいない／ありません Nihon ni 50 nen sunde iru kara, nihongo o joozu ni hanasu ni chigai nai/arimasen *Since he has lived in Japan for 50 years he must speak good Japanese*.

ordinal

This refers to the numbers which indicate the order things are in: "first, second" etc, as contrasted with the cardinal numbers–one, two–which show size or quantity.

Japanese has several ways of showing order, using separately or in combination: 番 ban, 第 dai, 目 me:

1 番 ban is a sign for number (cf 番号 bangoo number) and makes the ordinal when suffixed to a cardinal number + no: (一番 ichiban, 二番 niban, 三番 sanban) + me + no and the noun concerned. "Our first car" would be 一番目の車 ichiban me no kuruma.

2 第一の車 dai-ichi no kuruma could also mean *our first car*–or preferred car (if we have several). As noted under comparison 一番 ichiban + adjective or adverb is also used to make the superlative. However, 第一課 daiikka, 第二課 dainika, 第三課 daisanka *lessons one, two, and three*.

3 目の me no: 一つ目の石 hitotsu me no ishi *the first stone*; 三個目の石 san ko me no ishi *the third stone*. (Where ko is the counter for such small objects.)

With me the Japanese numbers may also be used, for things, not persons: 一つ目の hitotsu me no..., 二つ目の futatsu me no..., 三つ目の mittsu me no...

For persons, 一人目の hitori me no..., 二人目の futari me no... can be used.

participle

As noted under continuous the present participle is that part of the verb which in English ends in ...ing–as in "she is working". In Japanese the corresponding -te/-de form is used with iru to make a continuous present. In some languages, but not in Japanese, there is also a past participle–"given, defeated". Phrases which, in English, need the past participle can be rendered in Japanese, with transitive verbs, by using the present participle with aru to mean that something has been done: ドアは開けてあります doa wa akete arimasu *the door has been opened*–only slightly different from 開いています aite imasu the door is open. (See also perfect.)

particle

As noted in the notes to Unit 1, the many particles used in Japanese (many of them monosyllabic) are of two kinds: those that are part of the basic meaning of a sentence and those that are not. The first category are reviewed briefly, because they are so basic to the language. in the grammar notes to Unit 1. They include those which we call post-positions: へ e, から kara, まで made, の no, と to, に ni, で de and also those which otherwise link nouns with the sense of and/also: も mo, と to, や ya.

In addition, the spoken language has a number of particles, often added at the end of a sentence, which add emphasis or seek agreement. They include, ね ne, の no, わ wa, よ yo.

passive

The opposite of active; applied to those forms of the verb which indicate that an action is performed on the subject–eg "the cat is chased away". There is no object attached to a verb in the passive; the sufferer of the action–sometimes called the "patient"–is the subject of the verb–in this instance the cat.

In most languages only a transitive verb can have a passive, but oddly enough the passive of some intransitive verbs can be used idiomatically in Japanese to indicate that the subject of the verb has suffered a disadvantage. For such examples as "I was stolen from; I was subject to the visitation of…; I was 'died on'" etc (see under intransitive).

perfect

The tense which in some languages means that an action took place in the past which continues to have an effect in the present–eg "he has gone out"; in Japanese the same sense is rendered by phrases with kuru, as 出て来ました dete kimashita (see participle) or, eg in answer to a question "Is he here?", 出ています dete imasu meaning   not "he is going out" but *he has gone out*.

Appendix I

phrase   A group of words which grammatically and semantically go together but which do not include a finite verb (see clause) eg "on arrival" "in his place…"

plain form   Those forms of the Japanese verb—sometimes called "informal" or "abrupt"—which do not have the endings, for example -masu, typical of the formal or polite style, in which main verbs are in the -masu form while the verbs in subordinate clauses are normally in the plain form.

plural   Japanese does not have a general plural like that of European languages—house > houses, man > men; the plural meaning has mainly to be understood from the context. But in certain cases a plural is formed by doubling a word or by adding suffixes: 人々 hito-bito (people), 木々 kigi (trees–Unit 2); あなた達 anata-tachi (suffix 達 tachi) *you*, 田中さん達 Tanaka-san-tachi (the Tanakas); 私共 watashi-domo (I/we) 彼ら kare-ra (they). NB 友達 tomodachi is used as often in the singular as in the plural.

polite   Another term for the formal style as opposed to the plain.

post-positions   A term invented to make the point that the words which in many European languages convey relations of time, place, cause, etc, between nouns and are called prepositions (because they come before the noun they refer to) most often come after the noun in Japanese: examples are で de へ e に ni から kara まで made.

potential   That form of the Japanese verb which means "can, is able to…" It has the ending -eru and thus conjugates as a Group II verb; it is shown in our tables. Note that where the potential has an object this can bear either the o or the ga tag, but normally ga is used: 英語が話せません eigo ga hanasemasen *he/she etc cannot speak English*. (Cf under nominalisation 英語を話す事が出来ない eigo o hanasu koto ga dekinai *cannot speak English*.)

predicate   Formally, everything in a sentence which follows the subject: "The cat (subject) sat on the mat". In Japanese, the construction of pseudo-adjectives differs according to whether they are in "predicative" position—that is, part of the predicate (as in "the wine is excellent") or "attributive"–that is, attached to the noun ("This excellent wine"). The effect of this distinction on the use of pseudo-adjectives in Japanese is set out under attributive.

prepositions   Words like "in, on, after, with" in English, which essentially define a relation between nouns or pronouns and in English come before the noun to which they refer. As indicated under post-positions the equivalent particles in Japanese typically come after the noun to which they refer.

present   In Japanese the tense which uses the dictionary form in plain style and has the -masu ending in formal/polite style. Semantically it has both a present and future connotation. (See future.)

presumptive   Presumptive ("Dr Livingstone, I presume") best describes the combination of another verb with daroo/deshoo to mean may, or might, or might have: 書いただろう kaita daroo *may have written*.

probability   When the presumptive forms of the copula desu, だろう／でしょう daroo /deshoo are added to another verb, the connotation is that of a degree of probability: 来るだろう／でしょう kuru daroo (plain)/deshoo (polite) *he/she/they may come*.

A lesser degree of probability is expressed by the use of the dictionary form of the verb + かもしれない／しれません ka mo shirenai/shiremasen (literally) one cannot know (potential) whether. Thus 来るかもしれません kuru ka mo shiremasen *he may come*.

The idea that something is expected or due to happen is conveyed by the phrase はずです hazu desu after the statement in plain form: thus 八時に来るはずです hatchiji ni kuru hazu desu *they are due to arrive at 8*.

See obligation for にちがいない … ni chigai nai "must" in a logical inference.

pronoun   A word used as proxy for a noun–like "he, she, it they, them" and–when these words are used alone (ie not as demonstrative adjectives)–"this, that, those". Pronouns, particularly when they are the subject of a verb, are often not expressed in Japanese and are left to be understood from the

Appendix I

	context. (See grammar notes to Unit 6.)
pseudo-adjectives	Those adjectives which are not the true "Japanese" adjectives, which all end in i. The pseudo-adjectives require the suffix -na when they are used as attributes and add -ni to form the corresponding adverb.
qualify	By convention, an adjective is said to "qualify" the noun to which it is applied. By contrast adverbs are said to modify verbs, adjectives or other adverbs.
reading	Term used to translate the Japanese 読み方 yomikata (see Unit 4), indicating the sound which a given character bears, and thus its meaning, in a given context. The main distinction is between the **ON** reading or readings–音 **ON** (literally the "sounds") which came with the kanji when it was borrowed from the Chinese and the 訓 kun readings, which are the Japanese words which had the original meaning subsequently ascribed to the kanji. There can be several **ON** readings corresponding to imports made at different times or from different regions. (Just as in English "chattel" and "cattle", "chase" and "catch" derive from the same French words but were borrowed from different regions.)
	Conversely, a given kun reading may be attached to several different kanji according to context: for example tsukuru meaning to make (sandwiches) is represented by the kanji 作 in Unit 1, while tsukuru meaning to make (beer) is represented in Unit 5 by the different kanji 造.
relative clause	In English this is an adjectival clause which refers back to a given noun in an earlier part of the sentence. "This is the man *whom I saw*" "The thing *I am worried about*"–where the relative pronoun "which" or "that" is not expressed. Japanese has no relative pronouns like "who, whom, which, that" and therefore no true relative clause. Instead, Japanese uses an adjectival phrase or clause which simply precedes the noun to which it refers, with no other grammatical connection. Thus 私が見た人 watashi ga mita hito the 'I saw man' *the man whom I saw*. 心配な事 Shinpai na koto 'the worry thing' *the thing I am worried about*. For more detail about how Japanese handles relative clauses see under nested.
reported speech	The same as indirect speech.

romaji   The system of European letters into which Japanese is phonetically transcribed (romanised) for the benefit of learners or tourists. We mainly follow here the Hepburn system, which has become general; other systems have the advantage that they are nearer to the way the Japanese interpret their own phonetics, but these systems need more adjustment on the part of the learner. For example the syllable written シ in katakana is shown as SI in the system of transliteration called 訓令式 kunrei shiki "(government) instruction method", making it symmetrical with SA, SU, SE and SO–which is how Japanese sees this set of five syllables; but in practice the sound has to be pronounced more like SHI.

Similarly the katakana syllable チ, written as TI in kunrei shiki, has a pronunciation nearer to CHI, and katakana ツ TU sounds more like TSU. In the Hepburn system, these syllables are therefore written as SHI, CHI, TSU. However, the learner should still listen out for the way these syllables are said in Japanese, the consonants are by no means pronounced exactly as the Hepburn system might suggest.

simultaneous   What we call that form of the verb, or sometimes of an adjective, made by adding ながら -nagara to the stem, with the meaning that one action is done at the same time as another. (Cf 地図を見ながら chizu o minagara and ビールを飲みながら biiru o nominagara in Unit 2)

In a given context, the connotation may be more like "though doing (being) X…" than "while doing X". Thus, きれいながら利口ではありません kireinagara rikoo de wa arimasen *He/she is good-looking but not clever.*

stem   A convenient term for the verb or adjective stripped of its endings; thus kak- is the main stem of kak-u (write). However, Japanese recognises several stems; thus we separately distinguish the -masu stem; the negative stem, as in kaka-nai is the basis of the negative -nakereba form of the verb used in expressing obligation.

subject   In "the dog chases the cat", dog is the subject of the verb chase, and cat is the object. In Japanese the subject is followed by the tag wa if it is also the topic of the sentence, or by the tag ga, which also marks the subject of a subordinate clause. Very often in Japanese the subject is not expressed, and has to be understood from the context.

Appendix I

subordinate clause A clause which is not a main clause. Subordinate clauses can indicate time, place, reason (because), concession (although) etc and can also be noun clauses as part of indirect speech. The Japanese verb in a subordinate clause is normally in plain form.

superlative The highest degree of comparison–highest, best, most probable; see comparison.

suspensive When two adjectives are used together in Japanese the first has to be in this special form, which, for true adjectives, ends in -kute: 長くておもしろい nagakute omoshiroi *long and/but interesting*.
However, when the corresponding negative is used おもしろくなくて 長い omoshirokunakute nagai *not interesting but long*, the implication can be "too long to be interesting". This could also be translated by 長すぎておもしろくない nagasugite omoshiroku nai *being too long it is not interesting*.

In the same way the participle of a verb, used in parallel with a main verb, can be regarded as a suspensive form.

tense The means by which the time element is expressed in the grammar of verbs–and, in the case of Japanese, of the true adjectives. The basic tenses in Japanese are the present/future, and the past. Each of these also has a continuous form. Japanese does not have a perfect tense, as English has, which describes a state deriving from the past but having an effect in the present (I have shaved; he has learnt Japanese) but our grammar notes explain how Japanese expresses this concept.

transitive Used of a verb which takes, or can take, an object, and which can have a passive form; "to kill" is transitive but "to bark" is intransitive. Para 5(d) of the introductory notes to the tables lists some pairs of corresponding transitive and intransitive Japanese verbs. The entry intransitive gives examples of verbs like "die, rain", which are intransitive, but which in Japanese have passive forms with a special meaning.

verb A word which describes an action, like "take", "do" "insure" "drive" etc. As noted under other headings, verbs can be transitive or intransitive, they can be auxiliary, they can be in an active or passive form, in affirmative or negative form. Japanese verbs fall into two Groups: Group I has its stem ending in a consonant (including the lost w in such verbs as kau (kawu) to buy, and ou (owu) to pursue. The conjugation of Japanese verbs is set out in the tables following this Reference Grammar.

verbal noun

A verbal concept made into a noun, in English by adding "ing" to the verb: shaving is a bore, it is fun meeting new people. In Japanese the dictionary form + no wa/ga or koto/to iu koto does the same job, as shown under nominalisation.

Appendix 2
◇ ◇ Japanese Verbs & Adjectives ◇ ◇

(Asterisks refer to entries in the Reference Grammar)

1 The Tables which follow are necessarily a compromise between the conventions of European grammar and the Japanese perception of their own language. In particular some of the endings that we see as inflections* the Japanese see as auxiliary verbs* (like can, shall, would in English). Moreover there is often no precise term in English to describe the function of a given Japanese verb ending: for example, what we have called the hypothetical* form (eg kakeba) can mean either if or when. What we have called the simultaneous* form (eg kakinagara) is used for "while writing", but also sometimes when we should say "although writing…" or, in the case of an adjective, "though interesting…"

2 The West sees Japanese verbs as falling into two Groups according to the ending of their dictionary form—just as French infinitives end either in *-er*, *-re* or *-ir* and the verbs "conjugate" accordingly. Most Japanese verbs fall into Group I—that is, they have dictionary forms which end in a consonant + u or in a vowel + u, eg 書く kak-u *to write* 洗う ara-u *to wash*.

Table 1 shows the conjugation* of these verbs, that is, what endings (inflexions*) they take to express the various uses of the verb. Group I verbs are subject to regular phonetic changes in certain forms; these are set out in Table 2.

3 Group II comprises those verbs which have the dictionary form ending in e-ru or i-ru and so have the vowel e or i at the end of their stem, eg 出来る deki-ru *to be able*; 感じる kanji-ru *to feel*; 借りる kari-ru *to hire*; and 見る mi-ru *to see*.

Table 3 shows that these conjugate with slight differences from Group I. Happily, because Group II contains only verbs with dictionary form ending in e-ru and i-ru, all verbs with dictionary form ending in -aru, -oru, and -uru belong to Group I.

4 There is a slight catch about these two Groups; whereas with French the conjugation can be identified at a glance (though German "strong" verbs cannot), a first look at the Japanese verbs with dictionary form ending in -eru or -iru will not suffice to tell whether they belong to Group I or II. The best assumption for the learner is that verbs in -eru and -iru belong to Group II, subject, however, to a check on the few common exceptions listed in para 5 below. Sometimes there are pairs of verbs, of which the transitive verb of the pair is likely to belong to Group II.

5 These lists will help to check:
(a) Verbs with dictionary form ending in -eru but belonging to Group I: 減る heru *decrease* and 帰る kaeru *go back*.
(b) Verbs with dictionary form ending in -iru but belonging to Group I: 入る hairu *enter*, 走る hashiru *run*, 要る iru *be necessary*, 限る kagiru *limit*, 切る kiru *cut*, and 知る shiru *know*.

(c) Two or more verbs sounding the same (though with different characters and meanings) and belonging to different Groups, and thus taking different endings.

Common examples are: 要る *iru to need* (Group I irimasu); but いる *iru to be* (Group II imasu); 帰る kaeru *go back* (Group I kaerimasu); but 代える／替える kaeru *change* (Group II kaemasu); 切る *kiru cut* (Group I kirimasu); but 着る kiru *wear* (Group II kimasu).

(d) Pairs of verbs sharing the same character, but mainly with the Group I verb intransitive* and its fellow in Group II transitive*.

Examples:	集まる	atsumaru	Group I	*collect* (intransitive)
	集める	atsumeru	Group II	*collect* (transitive)
	入る	hairu	Group I	*go in* (intransitive)
	入れる	ireru	Group II	*to put in, pour* (transitive)
	始まる	hajimaru	Group I	*begin* (intransitive)
	始める	hajimeru	Group II	*begin* (transitive)
	決まる	kimaru	Group I	*be decided* (intransitive)
	決める	kimeru	Group II	*decide on* (transitive)
	曲がる	magaru	Group I	*turn* (mainly intransitive)
	曲げる	mageru	Group II	*turn* or *bend* something (transitive)
	負かす	makasu	Group I	*defeat* (transitive)
	負ける	makeru	Group II	*lose, be defeated* (intransitive)
混ざる／交ざる	混ざる／交ざる	mazaru	Group I	*mix, be mixed* (intransitive)
混じる／交じる	混じる／交じる	majiru	Group I	*mix, be mixed* (intransitive)
混ぜる／交ぜる	混ぜる／交ぜる	mazeru	Group II	*to mix (things)* (transitive)
	交える	majieru	Group II	*to exchange* (transitive)
	起こる	okoru	Group I	*to happen* (intransitive)
	起こす	okosu	Group II	*to cause* (transitive)
	止まる	tomaru	Group I	*to stop* (intransitive)
	止める	tomeru	Group II	*to stop* (transitive)
	分かる	wakaru	Group I	*distinguish* > *understand* (intransitive)
	分ける	wakeru	Group II	*share out* (transitive)

6 A few Japanese verbs are both transitive and intransitive–sometimes with different meanings. Examples

are:	運ぶ	hakobu	*transport* (transitive) *go well* (intransitive)
	張る	haru	*extend*
	間違う	ma-chi-gau	*to mistake* (transitive), *be mistaken* (intransitive)

7 Some intransitive Japanese verbs correspond most closely to English passives: we have noted kimaru above; another common example is 困る komaru *to be embarrassed* or *worried*

8 To revert once more to the comparison with French, whereas there are several dozen French irregular verbs, Japanese has only two: する suru *to do* and 来る kuru *to come*. These are displayed in Tables 4 and 5 below. In addition, ある aru (to be) and です desu (copula*) have some unexpected forms and/or are deficient in some parts. These verbs are set out, for reference, in Table 6.

9 The conjugation of the Japanese adjectives is set out in Table 7.

Appendix 2

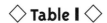

◇ Table I ◇

GROUP I VERBS
Verbs with endings in KU/GU/SU/BU/MU/NU/TSU/U/RU
Example 書く ka-ku *write*

FORM	AFFIRMATIVE		NEGATIVE	
	PLAIN	POLITE	PLAIN	POLITE
Present/future	kaku	kakimasu	kakanai	kakimasen
"-masu stem"	kaki			
Pres. Participle "(am, is, are) writing"	kaite*		kakanaide kakanakute	
Past "wrote"	kaita*	kakimashita	kakanakatta	kakimasen deshita
Hypothetical "if/when I write"	kaku nara kakeba kaita(na)ra*		kakanai nara kakanakereba kakanakatta(na)ra	
Iterative "often writing"	kaitari*		kakanakattari	
Simultaneous "while writing"	kakinagara			
Intentional "will write"	kakoo	kakimashoo	kakumai	
Imperative "write!"	kake	kakinasai	kaku na	
Request	kaite	kaite kudasai	kakanaide	kakanaide kudasai
Desiderative "I want to write"	kakitai	kakitai desu	kakitaku nai	kakitaku nai desu/ arimasen
"He wants to write"	kakitagaru	kakitagarimasu	kakitagaranai	kakitagarimasen
Potential "can write"	kakeru	kakemasu	kakenai	kakemasen
Passive "is written"	kakareru	kakaremasu	kakarenai	kakeremasen
Causative "make/let (someone) write"	kakaseru	kakasemasu	kakasenai	kakasemasen
Causative Passive (alternative) "cause (something) to be written"	kakasareru kakaserareru	kakasaremasu kakaseraremasu	kakasarenai kakaserarenai	kakasaremasen kakaseraremasen

*These forms of the verb have the phonetic changes set out in Table 2 below.

Note 1 The desiderative form of the verb (I want to…) carrying the ending -tai is in fact and in form an adjective. It therefore has all the other endings associated with the Japanese adjective and listed in Table 7. The form in -tagaru, however, is a verb in its own right with a full conjugation; in contrast to -tai it means that a third person (not the speaker) wants to do something.

Note 2 The potential, passive, causative and causative passive are shown here as parts of the verb which is being listed, but it will be seen that all four forms are also verbs belonging to Group II and thus capable of full conjugation in their own right as in Table 3.

◇ Table 2 ◇

PHONETIC CHANGES

In those parts of the Group I verbs marked *

in Table 1 the last consonant of the dictionary form is changed as follows:

ENDING	EXAMPLE	PARTICIPLE	PAST	HYPOTHE-TICAL	ITERATIVE
-ku	kaku *write* Exception iku *go*	(ka) ite itte	(ka) ita itta	(ka) ita(na)ra itta(na)ra	(ka) itari ittari
-gu	isogu *be in a hurry*	(iso) ide	(iso) ida	(iso) ida(na)ra	(iso) idari
-su	osu *push*	(o) shite	(o) shita	(o) shita(na)ra	(o) shitari
-bu	yobu *call*	(yo) nde	(yo) nda	(yo) nda(na)ra	(yo) ndari
-mu	yomu *read*	(yo) nde	(yo) nda	(yo) nda(na)ra	(yo) ndari
-nu	shinu *die*	(shi) nde	(shi) nda	(shi) nda(na)ra	(shi) ndari
-tsu	matsu *wait*	(ma) tte	(ma) tta	(ma) tta(na)ra	(ma) ttari
-u* * *	kau *buy* omou *think* iu *say*	(ka) tte (omo) tte (i) tte	(ka) tta (omo) tta (i) tta	(ka) tta(na)ra (omo) tta(na)ra (i) tta(na)ra	(ka) ttari (omo) ttari (i) ttari
-ru	hairu *enter*	(ha) itte	(ha) itta	(ha) itta(na)ra	(ha) ittari

* The verbs ending in a vowel + u would have made, for example, kaanai (from ka-u). However, this combination led to the emergence of a virtual semi-vowel w between the vowel ending and the u: ka(w)u, i(w)u, omo(w)u; this (w) was assimilated to the te and ta of the ending, as with tsu and ru, to give the suffixes -tte, -tta, etc. The w appears as such in the forms omowanai, kawanai, iwanai.

Appendix 2

◇ Table 3 ◇

GROUP II VERBS
Verbs with vowel stem
Example 見る mi-ru *to see*

FORM	AFFIRMATIVE		NEGATIVE	
	PLAIN	POLITE	PLAIN	POLITE
Present/future "-masu stem"	miru mi	mimasu	minai	mimasen
Pres. Participle "(am, is, are) seeing"	mite		minaide minakute	
Past "saw"	mita	mimashita	minakatta	mimasen deshita
Hypothetical "if/when I see"	miru nara mireba mita(na)ra		minai nara minakereba minakatta(na)ra	
Iterative "often seeing"	mitari		minakattari	
Simultaneous "while seeing"	minagara			
Intentional "will see"	miyoo	mimashoo	mimai	
Imperative "see!"	miro	minasai	miru na	
Request	mite	mite kudasai	minaide	minaide kudasai
Desiderative "I want to see"	mitai		mitaku nai	mitaku nai desu/ arimasen
"He wants to see"	mitagaru	mitagarimasu	mitagaranai	mitagarimasen
Potential "can see"	mirareru	miraremasu	mirarenai	miraremasen
Passive "is seen"	mirareru	miraremasu	mirarenai	miraremasen
Causative "make/let (someone) see"	misaseru	misasemasu	misasenai	misasemasen
Causative Passive (alternative) "cause (something) to be seen"	misaserareru	misaseraremasu	misaserarenai	misaseraremasen

Note 1 The form ending in -tai is an adjective and has the endings of Table 7.

Note 2 The potential, passive, causative, and causative passive are verbs in their own right and conjugate like any other verbs of Group II.

Aid to memory In the present tense of the -ru Group the potential and the passive are the same, and have two r's before the -masu ending > mirare-masu; the causative has two s's > misase-masu; and the causative passive has two s's and two r's > misaserare-masu.

◇ Table 4 ◇

IRREGULAR VERBS
する SURU and くる KURU
AFFIRMATIVE

FORM	SURU		KURU	
	PLAIN	POLITE	PLAIN	POLITE
Present/future	suru	shimasu	kuru	kimasu
"-masu stem"	shi		ki	
Pres. Participle	shite		kite	
Past	shita	shimashita	kita	kimashita
Hypothetical	suru nara		kuru nara	
"if/when"	sureba		kureba	
	shita(na)ra		kita(na)ra	
Iterative "often…"	shitari		kitari	
Simultaneous	shinagara		kinagara	
"while…"				
Intentional	shiyoo	shimashoo	koyoo	kimashoo
Imperative	shiro	shinasai	koi	kinasai
Request	shite	shite kudasai	kite	kite kudasai
Desiderative	shitai	shitai desu	kitai	kitai desu
	shitagaru	shitagarimasu	kitagaru	kitagarimasu
Potential "I can…"	(dekiru)	(dekimasu)	korareru	koraremasu
Passive "is done"	sareru	saremasu	korareru "suffers the visitation of…"	koraremasu
Causative "make/let (someone) do"	saseru	sasemasu	kosaseru	kosasemasu
Causative Passive (alternative) "cause (something) to be done"	saserareru	saseraremasu	kosaserareru	kosaseraremasu

Appendix 2

◇ Table 5 ◇

IRREGULAR VERBS
する SURU and くる KURU
NEGATIVE

FORM	SURU		KURU	
	PLAIN	POLITE	PLAIN	POLITE
Present/future "-masu stem"	shinai	shimasen	konai	kimasen
Pres. Participle	shinaide shinakute		konaide konakute	
Past	shinakatta	shimasen deshita	konakatta	kimasen deshita
Hypothetical "if/when"	shinai nara shinakereba shinakatta(na)ra		konai nara konakereba konakatta(na)ra	
Desiderative "I do not want to…" "He doesn't want to…"	shitaku nai shitagaranai	shitaku nai desu shitaku arimasen shitagarimasen	kitaku nai kitagaranai	kitaku nai desu/ arimasen kitagarimasen
Iterative "often not…"	shinakattari		konakattari	
Intentional	surumai		kurumai	
Imperative	suru na		kuru na	
Request	shinaide	shinaide kudasai	konaide	konaide kudasai
Potential "I cannnot…"	(dekinai)	(dekimasen)	korarenai	koraremasen
Passive "is not done"	sarenai	saremasen	korarenai	koraremasen
Causative "make/let (someone) not do"	sasenai	sasemasen	kosasenai	kosasemasen
Causative Passive (alternative) "cause (something) not to be done"	saserarenai	saseraremasen	kosaserarenai	kosaseraremasen

◇ Table 6 ◇

DEFICIENT/INCOMPLETE VERB
Example です desu *the copula*

FORM	AFFIRMATIVE		NEGATIVE	
	PLAIN	POLITE	PLAIN	POLITE
Present				dewa/ja nai desu
	da (na)*	desu	nai	dewa/ja arimasen
Pres. Participle	de		dewa/ja nakute	
Past	datta	deshita	dewa/ja nakatta	de wa/ja arimasen deshita
Hypothetical			dewa/ja nakereba	
	nara		dewa/ja nai nara	
	datta(na)ra		dewa/ja nakatta(na)ra	
Iterative	dattari		dewa/ja nakattari	
("presumptive")**	daroo	deshoo	dewa/ja nai daroo	dewa/ja nai deshoo

*Na has to be used before **node, noni,** and **no**

**This form of the copula is added to other verbs to give the meaning of "will /may perhaps…" (as in Unit 2)

DEFICIENT/INCOMPLETE VERB
Example ある aru *to be*

Present	aru		nai	nai desu
"-masu stem"	ari	arimasu		arimasen
Pres Participle	atte		nakute/naide	
Past	atta	arimashita		arimasen deshita
			nakatta	nakatta desu
Hypothetical	aru nara		naranai nara	
	areba		nakereba	
	attara		nakatta(na)ra	
Iterative	attari		nakattari	
Simultaneous*	arinagara		nainagara	
(Presumptive)	aroo	arimashoo	arumai	nai deshoo
Imperative	are			
Desiderative	aritai	aritai desu	aritakunai	aritakunai desu
				aritaku arimasen

*With this verb the meaning is "although…"

Appendix 2

◇ Table 7 ◇

ADJECTIVES

The Japanese adjective proper–ie those which end in -i–shares some forms with the verb. Examples are 早い **haya-i** *early,* 寒い **samu-i** *cold,* and 面白い **omoshiro-i** *interesting.*

This is not so for the pseudo-adjectives, which are formed by the addition of **-na** to what are sometimes called adjectival nouns*; eg 静かな町 **shizuka-na machi** *a quiet town.*

The Japanese adjective standing alone corresponds to the plain form of the verb; thus 早い **haya-i** *it is early.* The polite equivalent is formed by adding **desu.**

Example 早い **hayai** *early*

FORM	AFFIRMATIVE		NEGATIVE	
	PLAIN	POLITE	PLAIN	POLITE
Present/future	hayai	hayai desu	hayaku nai	hayaku arimasen hayaku nai desu
Pres. participle "it being early"	hayakute		hayakunakute	
Past "it was early"	hayakatta	hayakatta desu	hayakunakatta	hayakunakatta desu
Hypothetical "if it is early" "if it were early" "if it had been early"	hayai nara hayakereba hayakatta(na)ra hayakatta nara		hayakunainara hayakunakereba hayakunakatta(na)ra	
Presumptive "it may be early"	hayakaroo	hayai deshoo	hayaku nakaroo	hayaku nai deshoo
Adverbial "(he got up) early"	hayaku		hayaku naku	
Simultaneous "though early [it was warm]"	hayainagara			

◇ ◇ The Anomalous Readings ◇ ◇

The following are examples of anomalous readings called JUKUJI KUN (熟字訓), which you may come across in daily use.

JUKUJI KUN are kanji compounds of which both the reading and the meaning apply, arbitrarily, to the compound as a whole. That is, neither component of the JUKUJI KUN has either a pronunciation or a meaning of its own.

明日	あす、あした	tomorrow
今日	きょう	today
今年	ことし	this year
昨日	きのう	yesterday
今朝	けさ	this morning
大人	おとな	adult
田舎	いなか	countryside
土産	みやげ	souvenir
上手	じょうず	good at
下手	へた	weak in
一人	ひとり	one person
二人	ふたり	two people
一日	ついたち	the first day of a month

Indexes

索引

Word List

	WORD	READING	ENGLISH	UNITS
あ	間	あいだ	among, in between	8
	相手	あいて	partner, the other party	3.5
	アインシュタイン		Einstein	7
	(〜に) (会う)	(〜に) あう	to meet	10
	赤字	あかじ	deficit, red figures	11
	赤字財政	あかじざいせい	deficit financing	11
	明るい	あかるい	bright	2
	朝	あさ	(in the) morning	2.3
	朝早く	あさはやく	early (in the) morning	3
	アジア		Asia	11
	明日	あした、あす	tomorrow	1
	新しい	あたらしい	new	7.8
	辺り	あたり	surroundings, neighbourhood	2
	当たり役	あたりやく	right role (effective)	6
	(厚い)	あつい	(literally) thick, (of trust) deep	6
	(〜を) 扱う	あつかう	to deal with, to manage	12
	(〜を) 集める	あつめる	to collect	8
	(〜に／〜を) 当てる	あてる	to hit (the right point) (focus) -transitive	12
	あなた		you	10
	兄	あに	older brother	2
	あまりにも		too much, excessively	5
	(〜に) 甘んじる	(〜に) あまんじる	to be content (with)	9
	雨	あめ	rain	2
	アメリカ人	アメリカじん	the/an American	10
	(危ぶまれる)	あやぶまれる	to cause anxiety, to be feared	9
	洗う	あらう	to wash	2
	(争う)	あらそう	to argue, to dispute	5
	(表す)	あらわす	to represent, to show, to express	4.7
	(現れる)	あらわれる	to appear	10
	(有る) (ある)		to have, to exist	1.2.4-10.12
	ある	ある	a certain	10
	(て／である)		to be done by someone (with intention)	4
	(歩く)	あるく	to walk	2
	ある程度	あるていど	to some extent	9
い	(良い) (いい、よい)	いい (neg. よくない)	good	2.3.10.12
	好い	よい、いい	good	2
	(言う)	いう	to say	1.2.10-12
	言うまでもない	いうまでもない	it goes without saying…	11
	家	いえ/うち	house, home	2.3.10

	WORD	READING	ENGLISH	UNITS
い	以下	いか	below	4
	(〜に／へ) 行く	いく	to go	1-3.10
	いくつか (の)		some, several	4.10.11
	いくら		how much	10
	意見	いけん	opinion	6
	以降	いこう	after	9
	(維持する)	いじする	to maintain	9
	〜以上 (の) …	〜いじょう (の) …	beyond…, more than…	4.5.8
	いずれにしても		in any case	12
	急いで	いそいで	in a hurry	10
	忙しさ	いそがしさ	being busy	2
	(〜に) 至る	(〜に) いたる	to reach	8
	一	いち	one	8
	一日	いちにち	one day	3
	一日中	いちにちじゅう	all day	2
	一倍半	いちばいはん	one and a half times	5
	一部	いちぶ	a part	11
	一角	いっかく	a corner, a spot	10
	(一致する)	いっちする	to agree	6
	いつも		always	4.5
	一歩	いっぽ	a step	7
	一方	いっぽう	while, on the other hand	7.11
	田舎	いなか	countryside	1.5
	犬	いぬ	dog	1.2
	今	いま	now	4.5.10
	今や	いまや	(by) now	8
	意味	いみ	meaning, significance	4
	(意味する)	いみする	to mean, to imply	8
	妹	いもうと	younger sister	2
	(いる)		to exist	1-3.5.6.9
	(〜て／で) いる		(have been) …ing	1.3-5.7.9.11.12
	(〜て／で) いる		to be in the state of…	3-10
	(入れる)	いれる	to include, to pour	2
	色々な	いろいろな	various	3.4.5
	所謂	いわゆる	so-called	7
	因果関係	いんがかんけい	the relation of cause and effect	10
う	ウィルビー		Willoughby	10
	上	うえ	top, above	2.3
	(受け取る)	うけとる	to receive	6

Word List

	WORD	READING	ENGLISH	UNITS
う	牛	うし	bull, cow, ox cattle	2
	後ろ	うしろ	behind	4
	家	うち／いえ	house, home	2.3.10
	（打ち出す）	うちだす	to hammer out	11
	写し	うつし	copy	6
	（生まれる）	うまれる	to be born	10
	海	うみ	the sea	5
	売り手	うりて	seller	9
	（売る）	うる	to sell	5
	（上回る）	うわまわる	to exceed	9
	上向き	うわむき	upwards, rising	9
	運転手	うんてんしゅ	driver	10
	運動する	うんどうする	to exercise, to move	7
え	英語	えいご	English language	3
	英国	えいこく	Britain, (England)	5
	英国人	えいこくじん	the/a British (English)	5
	英国の	えいこくの	British, Britain's	5
	エネルギー		energy	7
	（選ぶ）	えらぶ	to choose, to select, to elect	8
	円	えん	Yen	1.12
	円高	えんだか	strong Yen	11
	演算	えんざん	operation with figures	12
	援助金	えんじょきん	subsidy	12
お	（負う）	おう	to carry, to suffer	9
	往復	おうふく	return journey	10
	往復切符	おうふくきっぷ	return ticket	10
	応用	おうよう	application	12
	（多い）	おおい	many, much	5
	大金持	おおがねもち	very rich person	10
	大きな	おおきな	big, large	1.9
	多くの〜	おおくの	a lot of…	3.5
	大蔵省	おおくらしょう	Ministry of Finance	9.11
	大麦	おおむぎ	barley	5
	丘	おか	hill	2
	お客	おきゃく	client, guest	3.10
	（起きる）	おきる	to wake up, to occur	3.6
	（〜て／で おく）		to do for preparation	5
	奥さん	おくさん	wife (respect form)	3

	WORD	READING	ENGLISH	UNITS
お	(送る)	おくる	to send	3.6
	(行う)	おこなう	to carry out, to do	6.9.11
	起こり	おこり	the origin	4
	(収める)	おさめる	to obtain, to win	9
	汚職	おしょく	corruption	8
	恐らく	おそらく	probably	12
	(落ち込む)	おちこむ	to sink below	11
	お茶	おちゃ	tea, green tea	2
	夫	おっと	husband (plain form)	1
	お父さん	おとうさん	father	3
	男の人	おとこのひと	man/men	3
	同じ	おなじ	same	3.8
	同じ様な	おなじような	similar	12
	同じ様に	おなじように	similarly	9
	お願いする	おねがいする	to ask a favour	10
	(帯びる)	おびる	to carry, to wear	7
	オペレーティング・システム		operating system	12
	思いも寄らない	おもいもよらない	unexpected	8
	(思う)	おもう	to think	1.9
	面白い	おもしろい	interesting	4.5
	主な	おもな	main	5.8.9
	主に	おもに	mainly	4.8
	(下りる)	おりる	to go down	2
	音	おん	On ("a sound")	4
	女の子	おんなのこ	girl	2
	音読み	おんよみ	On reading	4
	(終わる)	おわる	to end, to finish	6.9
か	か		(question marker)	1.3.6.8-10.12
	か		either…or	6
	が		(subject marker)	1-12
	が		(object marker)	2.6.9.12
	が		and/but	1-8.10
	回	かい	suffix for times	1.8
	海外	かいがい	overseas	11
	改革	かいかく	reform	8
	会議	かいぎ	conference	12
	外国	がいこく	foreign country	3.11
	会社	かいしゃ	firm, company	3.10.12
	買い手	かいて	buyer	9

Word List

	WORD	READING	ENGLISH	UNITS
か	開発	かいはつ	development	9.12
	回復	かいふく	recovery	11
	(介抱する)	かいほうする	to care the sick, to tend	10
	開放	かいほう	opening	11
	(買う)	かう	to buy	1
	(帰る)	かえる	to go/come back (home)	2.3
	価格	かかく	price	9
	かかる		to cost	10
	かかわり		concern, connection	6
	(書く)	かく	to write	3.6
	各	かく	each…	8
	拡大	かくだい	expansion	11
	(獲得する)	かくとくする	to acquire	8
	過去	かこ	past	10
	火山	かざん	volcano	2
	(賢い)	かしこい	wise	12
	貸し出し	かしだし	loan, lending	9
	一夫	かずお	Kazuo (man's name)	1
	風	かぜ	wind	2
	(加速する)	かそくする	to accelerate	7
	ガソリン		petrol, gasoline	1
	〜方	〜かた	how to…/method of…	4
	形	かたち	form, shape	4
	価値	かち	value	9
	課長	かちょう	section chief	3
	家長	かちょう	head of a family	3
	学校	がっこう	school	3
	かつ		and, also	10
	活動	かつどう	activity	11
	角	かど	corner	2
	〜かどうか		whether… or not	5.12
	かなり		fairly, quite	3
	可能性	かのうせい	possibility	8.10
	(可能な)	かのうな	possible	10
	過半数	かはんすう	majority	8
	株価	かぶか	share price	9
	(かもしれない)	かもしれない	may be…, might be…	6.11
	通う	かよう	to go regularly	3
	から		from	3.4.7.8.10
	から		since, from	3.7.

	WORD	READING	ENGLISH	UNITS
か	から		because, as	4.10
	から		from (components, ingredients)	4.5.7.8
	(〜て／で) から		after …ing	2.6
	彼	かれ	he	3.6.10
	ガレージ		garage	1
	川	かわ	river	2
	可哀相な	かわいそうな	pitiful, poor	10
	(〜の) 代わりに	(〜の) かわりに	instead, instead of	2.3.12
	替わる	かわる	to be replaced	6
	官界	かんかい	officialdom	11
	考え	かんがえ	thought, idea	6
	(考え事をする)	かんがえごとをする	to think	3
	(考える)	かんがえる	to think, to consider	7.12
	関係	かんけい	relation	6-10
	漢語	かんご	word from the Chinese	4
	韓国	かんこく	the Republic of Korea	5
	漢字	かんじ	Kanji	4
	〜に関して	〜にかんして	regarding…	9
	完成 (する)	かんせい (する)	completion (to complete)	12
	関税	かんぜい	tariff, customs duty	11
	官僚	かんりょう	official, bureaucrat	8.11
	緩和	かんわ	easing	11
き	木	き	tree	2.4
	木々	きぎ	trees	2
	企画	きかく	plan, scheme, project	12
	機関	きかん	organization	12
	企業	きぎょう	enterprise, firm	8.11
	(聞く)	きく	to hear, to listen, to ask	1.3.10
	起源	きげん	origin	4
	危険性	きけんせい	risk, dangerous tendency	8
	機構	きこう	organization, mechanism	11
	記事	きじ	article (in newspaper, etc)	6
	記者会見	きしゃかいけん	press conference	6
	技術	ぎじゅつ	technology, technique	12
	規制	きせい	regulation	11
	奇跡	きせき	miracle	9
	北	きた	north	2
	(〜て／で) (来た)	(〜て／で) (きた)	to have been …ing	4.9.10.12
	(期待する)	きたいする	to expect	9

Word List

	WORD	READING	ENGLISH	UNITS
き	汚い	きたない	dirty	2
	切符	きっぷ	ticket	10
	（機能する）	きのうする	to function	12
	寄付	きふ	contribution, donation	8
	気分	きぶん	feeling	2
	基本粒子	きほんりゅうし	basic particle	7
	（～に）（決める）	（～に）きめる	to decide (on)	10
	逆説	ぎゃくせつ	paradox	10
	休暇	きゅうか	vacations	9
	九十	きゅうじゅう	ninety	4
	（急変する）	きゅうへんする	to change suddenly	8
	（急落する）	きゅうらくする	to drop sharply	9
	今日	きょう	today	2
	業界	ぎょうかい	trade circles	12
	（協議する）	きょうぎする	to discuss	8
	競争	きょうそう	competition	8
	競争力	きょうそうりょく	competitive power	9
	（共通な）	きょうつうな	common	4
	共同債権買収機構	きょうどうさいけんばいしゅうきこう	cooperative organization for the purchase of debts	11
	局外者	きょうくがいしゃ	outsider	12
	巨大な	きょだいな	huge, gigantic	7
	極めて	きわめて	extremely, very	12
	金	きん	gold	4
	銀行	ぎんこう	bank	9.11
	近所（の人）	きんじょ（のひと）	neighbourhood (neighbour)	10
く	クォーク		quark	7
	草	くさ	grass	2
	崩す	くずす	to destroy	11
	口	くち	mouth	4
	国	くに	county, state	5.11.12
	区別（を）する	くべつ（を）する	to distinguish	4
	組み合わせ	くみあわせ	combination	4.8
	（組み合わせる）	くみあわせる	to combine	4
	雲	くも	cloud	2
	～位	～くらい（ぐらい）	approximately	4
	比べる	くらべる	to compare	5
	グルオン		gluon	7
	グループ		group	4
	車	くるま	car, vehicle	1.2

	WORD	READING	ENGLISH	UNITS
く	黒字	くろじ	surplus (black figures)	11
	(加える)	くわえる	to add	7
	訓	くん	Kun	4
け	計画	けいかく	plan	12
	景気	けいき	business conditions	11
	経済	けいざい	economy	9.11
	経済活動	けいざいかつどう	economic activity	11
	経済対策	けいざいたいさく	economic measure	11
	ケインズ		Keynes	11
	結果	けっか	result	12
	結果的に	けっかてきに	in the result	11
	決して～ない	けっして～ない	never…	12
	(決定できる)	けっていできる	to be able to decide	6
	(決定的な)	けっていてきな	decisive	10
	下落	げらく	fall (in prices)	9
	元気な	げんきな	healthy, lively	1
	研究する	けんきゅうする	(to) research	7.10.12
	研究会社	けんきゅうがいしゃ	research company	10
	研究開発	けんきゅうかいはつ	research and development	12
	研究機関	けんきゅうきかん	research organization	12
	献金	けんきん	donation	8
	現在	げんざい	(at) present, now	7.9
	原子	げんし	atom	7
	原子核	げんしかく	atomic nucleus	7
	(減少する)	げんしょうする	to decrease (intransitive)	9
	減税	げんぜい	tax cut	11
	元素	げんそ	(chemical) element	7
	原則	げんそく	principle	12
	見地	けんち	viewpoint	7
	元老	げんろう	elder statesman	6
こ	小犬	こいぬ	puppy	1
	工	こう	construction, craft	4
	合意	ごうい	agreement	8
	後援会	こうえんかい	support association	8
	交換	こうかん	exchange	7
	公共投資	こうきょうとうし	public investment	11
	光子	こうし	photon	7
	公式	こうしき	formula	7

Word List

	WORD	READING	ENGLISH	UNITS
こ	(構成する)	こうせいする	to compose, to form	7
	構造	こうぞう	structure	7
	(交代する)	こうたいする	to alter, to take turns	8
	校長 (先生)	こうちょう (せんせい)	head teacher	3
	公定歩合	こうていぶあい	official bank rate	11
	購入	こうにゅう	purchase	9
	候補者	こうほしゃ	candidate	8
	戸外	こがい	outdoors	1
	国事	こくじ	affairs of the state	6
	国土	こくど	national territory	2
	国内	こくない	within a country	5
	互恵関係	ごけいかんけい	reciprocal relation	8
	ここ		here, this place	1
	ここに		hence	7
	五十万	ごじゅうまん	500 thousands	1.10
	個人	こじん	individual, private	11
	国会	こっかい	the Diet	6.8
	国会議員	こっかいぎいん	member of the Diet	8
	事、こと	こと	fact, matter	1.3-12
	～事がある	～ことがある	sometimes it happens that…	6
	～事もある	～こともある	sometimes it also happens that…	6.9
	(～た／だ) 事がある	(～た／だ) ことがある	to have an experience of…	10
	～事が出来る	～ことができる	to be able to…	3.5.12
	～事になる	～ことになる	to become that…	8.12
	異なる	ことなる	different	7
	子供	こども	a child, children	1-3
	この～		this…	1.4.8.10.12
	この間	このあいだ	recently	1
	このために		because of this	5
	このような		this sort of…	4
	５００億	ごひゃくおく	500×10^8	12
	五分の三	ごぶんのさん	three-fifths	8
	小麦	こむぎ	wheat	5
	米	こめ	rice	5.11
	ゴルフ		golf	3
	これ		this	8.9
	これから		from now on	4
	雇用	こよう	employment	9
	今月	こんげつ	(in) this month	1
	今後	こんご	from now on	8

	WORD	READING	ENGLISH	UNITS
こ	今世紀	こんせいき	(in) this century	7
	コンピューター		computer	12
	根本的	こんぽんてき	fundamental, basic	12
さ	座	ざ	seat	8
	〜才	〜さい	age, suffix for age	1
	財界	ざいかい	financial circles	11
	最近	さいきん	recent times	10
	債権	さいけん	claim, credit	11
	最後の	さいごの	last, final	12
	最終的	さいしゅうてき	the final	12
	財政	ざいせい	finance	11
	魚	さかな	fish	5
	（下がる）	さがる	to fall, to decline	9
	削減（する）	さくげん（する）	reduction, to reduce	9.11
	酒	さけ	alcoholic drinks	10
	（避ける）	さける	to avoid	11
	（下げる）	さげる	to lower, to reduce	11
	（定かな）	さだかな	certain, sure	12
	さて		"to come to the point…"	10
	作動する	さどうする	to run, to operate (intransitive)	12
	（妨げる）	さまたげる	to obstruct, to hinder	11
	さらに		further, in addition	5
	サラリー		salary	1
	サラリーマン		office-worker	1.3
	〜さん		Mr. Ms. Mrs. Miss etc.	1.2.3
	三	さん	three	1
	三億人	さんおくにん	three hundred million people	5
	三十	さんじゅう	thirty	1.8
	三十五万	さんじゅうごまん	350,000	1
	三十八	さんじゅうはち	38	8
	算術	さんじゅつ	arithmetic calculation	12
	サンドイッチ		sandwich	1.2
	三番目（の）	さんばんめ（の）	the third	8
し	寺	てら、〜じ	buddhist temple	4
	しか〜ない		only…	5.6.9
	しかし		but, however	4.6.10-12
	しかしながら		however	12
	（仕方がない）	しかたがない	cannot be helped	1

Word List

	WORD	READING	ENGLISH	UNITS
し	時間	じかん	time	3.10.12
	資金	しきん	fund	12
	刺激	しげき	stimulus, incentive	12
	思考	しこう	thought	12
	仕事 (を) (する)	しごと (を) (する)	(to) work	3.4.6
	(指示する)	しじする	to instruct	12
	市場	しじょう	market	9.11
	市場開放	しじょうかいほう	opening the market	11
	～自身	～じしん	…self	6.10
	指数	しすう	index	11
	自然言語	しぜんげんご	natural language	12
	子孫	しそん	descendant	10
	事態	じたい	situation	8
	(実現する)	じつげんする	to come true (intransitive)	10
	実行する	じっこうする	to carry out	12
	実際 (に)	じっさい (に)	in fact, really	9.12
	実証 (する)	じっしょう (する)	proof, to prove	7
	実体	じったい	substance, entity	7
	(知っている)	しっている	to know	1.3.4.6
	じっと		steadily, patiently	3
	質問	しつもん	question	6
	(失敗) (する)	しっぱい (する)	failure, to fail	6.12
	質量	しつりょう	mass	7
	品	しな	goods	5
	(死ぬ)	しぬ	to die	10
	自分	じぶん	oneself	3.6.10
	四方	しほう	four directions, all around	5
	資本収益	しほんしゅうえき	return to capital	9
	島国	しまぐに	island country	5
	～て／で しまう		to have done something / irreparable	2.9.10
	自民党	じみんとう	L.D.P. (abbr.)	8
	ジム		Jim	10
	事務次官	じむじかん	Permanent Secretary	6
	(示す)	しめす	to show, to express, to point out	4.7
	地元	じもと	locality	8
	社員	しゃいん	company employee	10.12
	社会党	しゃかいとう	Socialist Party	8.11
	社長	しゃちょう	president of a company	3
	十、１０	じゅう	ten	3.12
	周囲	しゅうい	circumference, around	7

	WORD	READING	ENGLISH	UNITS
し	十一区	じゅういっく	eleven regions	8
	自由化	じゆうか	liberalization	11
	習慣化（する）	しゅうかんか（する）	becoming a habit	8
	衆議院	しゅうぎいん	House of Representatives	8
	１９	じゅうきゅう、じゅうく	19	7
	終身雇用	しゅうしんこよう	life-time employment	9
	住宅	じゅうたく	housing, residence	9
	十二億	じゅうにおく	twelve hundred million	5
	（十分な）	じゅうぶんな	enough	1
	十分に	じゅうぶんに	enough (adverb)	5
	自由民主党	じゆうみんしゅとう	Liberal Democratic Party	8
	重力	じゅうりょく	gravity	7
	（縮小する）	しゅくしょうする	to reduce	9
	首相	しゅしょう	prime minister	6
	主食	しゅしょく	main food, staple food	5
	出現する	しゅつげんする	to emerge, to turn up	8
	〜種の	〜しゅの	…kinds of	7
	需要	じゅよう	demand	11
	需要主導の	じゅようしゅどう（の）	demand-led	11
	準備金	じゅんびきん	reserve fund	9
	上昇する	じょうしょう（する）	rise, to rise	9
	生じる	しょうじる	to be brought about	7
	上手な、上手に	じょうずな、じょうずに	good at (well), skilful(ly)	3.6
	使用する	しようする	to use	4
	小選挙区制	しょうせんきょくせい	small (single) constituency system	8
	焦点	しょうてん	focus	12
	少年	しょうねん	boy	10
	消費者	しょうひしゃ	consumer	9.11
	消費税	しょうひぜい	consumption tax	11
	（証明）（する）	しょうめい（する）	proof, to prove	7.10
	将来	しょうらい	(in) future	6.9
	初頭	しょとう	(at) the beginning	7
	処理する	しょりする	to deal with, to manage	12
	書類	しょるい	document	6
	（調べる）	しらべる	to check, to examine	6
	白い	しろい	white	1
	人口	じんこう	population	5
	人工知能	じんこうちのう	artificial intelligence	12
	進出	しんしゅつ	advance, entry (market, business)	11
	新人	しんじん	new man, new comer	6

Word List

	WORD	READING	ENGLISH	UNITS
し	真の	しんの	true	7
	心配な	しんぱいな	worrying	5.6
	人脈	じんみゃく	human network in a specific group	9
	信用	しんよう	trust, confidence	6
す	水準	すいじゅん	standard, level	11
	推論する	すいろんする	to reason, to deduce, to infer	12
	数字	すうじ	figure, numeral	12
	数理論	すうりろん	mathematical theory	7
	（〜すぎる）		to be too…	3
	すぐ		immediate	3.5
	すぐ（に）		immediately	3.11
	優れた	すぐれた	excellent	9
	少し	すこし	a little, a few	2.9
	（進める）	すすめる	to promote	9
	ずっと		far more, all the time	5.9
	即ち	すなわち	in other words, i.e.	7
	すべて（の）		all	6
	スポーツ		sport	3
	（する）		to do, to play	2.3.5.6.10
	（座る）	すわる	to sit	10
	（住んでいる）	すんでいる	to live	1.5
せ	正	せい	plus (prefix)	7
	政界	せいかい	political circles	11
	生活（を）（する）	せいかつ（を）（する）	living, life, to lead a daily life	3
	〜世紀	〜せいき	(in) …th century	7
	政権	せいけん	political power	8
	制限	せいげん	restriction	8
	政権交代	せいけんこうたい	change of political power	8
	成功	せいこう	success	9.12
	政策	せいさく	policy	6
	政治	せいじ	politics	8
	政治献金	せいじけんきん	political donation	8
	製造業者	せいぞうぎょうしゃ	manufacturers	9
	制度	せいど	system	8
	政党	せいとう	political party	8
	正統派	せいとうは	orthodox	11
	製品	せいひん	manufactured goods	9
	政府	せいふ	government	8.9

	WORD	READING	ENGLISH	UNITS
せ	政府援助金	せいふえんじょきん	state subsidy	12
	（声明する）	せいめいする	to declare, to announce	6
	世界	せかい	world	9.11
	責任	せきにん	responsibility	6
	石油	せきゆ	petroleum	5
	世代	せだい	generation	12
	積極的に	せっきょくてきに	positively	9
	説明（する）	せつめい（する）	explanation, to explain	4.6.7.10
	（設立する）	せつりつする	to establish	11.12
	狭い	せまい	narrow, small (space)	5
	１９９１年	せんきゅうひゃくきゅうじゅういちねん	the year 1991	9
	１９９３年	せんきゅうひゃくきゅうじゅうさんねん	the year 1993	8
	１９９２年	せんきゅうひゃくきゅうじゅうにねん	the year 1992	12
	１９９４年	せんきゅうひゃくきゅうじゅうよねん	the year 1994	8
	１９３０年代	せんきゅうひゃくさんじゅうねんだい	1930's	7
	１９３７年	せんきゅうひゃくさんじゅうしち/ななねん	the year 1937	10
	１９８２年	せんきゅうひゃくはちじゅうにねん	the year 1982	12
	選挙	せんきょ	election	8
	選挙区	せんきょく	constituency	8
	選挙制度	せんきょせいど	electoral system	8
	全国	ぜんこく	the whole country	8
	千五百	せんごひゃく	1500	4
	先生	せんせい	teacher	3
	先祖	せんぞ	ancestor	10
	選択	せんたく	choice	11
	１０２４	せんにじゅうよん	1024	12
	前半	ぜんはん	(in)the first half	8
	戦略	せんりゃく	strategy	12
そ	（～そうだ）		we hear… they say…	4
	そうでなければ		if it is not so	3
	そうなら		if it is so	8
	総合	そうごう	synthetic, all round	11
	相対性理論	そうたいせいりろん	the Theory of Relativety	7
	相談する	そうだんする	to consult	6
	総定数	そうていすう	total fixed number	8
	相当額	そうとうがく	corresponding amount	11
	促進	そくしん	promotion, encouragement	11
	速度	そくど	velocity	7
	そこ		there, that place	5.10

Word List

	WORD	READING	ENGLISH	UNITS
そ	阻止する	そしする	to obstruct, to hinder	11
	租税	そぜい	taxation	11
	措置	そち	measure	11
	外	そと	outside, outdoor	2
	その〜		that…, the…	3.4.6.7.10.12
	その上	そのうえ	on top of that	5
	その他の	そのた／ほかの	other	11
	そのため		because of that	9
	そば		near	2.1
	祖父	そふ	grandfather	10
	ソフトウェア		software	12
	それ		that, it	3.4.10.11
	それから		and then, after that	2
	それ自体	それじたい	itself	10
	それぞれ（の）		each	6.7
	それで		therefore	1.2.4.5
	それとも		or, else	8
	存在する	そんざいする	to exist	7.10
	そんな		such(a)	3.6
た	だ		is,are (copula)	1-4.7-10.12
	他（の）	た／ほか（の）	others, other	6.11.12
	〜たい		to want to…	2.3.5.10
	（〜に）対応できる	（〜に）たいおうできる	to be able to react (to)	12
	対外的に	だいがいてきに	externally	11
	大学	だいがく	university	3
	大企業	だいきぎょう	large enterprise	9
	耐久消費財	たいきゅうしょうひざい	durable consumer goods	9
	第五世代	だいごせだい	the Fifth Generation	12
	対策	たいさく	measure	11
	大事な	だいじな	important	6
	貸借対照表	たいしゃくたいしょうひょう	balance sheet	9
	大丈夫	だいじょうぶ	all right, fine	10
	大臣	だいじん	minister	6
	（大好きな）	だいすきな	very fond of	1.2
	（大切な）	たいせつな	important	3.6
	第二の	だいにの	the second	5.8
	大分	だいぶ	for some time, a lot	2
	タイム・トラベル		time travel	10
	（平らな）	たいらな	flat	4

	WORD	READING	ENGLISH	UNITS
た	タウ粒子	タウりゅうし	Tauon	7
	（高い）	たかい	expensive, high, tall	1-3.9
	互いに	たがいに	to each other, to one another	5
	たくさん、沢山（の）	たくさん（の）	many, much, a lot	3-5.10
	タクシー		taxi	10
	（〜たくてたまらない）		to be eager to...	10
	巧みに	たくみに	skilfully	9
	だけ		only	2.7.12
	〜だけでなく		…not only…	5.11
	ターゲット		target	7
	（出す）	だす	to take out	2
	多数の	たすうの	large number of	4.6
	（助ける）	たすける	to help	3.6
	ただ		only	3.12
	（正しい）	ただしい	right, correct	12
	立つ	たつ	to stand	1
	だった		was, were (copula)	7-10.12
	例えば	たとえば	for example	4.7.12
	田中	たなか	Tanaka (family name)	1.2.3
	谷	たに	valley	2
	谷川	たにがわ	valley stream	2
	束	たば	bundle	7
	旅（する）	たび（する）	travel, journey (to travel)	10
	旅人	たびびと	traveller, tourist	10
	多分	たぶん	perhaps	4.5
	（食べる）	たべる	to eat	2.4.5
	（だめな）		no good	10
	〜のために		because of…	10
	〜ために		in order to…	1.4.10
	〜のために		for the purpose of	7
	（〜に）（頼る）	（〜に）たよる	to rely	11.12
	(た/だり、〜た/だり) する		do…and do, among other things	3
	〜だろう		it may be that	11
	〜だろうか		will it be? would it be?	8.12
	（〜のではない）だろうか		will it not be? would it not be?	12
	談合	だんごう	collusion	11
	単純化	たんじゅんか	simplification	11
	単純多数方式	たんじゅんたすうほうしき	simple majority (system)	8
	団体	だんたい	group	8
	担当者	たんとうしゃ	responsible person	6

Word List

	WORD	READING	ENGLISH	UNITS
た	担保	たんぽ	collateral, security (eg for a loan)	11
ち	近く	ちかく	neighbourhood	5
	力	ちから	force, power	7.8
	竹林	ちくりん	bamboo grove	2
	地図	ちず	map, plan	2
	父	ちち	father (plain form)	2
	父親	ちちおや	father	10
	着実に	ちゃくじつに	steadily	9
	(〜に) 着手する	(〜に)ちゃくしゅする	to launch	12
	ちゃん		term of endearment (with the first name)	10
	中央	ちゅうおう	the centre	8
	中央銀行	ちゅうおうぎんこう	the Central Bank	9
	中国	ちゅうごく	China	4.5.11
	中国の	ちゅうごくの	Chinese (China's)	4.5
	中古の	ちゅうこの	used, second hand	1
	中性子	ちゅうせいし	neutron	7
	長	ちょう	chief,seniority (suffix)	3
	長期貸し出し	ちょうきかしだし	long term loan	9
	長時間	ちょうじかん	(for) a long time (hours)	3
	調整	ちょうせい	regulation, adjustment	9
	ちょうど		just, exactly	2
	直接	ちょくせつ	directly	6
	直接的	ちょくせつてき	direct	10
	直接税	ちょくせつぜい	direct tax	11
	直接労働力	ちょくせつろうどうりょく	direct labour force	9
	(〜に) (直面する)	(〜に) (ちょくめんする)	to face, to confront	11
	貯蓄率	ちょちくりつ	rate of saving	9
つ	(追求する)	ついきゅうする	to pursue	12
	(〜の) 付いた	(〜の) ついた	provided with…	12
	(〜に) 次いで	(〜に) ついで	after…, ranking next to…	5
	通産省	つうさんしょう	Ministry of International	12
	通商産業省	つうしょうさんぎょうしょう	Trade and Industry	12
	通常の	つうじょうの	usual	12
	(使う)	つかう	to use	4.5
	(仕える)	つかえる	to serve, to attend on	3
	月	つき	month, monthly	1
	〜付き	〜つき	with…, bearing…	11
	次の	つぎの	next	7

	WORD	READING	ENGLISH	UNITS
つ	(付く)	つく	to attach (intransitive)	3.4.8
	机	つくえ	desk	3
	(作る)	つくる	to make	1.2.5.12
	(造る)	つくる	to make (alcohol, etc)	5
	続く	つづく	to continue (intransitive)	7
	続く〜	つづく	ensuing, following	8
	(続ける)	つづける	to continue (transitive)	5.6
	(〜続ける)	〜つづける	to continue …ing	5
	包み	つつみ	wrapping, packet	2
	(包む)	つつむ	to wrap	1
	(〜に) つながる		to connect (to)	9.11
	常に	つねに	always	9
	つまり		in short	4.10
	(〜つもりだ)		to intend to…	1
	強い	つよい	strong	7
	強まる	つよまる	to become strong(er)	8
	(連れて行く)	つれていく	to take (somebody)	10
て	手	て	hand	2.4
	で		instrument	1.4.6-8
	で		place of action	2.3.5.6.12
	で		extent	3.5-11.12
	で		components–made of	4
	(提供する)	ていきょうする	to provide, to offer	12
	定数	ていすう	fixed number	8
	手紙	てがみ	letter	3
	(〜に) 適した	(〜に) てきした	to fit, to suit	12
	(〜で出来ている/〜から出来た)	〜でできている/〜からできた	to be made of…	4
	できる		to be able to do	3.5.6.9
	でした		it was, they were (copula).	2.10
	でしょう		it may be that… it is supposed that…	2.4.5
	でしょうか		will it be that…? would it be that…?	3
	です		is, are (copula)	1-6.10
	(出て来る)	でてくる	to come out	1.10
	手に入る	てにはいる	to come into one's posession	5
	〜ではない		is not…, are not…	6.12
	でも		but	2
	寺	てら	Buddhist temple	3.4
	テレビ		television	2.6
	出る	でる	to go out, to come out (as)	1.3

Word List

	WORD	READING	ENGLISH	UNITS
て	展開	てんかい	development	7
	転換	てんかん	turnover	9
	天気	てんき	weather	2
	電気	でんき	electricity	7
	電子	でんし	electron	7
	電磁場	でんじば	electro-magnetic field	7
	電弱力	でんじゃくりょく	electro-weak force	7
	伝統的	でんとうてき	traditional	11
	(電話 (を) する)	でんわ (を) する	(to) telephone, (to) call	3
と	と		and (to connect two words)	1.2.4.5.7-12
	と		together with	3.5.6.8.9
	と		if, when, whenever	3.5.6.10.11
	と		quotation-indirect speech	1.2.7.9-12
	と		tag-for what are becomes（〜となる）	8.12
	と		different from	7.8
	〜という…		…that is…	4.10
	〜と言う…	〜という…	…called…	4.7.12
	〜と言う事	〜ということ	the fact/statement that…	2.3.10
	〜と言える	〜といえる	it can be said that…	11
	ドイツ		Germany	9
	党	とう	political party	8
	どう		how, what	10
	(同意する)	どういする	to agree	8.11
	統一	とういつ	unification	7
	統一理論	とういつりろん	unifying theory	7
	東京	とうきょう	Tokyo	1.2
	当局	とうきょく	the authorities concerned	9
	(統合する)	とうごうする	to put together	7
	投資	とうし	investment	11
	投資家	とうしか	investor	9
	(〜と) 同時に	(〜と) どうじに	at the same time (as)	11
	当座	とうざ	for the time being	9
	当然	とうぜん	natural	9
	〜と同様に	〜とどうように	in the same way as	9
	東南アジア	とうなんアジア	South East Asia	5
	導入	どうにゅう	introduction	8
	(答弁する)	とうべんする	to respond	6
	通す	とおす	to keep (one's way) to insist on	6
	〜通りに	〜とおりに	as the same way as…	12

	WORD	READING	ENGLISH	UNITS
と	〜(の)とき、(時)	とき	when…	3.4
	時々	ときどき	sometimes	3
	特色	とくしょく	characteristic	8
	特定の	とくていの	specific	12
	特別措置	とくべつそち	special measures	11
	特別な	とくべつな	special	6
	独立している	どくりつしている	to be independent	9
	どこ		where	1.6
	どこでも		wherever	5
	所／ところ	ところ	place, scene	1.4
	た／だ ところの〜		have just done	10
	ところが		but, however	8.9
	年上	としうえ	older	1
	〜として／とした		as, in the capacity of…	4.11.12
	(〜とする)		to regard as…	9
	(〜う)(とする)		to try to…	5.7
	土地	とち	land, earth	5.9
	どちらも		both sides	5
	どの〜		which…	11
	止める	とめる	to stop, to park (trans.)	1.2.10
	〜共	〜とも	both…	5
	友達	ともだち	friend	3
	(伴う)	ともなう	to accompany, to involve	8
	土曜日	どようび	Saturday	1
	ドライブ(する)		(to go for a) drive	1.2
	トラベル・マシン		travel machine	10
	鳥	とり	bird	4
	取り囲む	とりかこむ	to surround	5
	ドル		Dollars	10
	どんな		what sort of…	3.8
な	無い	ない	not to have, not to exist, not available	6.12
	内閣	ないかく	the Cabinet, the governement	6.8
	内閣改造	ないかくかいぞう	Cabinet reshuffle	6
	内需	ないじゅ	domestic demand	11
	内需拡大	ないじゅかくだい	expansion of domestic demand	11
	内部	ないぶ	the inside, the inner part	7
	(〜の)中	(〜の)なか	in…, among…	2.9.11
	長い目でみると	ながいめでみると	taking a long term view	11
	〜ながら		(suffix of simultaneous form of the verb)	2.12

Word List

	WORD	READING	ENGLISH	UNITS
な	ながら		although…	9
	（なければ）ならない／いけない		must…, to have to…	3.6.10
	長々と	ながながと	very long, at length	3
	長年	ながねん	for many years	9.12
	長引く	ながびく	dragging on	11
	（納得がいく）	なっとくがいく	to be convinced	10
	等／など		and so on	3.6.11.12
	７０	ななじゅう, しちじゅう	seventy	7
	七十五	ななじゅうご, しちじゅうご	75	2
	何	なに	what	6
	（〜な）ら		if it is, if it were	5.10
	成り立ち	なりたち	origin	4
	（〜に）（成る）	（〜に）なる	to become, to come to…	1.2.5.6.8.10.11
	（〜から）（成る）	（〜から）なる	to be consist of…	7.8
	（〜と）（成る）	（〜と）なる	to become	8.12
	何名か	なんめいか	several (people)	8
に	に		place–where sombody is or resides	1-5
	に		ownership and belonging	1.4.7.8.10
	に		time, occasion	1.3.5-8.11.12
	に		destination	2.3.6.9.10.12
	に		result of change	1.5-8.10.12
	に		indirect object	1.3.4.6-8.10-12
	二、2	に	two	8.12
	〜において		as for, in point of	9
	二、三	にさん	two or three	3
	西	にし	west	4
	二千五十年	にせんごじゅうねん	the year	10
	〜に対する		in relation to…, against	8.9.11
	日曜日	にちようび	Sunday	1.2
	〜について		regarding	4.6
	日経	にっけい	Japanese Economy (abbr.) NIKKEI	9
	日経株価指数	にっけいかぶかしすう	Japanese share price index	9
	〜にとって		for, to	3.4.11
	担う	になう	to carry, to undertake	7
	二倍	にばい	twice as much, many	5
	日本	にほん／にっぽん	Japan	2.4.5.8.9.11
	日本人	にほん／にっぽんじん	the/a Japanese	2.4.5.11
	日本の	にほん／にっぽんの	Japanese, Japan's	3-5.8.9.11
	日本国内	にほんこくない	within Japan	5

	WORD	READING	ENGLISH	UNITS
に	日本銀行	にっぽんぎんこう	Bank of Japan	9
	日本経済	にほん／にっぽんけいざい	the Japanese economy	9.11
	～にもかかわらず		in spite of…	3
	ニュートリノ		Neutrino	7
	ニューラル・ネットワーク		neural network	12
	～による		due to…	8
	～によって（は）		depending on…	6
	～によって		by means of…	7
	人	にん	counter for people… eg san-nin, yo-nin	3.5.12
	人気がある	にんきがある	popular	6
	人間	にんげん	man, the human race	12
	任務	にんむ	duty, task	6
ぬ	抜きん出た	ぬきんでた	stood out, excelled	9
ね	年二回	ねんにかい	twice a year	1
	～年	～ねん	the year…	4.8-10.12
	～年（間）	～ねん（かん）	for …years	3.8.12
	～年代	～ねんだい	1930's etc.	7
の	の		(to express possession, belonging)	1-12
	の		(to be used for apposition)	1.2.5
	の		(to put figures as a prefix modifier)	1-5.7.8.12
	の		(to put a preceding word as a modifier)	1.2.4-12
	の		(nominalization)	1.5.6
	の		(subject marker in a noun modifying clause)	6.10.12
	脳	のう	brain	12
	農産物	のうさんぶつ	agricultural products	11
	～のです/だ/でしょう		(to put the effect of stress and justification	3-5.10.12
	能率的な	のうりつてきな	efficient	11
	能力	のうりょく	ability	12
	残り	のこり	remainder, the rest	8
	～ので		as, since	1-3.6.10
	～のに		although…	2
	伸びる	のびる	to expand, to increase	11
	述べる	のべる	to mention	6
	（上る）	のぼる	to rise, to go up	2.4
	（～に上る）	～にのぼる	to reach, to go up to	12
	（飲む）	のむ	to drink	2.3

Word List

	WORD	READING	ENGLISH	UNITS
は	は		(topic marker)	1-12
	は		(highlight marker)	1-12
	バー		bar	3
	(〜ば)		…if	6
	場合	ばあい	case, occasion	6
	〜倍	〜ばい	…times as much	5
	媒介	ばいかい	mediation	7
	買収	ばいしゅう	purchase	11
	廃止	はいし	abolition	11
	(入って来る)	はいってくる	to come into	4
	(入る)	はいる	to enter, to contain	2.3.6
	(吐く)	はく	to vomit	2
	(始まる)	はじまる	to begin (intransitive)	6
	(〜始める)	〜はじめる	to begin to… (transitive)	2
	場所	ばしょ	place	10
	(走る)	はしる	to run	2
	〜はず (だ)		to be likely to	4.6
	パーセント		per cent	2.4.9
	畑	はたけ	field	2
	働き中毒	はたらきちゅうどく	workaholic	9
	(働く)	はたらく	to work	3
	8	はち	eight	9
	(発見する)	はっけんする	to discover	7.10
	(発表する)	はっぴょうする	to announce	12
	ハードウェア		hardware	12
	話 (を) (する)	はなし (を) する	story, talk, to tell a story	3
	話し合い	はなしあい	discussion	6
	話す	はなす	to speak, to talk	3
	母	はは	mother (plain form)	1.2
	早い	はやい	early	2
	林	はやし	woods	2
	(払う)	はらう	to pay	1.10.12
	パラレル・プロセッサー		parallel processor	12
	バランス		balance, equilibrium	11
	反映する	はんえいする	to reflect	11
	(反対する)	はんたいする	to oppose, to object	11
	半年	はんとし	half a year	1
	半値	はんね	half price	9
	万有	ばんゆう	universa, of everything	7
	万有理論	ばんゆうりろん	"theory of everything"	7

	WORD	READING	ENGLISH	UNITS
ひ	日	ひ	a day, the Sun	2.4
	非〜	ひ〜	non	8
	延いては	ひいては	furthermore	9.11
	非関税障壁	ひかんぜいしょうへき	non tariff barrier	11
	比較	ひかく	comparison	5
	比較的	ひかくてき	relatively	9
	東	ひがし	east	4
	光	ひかり	light	7
	引き上げる	ひきあげる	to raise	11
	引き下げ	ひきさげ	reduction	11
	低い	ひくい	low	9.11
	（ひく）		to run over	10
	ピクニック		picnic	2
	非自民	ひじみん	non-LDP	8
	非常に	ひじょうに	very	11
	秘書官	ひしょかん	private secretary	6
	左	ひだり	left	4
	左手	ひだりて	left hand	4
	羊	ひつじ	sheep	5
	必要な	ひつような	necessary	7
	（否定する）	ひていする	to deny	10
	人	ひと	person, people	3.5.6.10
	人々	ひとびと	people	10
	一度	ひとたび／いちど	once	9
	一つ	ひとつ	one (inanimate thing)	2.4.5.9
	一つも〜（ない）	ひとつも〜（ない）	not a single…	2
	一つ一つ	ひとつひとつ	each one	4
	百五十	ひゃくごじゅう	150	2
	１００人	ひゃくにん	100 people	12
	票	ひょう	vote	8
	標準モデル	ひょうじゅんモデル	the Standard Model	7
	ビール		beer	2.3.5
	比例代表制	ひれいだいひょうせい	proportional representaion system	8
	広さ	ひろさ	area,size	5
ふ	負	ふ	negative (prefix)	7
	ファイル		file	6
	深い	ふかい	deep	9
	不可能な	ふかのうな	impossible	10
	不況	ふきょう	recession	9.11

Word List

	WORD	READING	ENGLISH	UNITS
ふ	不況対策	ふきょうたいさく	measures against recession	11
	複合	ふくごう	compound	7
	〜を含めた	〜をふくめた	including…	11
	負債	ふさい	debt	9
	部首	ぶしゅ	radical	4
	不信	ふしん	doubt, distrust	9
	二つ	ふたつ	two (things)	4.5
	二人	ふたり	two (people)	1
	部長	ぶちょう	department chief	3
	普通銀行	ふつうぎんこう	ordinary bank	9
	物質	ぶっしつ	matter, substance	7
	物体	ぶったい	object, matter	7
	不動産	ふどうさん	(immoveable) property, real estate	9.11
	（太る）	ふとる	to get fat	3
	部分	ぶぶん	part	4
	部門	ぶもん	department	6
	不利な	ふりな	disadvantageous	11
	不良貸し出し	ふりょうかしだし	bad debt, (bad loans)	9
	不良債権	ふりょうさいけん	(bad claim), bad debts	11
	古里	ふるさと	one's native place	3
	プログラム		program	12
	プログラミング		programming	12
	プロジェクト		project	12
	プロトタイプ		prototype	12
	プロトタイプ・マシン		prototype machine	12
	〜分	〜ぶん	a share of…, a portion of…	1
	分子	ぶんし	molecule	7
へ	へ		to	1-3.10
	へ		towards	2.7.8.10-12
	平行世界	へいこうせかい	parallel universe/world	1
	米国	べいこく	U.S.A.	5
	並列推論マシン	へいれつすいろんマシン	parallel inference machine	12
	米ドル	べいドル	U.S. dollar	11
	べき（だ）		ought to…	6
	（〜と）別個	（〜と）べっこ	different matter/thing (from)	7
	別々の	べつべつの	separate	7
	便宜	べんぎ	facilities, benefit	8
	便宜を図る	べんぎをはかる	to provide with benefits	8
	返答	へんとう	reply	6

	WORD	READING	ENGLISH	UNITS
ほ	(〜の) 方	(〜の) ほう	direction of…	2
	貿易	ぼうえき	(foreign) trade	5.11
	貿易相手	ぼうえきあいて	trading partner	5
	貿易相手国	ぼうえきあいてこく	country which is a trading partner	5.11
	貿易 (収支) 黒字	ぼうえき (しゅうし) くろじ	trade surplus	11
	貿易収支	ぼうえきしゅうし	trade balance	11
	〜方がよい／いい	〜ほうがよい／いい	it is better…	12
	方法	ほうほう	way, method	10
	報酬	ほうしゅう	reward	9
	(訪問する)	ほうもんする	to visit	10
	他 (の)	た／ほかの	other (than)… apart from…	1.2
	(〜の) 他	(〜の) ほか	other…	6.11.12
	補助金	ほじょきん	subsidy	8
	ボス		boss	3
	〜ば、〜程	〜ば、〜ほど	the more…, the more…	11
	ほとんど		almost	4
	ほとんどの〜		most of…	3.4
	ボーナス		bonus	1
	本質的に	ほんしつてきに	essentially	12
	本当の	ほんとうの	true	8
ま	毎日	まいにち	every day	2
	前	まえ	before, former days	8
	〜前	〜まえ	…ago, before	4.9
	〜の前	〜のまえ	in front of…,	3
	正子	まさこ	Masako (woman's name)	1
	まず		first of all	6
	ますます		more and more	5
	又	また	again, also	2.5.8
	まだ		still	2
	まだ (〜て／でいない)		to have not…yet done	10.12
	町	まち	town	1.3.10
	〜末	〜まつ	(at) the end of…	7
	真っ青	まっさお	dead white	10
	〜まで		till, so far as	4.6.8-11
	(学ぶ)	まなぶ	to learn	12
	(招く)	まねく	to invite, to cause	9
	丸一日	まるいちにち	the whole day long	3
	周り	まわり	surrounding	5
	(満足する)	まんぞくする	to be satisfied	12

Word List

	WORD	READING	ENGLISH	UNITS
み	(見える)	みえる	can be seen	2
	(見下ろす)	みおろす	to look down	2
	右	みぎ	right	4
	右手	みぎて	right hand	4
	見込む	みこむ	to expect	9
	短い	みじかい	short	12
	水	みず	water	2
	道	みち	road, passage	2
	三つ	みっつ	three (things)	4
	(見つけ出す)	みつけだす	to find out	7
	皆	みな	all	1.2
	(みなす)		to regard	7.10
	ミュー粒子	ミューりゅうし	Muon	7
	未来	みらい	future	10
	(見る)	みる	to see, to look, to watch	2.10
	(〜て／で) みる		to try …ing	10
	民間	みんかん	private (sector, etc.)	11
	民間投資	みかんとうし	private investment	11
	民主主義	みんしゅしゅぎ	democracy	8
む	(向かう)	むかう	to head, to go towards	2
	昔	むかし	old days, formerly	4.5
	麦	むぎ	wheat and barley	5
	向こう	むこう	over there	2
	虫	むし	insect	2
	矛盾	むじゅん	contradiction	10
	(〜と)(結び付く)	(〜と) むすびつく	to be bound (with)	8
	(結び付ける)	むすびつける	to bind	7
	村	むら	village	5
め	名手	めいしゅ	expert	6
	(明示する)	めいじする	to state clearly,	11
	名声	めいせい	reputation fame, good reputation	6
	命令	めいれい	order, command	12
	(目指す)	めざす	to aim	12
も	も		also	1.3-11
	も		(to highlight "even")	11
	〜も〜も		both… and…	5
	もう		already	2.3

	WORD	READING	ENGLISH	UNITS
も	もう〜		more…	12
	(〜て／〜で) も		even though…	6.9.12
	目的	もくてき	objective	3.11.12
	目標	もくひょう	target, objective	12
	木片	もくへん	piece of wood	4
	(もたらす)		to bring about, to cause	11
	文字	もじ (もんじ)	a character (for writing)	4
	もちろん		of course	6
	(持つ)	もつ	to hold, to have	4.5.7.10
	もっと		more	4.5
	モデル		model	7
	〜に基づく	〜にもとづく	to be based on…	9
	(求める)	もとめる	to seek for, to ask for	7.11
	物	もの	thing	5
	もはや (〜ない)		(not) any longer	7
	森	もり	forest	2
	門	もん	gate	1
	問題	もんだい	problem, subject	6
や	〜や		and, etc	7.8.9
	〜や否や	〜やいなや	as soon as… no sooner…than	9
	やがて		soon, after a while	10
	(約束する)	やくそくする	(to) promise	8
	役人	やくにん	an official	6
	安い	やすい	cheap	1.11
	〜易い	〜やすい	easy to…	4
	安く	やすく	cheaply, at a low price	5
	休み	やすみ	holiday, a day off	3
	(休む)	やすむ	to rest, to have a break .	2.4
	やっと		finally	2
	野党	やとう	political parties not in power, Opposition	8
	山	やま	mountain	2.5
	(止める)	やめる	to stop (transitive)	3
	(やる)		to do	3
ゆ	夕方	ゆうがた	(at) dusk (in) early evening	2
	夕刊	ゆうかん	evening paper	2
	有名な	ゆうめいな	famous	7
	有力な	ゆうりょくな	powerful, influential	6
	雪	ゆき	snow	2

Word List

	WORD	READING	ENGLISH	UNITS
ゆ	輸出	ゆしゅつ	export	11
	油田	ゆでん	oil field	5
	(許す)	ゆるす	to allow	2
よ	よ		(to emphasize what the listener does not know)	10
	良い／よい／いい	よい	good	2.10.12
	(〜に酔う)	〜によう	to get drunk with…	10
	(要求する)	ようきゅうする	to demand, to require	11
	陽子	ようし	proton	7
	要するに	ようするに	in effect	8
	要点	ようてん	importnat point	8
	〜様に	〜ように	to (indirect command)	10
	〜様に (する)	〜ように (する)	as…, in the same way as	2
	〜の様に／ように	〜のように	in the same way as… like…	3.5.12
	(〜ようにしておく)	〜ようにしておく	to be ready to…	5
	(〜ようになる)	〜ようになる	to reach the stage where	5
	羊肉	ようにく	mutton	5
	羊毛	ようもう	wool	5
	よく		often	3
	与党	よとう	party in power	8
	夜中	よなか	middle of the night	3
	(呼ぶ)	よぶ	to call, to cause, to invite	6.7.9.11
	(読む)	よむ	to read	2.3.4
	〜より (も)		than…	1.5.6.8.11
	ヨーロッパ		Europe	5
	弱い	よわい	weak	7
	弱まる	よわまる	to become weak	8
り	利益	りえき	profit	4
	率	りつ	rate	9
	(離党する)	りとうする	to resign from a political party	8
	理由	りゆう	reason	4.9
	粒子	りゅうし	particle	7
	(利用する)	りようする	to utilize	10
	流通	りゅうつう	distribution	11
	両国	りょうこく	both countries	5
	量子物理学者	りょうしぶつりがくしゃ	quantum physicist	10
	旅行	りょこう	travel, journey	10
	理論	りろん	theory	7

	WORD	READING	ENGLISH	UNITS
れ	例	れい	example	4
	レプトン		lepton	7
	連続的に	れんぞくてきに	serially, continuously	12
	連立	れんりつ	coalition	8
	連立政権	れんりつせいけん	coalition government	8
	連立七党	れんりつしちとう／ななとう	seven party coalition	8
ろ	労働者	ろうどうしゃ	worker	9
	労働力	ろうどうりょく	labour force	11
	6	ろく	6	7
	6月	ろくがつ	June	12
	論争	ろんそう	controversy	11
	論理型	ろんりがた	logic (type)	12
わ	若い	わかい	young	3
	（分かる）	わかる	to understand	3.4
	（分かれる）	わかれる	to be divided	8
	私	わたし／わたくし	I	10
	私達	わたしたち／わたくしたち	we	4
	（忘れる）	わすれる	to forget	2
	（～に渡る）	～にわたる	extending to…	8
	（～を割る）	～をわる	to become below…	8
	悪い事に	わるいことに	unfortunately	10
を	を		(object marker, including places)	1-12
	を		(used with certain verbs of motion)	2.7
ん	～んです		(to provide stress and justification to a statement)	3

Radical List

RADICAL	KANJI	MAIN MEANINGS (UNIT)	KANJI	MAIN MEANINGS (UNIT)
1 一	一	one (1.2.3.4.5.6.7.8.9.10.11)	与	give (8)
	万	ten thousands (1.7.10)	三	three (1.3.4.5.8.10)
	下	down, beneath (2.4.9.11)	互	mutual (5.8)
	五	five (1.2.4.8.10.12)	天	heaven (2)
	不	negative prefix (9.10.11)	可	good, approval (8.10)
	民	people (8.11)	正	correct (1.7.11.12)
	平	level (5.10)	百	a hundred (2.4)
	両	both (5)	否	no (9.10)
	画	picture, plan (12)	悪	bad (10)
2 丨	中	middle (1.2.3.4.5.7.8.9.11)	内	inside (5.6.7.8.11)
	央	centre (8.9)	由	reason (4.8.9.11.)
	世	world (7.9.10.11.12)	本	book, origin (2.3.4.5.7.8.9.11.12)
	出	go/come out (1.2.3.4.5.7.8.9.10.11)	向	towards (2.9)
	果	fruit, result (10.11.12)	表	surface, express (4.7.8.9.12)
3 丶	必	necessary (7)	半	half (1.5.8.9)
	求	seek, pursue (7.11.12)	単	simple,single (8.11)
	業	occupation, business (8.9.11.12)		
4 丿	九	nine (4.5.8.10)	丈	length (10)
	久	long time (9)	丸	round, circle, whole (3)
	千	a thousand (4)	夫	husband (1.10)
	少	a little, a few (2.9.10)	丘	hill (2)
	包	wrap (1.2)	末	end (7)
	失	loss (6.12)	未	not yet (10)
	争	to fight (5.8.9.11)	危	danger (8.9)
	年	year, age (1.3.4.5.7.8.9.10.12)	来	come (1.3.4.5.6.9.10.12)
	束	bundle (7.8)	東	east (1.2.4.5)
	重	weight (7)	島	island (5)
	奥	depth (3)	願	ask for wish (10)
	盾	shield (10)	省	Ministry, to omit (9.11.12)
5 乚	七	seven (2.8.10)		
6 亅	事	fact, matter (1.2.3.4.5.6.7.8.9.10.11.12)	才	talent, counter for age (1)
7 二	二	two (1.3.4.5.8.10)	元	origin, foundation (1.6.7.8)
8 亠	六	six (1)	夜	night (3)
	主	main (4.5.8.9.11)	変	change (8)
	忘	forget (2)	市	market (9.11)

RADICAL		KANJI	MAIN MEANINGS (UNIT)	KANJI	MAIN MEANINGS (UNIT)
		交	mix with (7.8)	哀	pity, misery (10)
		京	capital (1.2)	率	rate (9.11)
9	人 亻 入	人	person, human(1.2.3.4.5.6.9.10.11.12)	介	come between (7.10)
		以	with, through (4.5.8.9)	化	transform (8.11)
		他	other (1.2.6.11.12)	令	rule, command (12)
		付	attach (3.4.7.8.11.12)	仕	serve, do (1.3.4.6)
		代	substitute, generation (2.7.8.12)	企	plan, to plot (8.9.11.12)
		任	duty, to entrust (6)	伝	hand on (11)
		休	rest (2.3.4.9)	会	meet (3.6.8.10.11.12)
		合	agree, unite (4.6.7.8.11)	全	the whole (8)
		伴	accompany (4.8)	位	rank, approximately (4)
		含	contain (11)	伸	stretch (11)
		住	reside (1.5.9)	体	body (7.8.10)
		低	low (9.11)	作	make (1.2.5.12)
		何	what (6.8)	価	value, price (9)
		舎	house (1.5)	例	example (4.7.8.12)
		命	life, order (12)	供	offer, supply (1.2.3.12)
		使	use (4.5)	促	urge, encourage (11)
		係	relate, concern (6.7.8.9.10)	便	convenient (8)
		信	trust, believe (6.9)	保	maintain, keep (11)
		候	enquire after (8)	倍	multiply (5)
		値	value, price (9)	個	individual (7.11)
		借	borrow (9)	備	prepare, supply (9)
		債	debt (9.11)	働	work (3.9.11)
		僚	companion, colleague (8.11)	億	one hundred million (5.12)
		優	excellent(9)	今	now (1.2.4.5.7.8.10)
10	儿	先	previous, ahead (3.10)		
11	入	入	enter, in (2.3.4.5.6.8.9)		
12	八	八	eight (8)	公	formal, public (7.11)
		共	both, together (4.5.11)	普	general, usual (9)
		並	line up, ordinary (12)	益	profit (9)
		前	before,front (3.4.8.9)	分	divide, share, separate (1-8.10)
13	冂	円	circle, Yen (1.11.12)	同	same (3.8.9.11.12)
		周	circumference (5.7)		
14	冖	写	copy (6)		

Radical List

RADICAL		KANJI	MAIN MEANINGS (UNIT)	KANJI	MAIN MEANINGS (UNIT)
15	冫	次	next (5.6.7)	弱	weak (7.8)
18	刀 刂	切	cut (3.6.10)	刺	sting, pierce (12)
		制	restrain, control (8.11)	削	delete, curtail (9.11)
		割	divide (8)	別	distinction, different (4.6.7.11)
19	力	加	add (7)	力	force, power (6.7.8.9.11.12)
		助	help, aid (3.6.8.12)	労	labour (9.11)
		動	move (7.9.11.12)		
21	匕	北	north (2)		
22	匚	区	ward, section (4.8)	巨	huge, gigantic (7)
24	十	十	ten (1.2.3.4.5.8.10)	古	old (1.3)
		協	in harmony (8)	直	straight, direct (6.9.10.11)
		南	south (5)	真	truth, reality (7.10)
		準	water level (7.9.11)		
25	卜	上	top, above, on (1.2.3.4.5.6.8. 9.11.12)	点	point, marks (8.12)
27	厂	反	antithesis (11)	厚	thick (6)
		原	original (7.12)		
28	厶	弁	speech (6)	能	ability (8.10.11.12)
29	又	又	and, again (2.5.8)	友	friend (3)
		収	obtain, seize (9.11)		
30	口 口	口	mouth (4.5)	兄	older brother (2)
		右	right (4)	吐	vomit (2)
		呼	call, send for (6.7.9.11)	品	goods (5.9)
		員	member (8.10.12)	味	taste (4.8)
31	囗	四	four (1.5.8)	因	cause (10)
		団	association (8)	回	turn (1.8.9.11)
		囲	enclose (5.7)	図	plan, drawing (2.8)
		国	country, state (2.3.4.5.6.8.11.12)		
32	土 士 土	土	earth (1.2.5.9)	去	leave, past (10)
		寺	temple (4)	在	exist (7.9.10)
		地	land (2.5.7.8.9)	声	voice (6)
		売	sell (5.9)	型	type (12)
		基	foundation, basis (7.9)	場	place (6.7.9.10.11)
		報	reward, report (9)	壁	wall (11)

RADICAL		KANJI	MAIN MEANINGS (UNIT)	KANJI	MAIN MEANINGS (UNIT)
34	夂	処	manage (12)	各	each (8)
36	夕	夕	evening (2)	外	outside (1.2.3.11.12)
		多	many, much (3.4.5.6.8)	名	name (6.7.8.)
37	大	太	big, grow fat (3)	奇	miracle (9)
		大	big, large (1.2.3.5.6.7.9.10.11)		
38	女	女	female (2)	好	like (1.2)
		始	begin (2.6)	妨	obstruct (11)
		妹	younger sister (2)	媒	go between (7)
39	子	子	child (1.2.3.7.10)	存	exist (7.10)
		学	study, learn (3.10.12)	孫	grandchild (10)
40	宀	宅	home (9)	字	letter (4.11.12)
		安	cheap, safe (1.5.11)	完	completion (12)
		宜	good, just, proper (8)	官	office (6.8.11)
		定	fix, decide (6.8.10.11.12)	実	fruit, truth (7.9.10.12)
		客	guest (3.10)	家	home, house (2.3.9.10)
		寄	drop in approach (8)		
41	寸	導	guidance (8.11)		
42	小	小	little, small (1.5.8.9)	光	light (7)
	⺍	当	hit, apply (6.8.9.11.12)	党	party, faction (8.11)
		常	always (9.11.12)		
44	尸	局	bureau (9.12)	展	open, spread out (7)
46	山	山	mountain (2.4.5.10)	崩	destroy (11)
47	川	川	river (2)		
48	工	工	construction, craft (4.12)	巧	skill (9)
		功	merits (9.12)	左	left (4)
49	己	改	reform (6.8)		
50	巾	帯	wear (7)		
51	干	刊	publication (2)		
53	广	広	wide, large (5)	応	application (12)
		府	urban prefecture (8.9.12)	度	degree (7.8.9)
		座	seat (8.9.10)	廃	abolition (11)

Radical List

RADICAL		KANJI	MAIN MEANINGS (UNIT)	KANJI	MAIN MEANINGS (UNIT)
54	廴	延	extend, postpone (9.11)		
56	弋	式	form, ceremony (7.8)		
57	弓	引	pull (11)	強	strong (7.8)
58	ヨ	帰	return (2.3)		
59	彡	形	form, shape (4)		
60	彳	役	role (6)	彼	he (3.6.10)
		往	going (10)	待	wait (9)
		後	behind, after (4.8.12)	術	art, artifice (12)
		得	gain (8.10)	復	again, repeat (10.11)
61	心 忄	心	heart (5.6)	忙	busy (2)
		性	sex, nature (7.8.10)	急	hurry (8.9.10)
		恵	blessing (8)	恐	fear (12)
		態	state of affairs (8)	慣	get accustomed to (8)
62	戈	成	become, succeed (4.5.6.7.8.9.11.12)	戦	war (12)
63	戸	戸	door (1)	所	place (1.4.7.10)
		雇	employment (9)		
64	手 扌	手	hand (2.3.4.5.6.9.10.11.12)	払	pay (1.10.12)
		打	hit, strike (11)	扱	treat (12)
		択	select, choose (11)	指	finger (9.12)
		技	art, skill (12)	拡	enlarge (11)
		担	in charge of, carry (6.7.11)	招	invite (9)
		抱	hug (10)	挙	conduct, perform (8)
		持	have (4.5.7.9.10)	措	dispose of, put aside (11)
		抜	pull out (9)	接	contact (6.9.10.11)
		推	infer, guess (12)	換	exchange (7.9)
		援	help, rescue (8.12)	投	throw (9.11)
		提	carry in hands (12)		
65	支	支	branch, support (11)		
66	攵	政	government (6.8.9.11.12)	数	number (4.6.7.8.9.12)
67	文	文	writing, sentence (4)	対	opposite, against (7.8.9.11.12)
69	斤	新	new (6.7.8)		

RADICAL	KANJI	MAIN MEANINGS (UNIT)	KANJI	MAIN MEANINGS (UNIT)
70 方	方	direction (1.2.4.5.8.10.11.12)	放	release (11)
	旅	travel (10)		
72 日	日	sun, day (1.2.3.4.5.8.9.11)	早	early (2.3)
	易	easy (4.5.11)	昔	long ago, old times (5)
	昇	rise (9)	明	bright (1.2.4.6.7.10.11)
	映	reflect (11)	時	time, hour (3.4.10.12)
	替	exchange, convert (6)	量	quantity (7.10)
	景	view, scene (11)	最	utmost (10.12)
	暇	leisure (9)	曜	day of a week (1.2)
	題	topic, theme (6)		
74 月	月	moon, month (1.12)		
75 木 朩	木	wood, tree (2.4)	机	desk (3)
	村	village (5)	林	woods (2)
	相	aspect, mutual (3.5.6.7.10.11)	核	nucleus, core(7)
	株	shares, stocks, stub (9)	格	status, case (9)
	校	school (3)	根	root (12)
	森	forest (2)	様	style, manner (9.10.12)
	構	structure (7.11)	標	mark, sign (7.12)
	権	authority, power (8.11)	機	loom,machine (11.12)
	極	terrestrial/magnetic poles, extreme (9.12)		
77 止	止	stop (1.2.3.10.11)	歩	walk (2.7.11)
	整	order (9)		
78 歹	列	row, line (12)	死	death (10)
	残	remain, the rest (8)		
80 母 毋	母	mother (1.2)	毎	every (2)
	毒	poison (9)		
81 比	比	compare, ratio (5.8.9)	皆	all (1.2)
82 毛	毛	wool (5)		
84 气	気	spirit, mind (1.2.6.7.11)		
85 水 氵	水	water (2.11)	酒	sake, alcohol (10)
	沢	marsh, swamp (4.5.10)	流	flow (11)
	況	state of things (9.11)	深	deep (9)
	油	oil (5)	満	fill (12)
	派	faction, sect (11)	源	origin (4)
	活	vivid (3.11)	演	perform, play (12)

Radical List

RADICAL	KANJI	MAIN MEANINGS (UNIT)	KANJI	MAIN MEANINGS (UNIT)
	汚	dirty (2.8)	消	extinguish (9.11)
	決	decide(6.10.12)	済	settle (9.11)
	治	rule over (8)	渡	cross (8)
	法	law (10)	減	decrease (9.11)
	洗	wash (2)	漢	China (4)
	海	sea (5.11)	激	enraged (12)
86 火 灬	火	fire (2)	畑	field (2)
	然	to be so (9.12)	無	nothing (12)
	照	shine (9)		
87 爫	受	receive (6)		
88 父	父	father (2.3.10)		
90 爿	将	commander, nearly (6.9)		
91 片	片	scrap, piece (4)		
93 牛 牛	牛	cow (2)	物	thing, matter(5.7.10.11)
	特	special (6.8.11.12)		
94 犬 犭	犬	dog (1.2)	独	independent (9)
	献	donate (8)	獲	gain, obtain (8)
96 王	理	reason (4.7.9.10.12)	現	appear, present (7.8.9.10)
99 甘	甘	sweet (9)		
100 生	生	live (3.7.10)		
101 用	用	business, use (4.6.9.10.12)		
102 田	町	town (1.3.10)	思	think (1.8.9.12)
	界	world (9.10.11.12)	異	different (7)
	田	rice field (1.2.3.5)	略	omit, outline (12)
	男	male (3.9)		
105 癶	発	expose, shoot (7.9.10.12)		
106 白	白	white (1.2.4.5)		
	的	target, suffix to certain adj's & adv's. (3.9.10.11.12)		
109 目	目	eye (3.8.11.12)		

RADICAL	KANJI	MAIN MEANINGS (UNIT)	KANJI	MAIN MEANINGS (UNIT)
110 矛	矛	halberd (10)	務	duties (6)
111 矢	知	know (1.2.3.4.6.12)	短	short (12)
112 石	石	stone (5)	研	research (7.10.12)
	磁	magnetic (7)		
113 示 ネ	示	indicate, show (4.7.11.12)	社	company, shrine (3.8.10.11.12)
	祖	ancestor (10)		
115 禾	利	advantage, profit (9.10.11)	私	private (4.10)
	和	harmony (11)	租	tax, tribute (11)
	秘	secret (6)	程	extent (9.11)
	税	tax (11)	種	seed (7)
	積	accumulate (9)		
116 究	究	examine carefully (7.10.12)		
117 立	立	stand (1.4.8.9.11.12)	産	produce (9.11.12)
	競	compete (8.9)		
118 竹	竹	bamboo (2)	符	ticket (10)
	第	prefix to numerals (5.8.12)	策	plan (6.11)
	答	answer (6)	等	sort, plural suffix (6.11.12)
	算	calculation (12)		
119 米	米	rice (5.11)	粒	grain, particle (7)
120 糸 糸	紀	history, chronicle (7)	約	promise (8)
	納	pay (10)	純	pure (8.11)
	紙	paper (3)	素	simple, origin (7)
	終	end (6.9.12)	経	pass through (9.11)
	組	combine (4.8)	統	unite (7.11)
	結	bind, result (7.8.11.12)	続	continue (5.6.7.8.12)
	維	to keep (9)	総	whole, general (8.11)
	緩	loose (11)	縮	shrink (9)
122 罒	買	buy (1.9.11)	置	put, place (11)
123 羊	羊	sheep (5)	着	arrive, wear (9.12)
	義	right, justice (8)		
124 羽	習	learn (8)		
125 耂	老	old	者	person (6.8.9.10.11.12)
	考	think (3.6.7.12)		

Radical List

RADICAL	KANJI	MAIN MEANINGS (UNIT)	KANJI	MAIN MEANINGS (UNIT)
126 而	耐	endure (9)		
128 耳	取	take (5.6)	職	job (8)
129 聿	書	write (3.6)		
130 肉 月	肉	meat (5)	有	exist (4.5.6.7.10.12)
	脈	range of mountains, pulse (9)	脳	brain (12)
	期	term (9)	朝	morning (2.3)
131 臣	臣	subject (6)		
132 自	自	self (3.6.8.10.11.12)		
133 至	至	reach (8)	致	do (6)
138 艮	良	good (2.9.11)	即	at once (7)
139 色	色	colour (3.4.5.8)		
140 ⺾	若	young (3)	英	excellent, Britain (3.5)
	草	grass (2)	茶	tea (2)
	落	fall (9.11)	蓄	store, save (9)
	蔵	storage (9.11)		
142 虫	虫	insect (2)	衆	many (8)
144 行	行	go, carry out (1.2.3.6.9.10.11.12)		
145 衤	初	first, beginning (7)	補	supplement (8)
	製	manufacture (9)	複	duplicate (7)
146 西	西	west (4)	票	vote (8)
	要	main, necessary (7.8.11)		
147 見	見	see, watch (2.6.7.9.10.11)	親	parent (10)
	規	regulation (11)		
148 角	角	corner (2.10)		
149 言	言	say (1.2.3.4.7.10.11.12)	語	word, language (3.4.12)
	訓	Kun reading (4)	談	talk (6.11)
	許	allow, forgive (2)	論	theory (7.11.12)
	訪	visit (10)	調	examine (6.9)
	話	speak (3.6)	計	plan (12)

RADICAL	KANJI	MAIN MEANINGS (UNIT)	KANJI	MAIN MEANINGS (UNIT)
	記	chronicle (6)	読	read (2.3.4)
	設	establish (11.12)	課	section (3)
	証	proof (7.10)	謂	reason, history (7)
	説	explain (4.6.7.10)	議	discussion (8.12)
150 谷	谷	valley (2)		
151 豆	頭	head (7)		
154 貝	則	law (12)	負	defeat, suffer (7.9)
	財	finance, property (9.11)	責	responsible (6)
	敗	fail, defeat (6.12)	費	spend, fee (9.11)
	貿	purcase, exchange (5.11)	貯	save, preserve (9)
	貸	lend, loan (9)	資	capital (9.11.12)
	賢	wise (12)	質	quality (6.7.12)
	購	purchase (9)		
155 赤	赤	red (11)		
156 走	走	run (2)	起	wake up (3.4.6)
157 足	足	leg, foot (12)	跡	trace (9)
158 身	身	body (6.9.10)		
159 車	車	wheel, vehicle (1.2)	較	compare (5.9)
	転	turn round (9.10)	輸	send (11)
161 辰	農	agriculture (11)		
162 辶	込	crowded, include (9.11)	辺	surroundings (2)
	返	return (6)	近	near (5.10)
	述	mention (6)	送	send (3.6)
	逆	reverse, opposite (10)	追	pursue (12)
	速	fast, speed (7)	造	create (5.6.7.9)
	連	serial, coalition (8.10.12)	通	pass (3.4.6.9.11.12)
	進	promote advance (9.11)	達	reach (3.4)
	過	to past (8.10)	道	way, road (2)
	運	carry (7.10)	適	suit, appropriate (12)
	選	choose, select (8.11)	避	avoid (11)
163 阝	部	division, part (3.4.6.7.11)		

Radical List

RADICAL	KANJI	MAIN MEANINGS (UNIT)	KANJI	MAIN MEANINGS (UNIT)
164 酉	配	distribute (5.6)	酬	reward (9)
	酔	intoxicated, drunk (10)		
165 釆	番	number, order (8)		
166 里	里	village, country (3)	野	field, plain (8)
167 金	金	gold, money (4.8.9.10.12)	銀	silver (9.11)
168 長	長	long (3.9.11.12)		
169 門	門	gate (1.6)	問	question, problem (6.10)
	間	between, period (1.3.8.10.11.12)	開	open (7.9.11.12)
	閣	government office (6.8)	関	relation (6.7.8.9.10.11.12)
	聞	hear, listen (1.3.10)		
170 阝	阻	obstruct (11)	限	limit (8)
	院	institution (8)	降	get off, come down (9)
	険	steep, fierce (8)	陽	positive (7)
	際	occasion, edge (9.12)	障	obstruct (11)
172 隹	焦	focus (12)	離	leave (8)
	集	collect (8)		
173 雨	雨	rain (2)	雪	snow (2)
	雲	cloud (2)	電	electricity (3.7)
	需	demand (11)		
174 青	青	blue (10)		
175 非	非	non... (8.11)		
176 面	面	face (4.5.11)		
177 革	革	reform (8)		
178 韋	韓	the Republic of Korea (5)		
180 音	音	sound (4)	意	meaning (4.6.8.11)
181 頁	頼	rely on (11.12)	額	amount, frame (11)
	類	kinds (6)		
182 風	風	wind (2)		

RADICAL		KANJI	MAIN MEANINGS (UNIT)	KANJI	MAIN MEANINGS (UNIT)
184	食	食	eat, food (2.4.5)	飲	drink (2.3)
185	首	首	neck (4.6)		
189	高	高	high, expensive (1.2.3.9.11)		
195	魚	魚	fish (5)		
196	鳥	鳥	bird (4)		
199	麦	麦	wheat (5)		
203	黒	黒	black (11)		

Japanese Language Learning Materials from Kodansha International

ＮＨＫラジオ日本「やさしい日本語」　全４巻
LET'S LEARN JAPANESE   *Nobuko Mizutani, Ph.D.*
Basic Conversation Skills

A four-volume series of easy lessons in practical conversational Japanese from NHK's popular Radio Japan language program. Audio cassettes of the broadcasts are also available for individual or classroom study.

Volume I:	Text	paperback, 136 pages	ISBN 4-7700-1711-1
	Tapes	three audio cassettes, 195 mins.	ISBN 4-7700-1741-3
Volume II:	Text	paperback, 136 pages	ISBN 4-7700-1784-7
	Tapes	three audio cassettes, 195 mins.	ISBN 4-7700-1785-5
Volume III:	Text	paperback, 136 pages	ISBN 4-7700-1786-3
	Tapes	three audio cassettes, 195 mins.	ISBN 4-7700-1787-1
Volume IV:	Text	paperback, 152 pages	ISBN 4-7700-1788-X
	Tapes	three audio cassettes, 195 mins.	ISBN 4-7700-1789-8

日本語をハナス！
HANDY JAPANESE!   *Tom Gally*
Surviving with the Basics

Teaches enough language skills to communicate in everyday situations. Ideal for travelers, business people, and beginning students.
Paperback with audio cassette, 160 pages, ISBN 4-7700-1748-0

日本語で歌おう！
SING JAPANESE!   *Peter Tse*
The Fun Approach to Studying Japanese

Learn to croon popular Japanese standards with this innovative guide to the world of *karaoke*. Includes a 60-min. prerecorded cassette with twelve songs. For beginners and intermediate students.
Paperback with audio cassette, 168 pages, ISBN 4-7700-1866-5

手書き日本語読本
A READER OF HANDWRITTEN JAPANESE   *P. G. O'Neill*

100 pieces of correspondence illustrate the many styles of handwritten Japanese in common use—from clearly written characters to very demanding cursive script.
Paperback, 268 pages, ISBN 4-7700-1663-8

新聞の経済面を読む
READING JAPANESE FINANCIAL NEWSPAPERS
Association for Japanese-Language Teaching

An innovative and comprehensive textbook for business people who need direct access to the financial pages of Japanese newspapers.
Paperback, 388 pages, ISBN 0-87011-956-7

敬語読本
MINIMUM ESSENTIAL POLITENESS   *Agnes M. Niyekawa*
A Guide to the Japanese Honorific Language

Explains how to use polite and honorific Japanese, emphasizing how to avoid unintentional rudeness. Indispensable for business and everyday conversation.
Paperback, 168 pages, ISBN 4-7700-1624-7

Innovative Workbooks for Learning Japanese Kana & Kanji.

ひらがながんばって！
HIRAGANA GAMBATTE!   *Deleece Batt*
An entertaining and effective illustrated workbook for younger learners. Clever mnemonic devices make learning the *hiragana* syllabary fun and easy.
Paperback, 112 pages, ISBN 4-7700-1797-9

カタカナがんばって！
KATAKANA GAMBATTE!   *Deleece Batt*
This new, interactive workbook teaches *katakana* with *manga*-style art and nearly 100 mini-articles on Japanese society and culture.
Paperback, 112 pages, ISBN 4-7700-1881-9

ひらがな
LET'S LEARN HIRAGANA   *Yasuko Kosaka Mitamura*
A well-tested, step-by-step program for individual study of the *hiragana* syllabary.
Paperback, 72 pages, ISBN 0-87011-709-2

カタカナ
LET'S LEARN KATAKANA   *Yasuko Kosaka Mitamura*
The companion volume for learning the *katakana* syllabary used for foreign words and new terms.
Paperback, 88 pages, ISBN 0-87011-719-X

速習かなワークブック
KANA FOR BUSY PEOPLE   *Association for Japanese-Language Teaching*
Through simultaneous use of the eyes, ears and hands, this text and audio cassette tape makes learning *kana* easier for adult beginners.
Paperback with audio cassette, 80 pages, ISBN 4-7700-1616-6

はじめての漢字ブック
KANJI FROM THE START   *Martin Lam and Kaoru Shimizu*
A basic-level reader which teaches *kanji* reading and writing skills in 12 graded lessons. Includes a grammar glossary and index, and Japanese-English and English-Japanese word lists.
Paperback, 384 pages, ISBN 4-7700-1936-X

常用漢字完全ガイド
THE COMPLETE GUIDE TO EVERYDAY KANJI
Yaeko S. Habein and Gerald B. Mathias
An exhaustive guide to the 1,945 most frequently used Sino-Japanese characters in the Japanese language.
Paperback, 344 pages, ISBN 4-7700-1509-7